Comedy, Seriously

Comedy, Seriously

A Philosophical Study

Dmitri Nikulin

palgrave
macmillan

COMEDY, SERIOUSLY
Copyright © Dmitri Nikulin, 2014.

First published in 2014 by PALGRAVE MACMILLAN® in the United States—a division of St. Martin's Press LLC, 175 Fifth Avenue, New York, NY 10010.

Where this book is distributed in the UK, Europe and the rest of the world, this is by Palgrave Macmillan, a division of Macmillan Publishers Limited, registered in England, company number 785998, of Houndmills, Basingstoke, Hampshire RG21 6XS.

Palgrave Macmillan is the global academic imprint of the above companies and has companies and representatives throughout the world.

Palgrave® and Macmillan® are registered trademarks in the United States, the United Kingdom, Europe and other countries.

ISBN: 978-1-137-41513-4

Library of Congress Cataloging-in-Publication Data

Nikulin, D. V. (Dmitrii Vladimirovich)
    Comedy, seriously : a philosophical study / Dmitri Nikulin, New School.
        pages cm
    ISBN 978-1-137-41513-4 (alk. paper)
    1. Comedy—History and criticism—Theory, etc. 2. Philosophy. I. Title.

    PN1922.N55 2014
    809'.917—dc23

                                                          2013046854

A catalogue record of the book is available from the British Library.

Design by Amnet.

First Edition: May 2014

10 9 8 7 6 5 4 3 2 1

Contents

Preface

Philosophy likes to think of itself as confronting the most urgent challenges of modernity and as addressing the fundamental questions of human existence. Yet, while comedy plays an important role in shaping our lives, philosophy has for too long neglected a significant discussion of it. Although there have been many excellent critical studies of its history and poetics, of its different aspects and genres, philosophy has yet to take comedy seriously. It is the aim of the present text not only to offer a humble remedy to this omission but also to reveal the essential relation between philosophy and comedy. As I will show, comedy is in fact the very dramatization of philosophical reasoning, and, as such, it deserves a central place as a subject of philosophical inquiry.

Already in antiquity, Plato and Aristotle were suspicious of comedy for its depictions of people as vulgar and base. Nevertheless, as readers of Umberto Eco's *The Name of the Rose* will recall, Aristotle apparently dedicated a whole book of his *Poetics* to comedy. But because this book was unfortunately lost to posterity, philosophy still needs to produce a version of this text.

Not only was comedy neglected in ancient times—modern philosophy, too, has tended to dismiss comedy. Here, the reasons have to do with the modern preference for tragedy and its deep roots in the formation of modern subjectivity. The modern Cartesian subject thinks of itself as autonomous and fully rational. It constitutes itself as the center of all meanings, as the navel of its own spiritual world. Yet the self-sufficiency apparently enjoyed by the modern subject is characterized by solitude, monologue, and solipsism.[1] The "I" inevitably suffers in its isolation, even as it narcissistically takes this loneliness as a mark of its own nobility and sublimity. For, behind its majestic and heroic pretense, the isolated subject is petty and pathetic. In the tragic theatrical trial of its everyday life, the modern subject appears at once as accused, prosecutor, defender, and judge.[2] Similarly, as hero, producer, and director of its own tragic drama within philosophy, the modern subject is both protagonist and sole actor.[3] In this lonesome predicament, it always confronts its own end and, consequently, is oriented toward death. The modern subject wants, even needs, to die. And yet it cannot get rid of itself. Like Hamlet, the modern philosophical hero wants to commit suicide, but it cannot step outside of itself to commit the deed. Still under the spell of the Romantics, we too tend to define ourselves in terms of finitude and death.

The spell cast by the Romantics clouds our view of comedy in other ways. Indeed, the Romantic view of civilization epitomizes what I see as our (mis) understanding of both tragedy and comedy. Not only did the Romantics understand civilization in terms of a "quarrel between the Ancients and the Moderns," but they also privileged the Greek world over the Roman world. Figures such as August Schlegel and G. W. F. Hegel, for instance, argued that ancient tragedy—through which they thought the Greek world was revealed—was sublime but that comedy was not even beautiful. And in their consideration of comedy, both Schlegel and Hegel thought Old Comedy superior to New Comedy and Greek comedy superior to Roman comedy.

I want to argue, instead, that comedy speaks more acutely than tragedy to human existential, moral, political, and erotic needs. However, by *comedy* I mean primarily New Comedy and not Old Comedy, which, however, should not be altogether dismissed but rather radically reevaluated. As I hope to show, it is neither Sophocles nor even Aristophanes who is truly modern. Rather, it is the main representative of Greek New Comedy, Menander, and the Roman dramatists Plautus and, especially, Terence who established the comic genre that is still meaningful and alive today. New Comedy has survived throughout history, living on in the Renaissance and early modernity in Shakespeare and Molière, up to contemporary existential comedy and Woody Allen.

In what follows, when speaking about comedy, I thus refer to the type created by New Comedy, as it was first established in Menander and Terence, flourished in modern comedy, and still lives on in contemporary comedy. The comedy I am discussing has a descriptive dimension, since it presents many complexities and inequalities in our lives. It also has a normative dimension, since it diagnoses problems and pathologies, allows for the rectification of these problems, and eventually offers the possibility of achieving well-being shared with others. Since many comedies use a mixture of genres and media and keep experimenting with them, this understanding of comedy will not match all existing comedies. Yet deviation from a norm is itself a comic norm, which comedy often uses as a device.

Comedy is perennial because the very human condition is comical. For comedy is the only genre that allows for the realization of human well-being and freedom as being with others. Such freedom is never a given, yet it is always possible—as a task that can be accomplished together with others. Comedy is defined by its structure and by its ending—a good ending that only comes about through a diligent, persistent, and often unexpected shared action by everyone involved in a comedy. Well-being, then, is not an atemporal or transcendent good, somehow always there just waiting to be discovered. Rather, comic well-being, which *is* achievable, is an assertion of love and the good life that comes as a resolution of a conflict at the end. Yet, as life itself, this good is in need of constant reproduction, renewal, and reaffirmation. Therefore, unlike tragedy, which is the celebration of death, comedy is the celebration of life.

Yet the achievement of human good, the reliving of love, and the reproduction of life need a careful and consequential—"logical"—reasoning. This is why, in my account, comedy is a profoundly philosophical enterprise and philosophy is a comic enterprise. Unsurprisingly, however, modern philosophy has missed its affinity with comedy. For, from its very inception, modern philosophy was constituted as the monological thinking of a lonely self or as the self-directed account of an isolated subject whose only determination was thus being toward death, which is tragic. Nonetheless, as I aim to show, comedy is the reproduction of practical philosophical reason on stage. Because of its affinity with philosophy, which, as a Socratic enterprise, is a dialogical realization of being with others, comedy reproduces the structure of a philosophical argument in its very plot. Beginning with a "problem" that comes as a trespassing of the initial state of affairs, the action moves through a number of steps that are interrelated through complicated yet coherent moves, which result in the "solution" of the problem, not by an act of a *deus ex machina* but by the careful calculation and mutually responsive action of the participants. Yet among all the actors one figure becomes (often unwillingly) the center of action: the comedian *par excellence*, the practical thinker responsible for tying together all the loose ends and advancing the action toward the resolution in the good ending. Paradigmatically represented by a slave, a servant, or a maid, the central comic character enacts the "foolish wisdom," distinctly represented in Socrates, who always fools around and, seemingly not knowing anything, advances an argument toward a resolution. The main comic character is a philosopher onstage. Being in a socially subdued position, the comic thinker becomes the one who makes the advancement toward the good ending. Here, comedy displays its goodness once again in the comic practical realization of justice, which comes as freedom that is reached only at the end, and as a result of the unfolding of the comic action and plot, and which becomes a treasured achievement of love and life and especially of personal freedom for the dispossessed.

I have divided the book into three main parts.[4] The first part is "historical," as it presents an overview of the existing approaches to comedy. I begin in antiquity, moving from Aristotle to the fourth century CE Roman grammarian Aelius Donatus, and then discuss modernity, from Italian literary theoretical discussions of the sixteenth century to the Romantic debates of the nineteenth century and contemporary literature. The second part is "logical," as it discusses the structure of comic plot (*mythos*) and action. Here, I appropriate and apply Aristotle's idea of rhetorical topics, and I discuss the role and place of love within comedy. The third part is "ethical," as it discusses the comic character (*ēthos*) as the "thinker" in her role in the advancement of the plot and the achievement of a good, or happy, ending.

Comedy is not only performed but also read. Yet comic *drama* stresses shared action oriented toward a good ending—or, we might say, a happy ending—and a resolution of a given conflict. For these reasons, I am mostly interested in comedy as drama, not as literature. Further, I want to demonstrate that comedy can be understood on its own, not merely as the complement to or opposite of tragedy. The idea of a system and hierarchy of genres has its roots in antiquity; it was later supported by the sixteenth-century French poet Ronsard and further cultivated by the Romantics. But we do not have to understand comedy within a system of related genres and subdivisions—such as tragicomedy, melodrama, serious comedy, ironic comedy, domestic comedy, comedy of manners, comedy of characters, comedy of intrigue, high comedy, low comedy, farce, satire, burlesque, sarcasm, grotesque, etc. The voice of the comic muse Thalia can resound on its own, not solely in concert with her sisters.

In this book, I intend to provide a defense of comic reason. On the one hand, *tragic* reason grows out of the specifically modern notion of autonomous subjectivity—which, again, is lonely and self-reliant. On the other hand, *comic* reason reflects a life with others. People practice comic reason in reflective deliberation with others and through well-ordered dramatic action. I would like to show that such dramatic action is capable of achieving a good, or happy, ending that celebrates life, love, and freedom.

We might even say that comedy has only one plot: people act toward realizing their desire to be with those they love; whoever initially opposes this aspiration is reconciled to the others' well-being and, thereby, aids in their happiness; and, finally, the oppressed are liberated. In short, comedy is always the same as regards its realization of human good, yet each comedy reaches this good in a different way. Comedy thus exercises a life that can be mutually shared and enjoyed. The virtue of comedy, then, consists in its ability to bring events to a good end, one that comes about through the shared effort of a number of actors.

Philosophically speaking, we see the comic aspect of reason in the life of the mind that establishes, through a shared debate, the "good ending" of a well-constructed, justified argument. The complex plot of comedy is fundamentally rational in structure. According to the Roman grammarian Donatus, in a comic plot we begin with *premises* that establish an intrigue or a problem, from which we move to a *complication*. Through a number of justified steps of deliberation, we finally arrive at the *conclusion*, the resolution of the initial problem and the realization of the "good ending." Thus we see that a comic plot resembles a long and sophisticated logical or dialectical argument. And so comic plot is more a product of carefully calculated and demonstrative dialogical reason than of productive imagination; in the end, the action should arrive at a mutually acceptable and recognized state of affairs. The comic ending is, we should hope, possible. Yet it is never guaranteed. Unlike the tragic end of destined death, the comic ending, as life, needs to be renewed, reproduced, and achieved again and again.

The analogy and structural similarity between comic plot and sound logical argument is rather striking. Comedy, we could say, is the dramatization of philosophical reasoning.[5] The complexities of a comic plot initially appear daunting and irresolvable. To achieve a resolution of the conflict, the construction of a plot requires great dramatic skill. Similar to an argument, which can use various techniques or invent new ones, a good plot may borrow from other sources or devise new, dramatic moves. Further, while comic plot and logical argument are both understandable at any one step in their development, taken in their entirety they are difficult to remember. This is due to their overall complexity and the subtle transitions they make from point to point. Finally, both comedy and philosophy do justice to life and thought. They establish respectively plot or argument through a reflective, argumentative procedure that requires an *actor* or *thinker* who makes the resolution of the conflict or the conclusion of the argument possible. In brief, one could say that comedy accomplishes with dramatic action what philosophy does with arguments. We might say that philosophical argument and comic plot are *intentionally* isomorphic in their structure. In this sense, comedy is philosophical and philosophy is comic. We might even say that comedy is born out of the spirit of philosophy, that it bears certain features explicable only through its initial proximity to philosophy.[6] To use a phrase, comedy is "*philosodia*," the philosopher's song.

Comedy is shared with others, practiced "in conversation" with others as participants. Comedy sees well-being—what Aristotle called *eudaimonia* (happiness)—as being with others. While it may at times be toilsome, comedy nevertheless overcomes suffering and brings us to a common end through joint effort and shared action. While tragedy celebrates death and human finitude, comedy celebrates life and its renewal. Hidden behind the mask of seemingly improper vitality and inexcusable fun, comedy often involves absurd actions and irrational decisions that are moral yet never moralistic.

Hence, comedy depicts and reproduces a life of well-being, and at the same time, comedy serves as this life's normative guide.

Comedy is always engaging and never boring, for it exercises and displays the life of the mind in dramatic action. Boredom, after all, is a sign of the modern tragic subject. As monological and autonomous, the subject inevitably becomes tired of itself in its lonely predicament. It does not even notice its own tedious, monotonous repetition. In its bored and isolated condition, the subject resembles, so Friedrich Schleiermacher retorts to Johann Gottlieb Fichte, the image of a sock knitting itself. Only in being with and talking to others can we stave off the boredom that is symptomatic of the isolated subject.

Comedy is built around an action that engages everyone on- and offstage. It is entertaining and often uses jokes, puns, and laughter. Yet comedy is not defined by such devices. Rather, it is determined by a structure directed toward a good ending. That is to say, comic being is oriented toward happiness, an orientation that is ever to be achieved. It is not, therefore, a contradiction to speak seriously about comedy. Comedy *is* a serious matter. Comedy is always moral: it carries the message of the possibility of human equality, freedom, and well-being. But at the same time, comedy is not moralistic. Rather, it is anarchic and often ironic. Moralism always hides a particular interest or agenda—usually of asserting oneself at the expense of others—behind a seemingly moral message. Instead, comedy likes to laugh heartily, to be indecent, and, at times, not to tell the whole truth. Such elements are not always vices but may be comic devices that help to steer the action toward a good or happy ending. In a moral, but nonmoralistic, interpretation of comedy, the characters are not abstract representatives of masked moral (or immoral) positions. On the contrary, the moral interpretation of comedy sees characters as people who, in turn, achieve themselves in dramatic comic action with others.

One of the most important characters of comedy, omnipresent in New Comedy, is the clever slave (*servos*), servant, valet, or maid. The clever slave figures prominently in Menander, Plautus, and Terence, and later in Shakespeare, Ben Jonson, and Molière, up to his or her contemporary transformations. The slave is a version of the culturally omnipresent, universal figure of the fool and appears in many guises: the jester, trickster, prankster, buffoon, clown, alazon, or eiron. In comedy, it is the fool who is wise, often without even knowing it. Through a series of deliberate actions, which resemble the steps of reasoning in a philosophical argument, the slave rescues others from an apparently irresolvable situation and leads everybody to a resolution of the conflict. The slave is the mastermind behind the development of the comic plot, the "director" of the intrigue who plans and stages a whole new dramatic frame in order to trick the seemingly wise and steer the action toward a fulfilling end.

Taking the slave into consideration, we can see how the comic figure is a philosopher. The slave is the "thinker." Indeed, the slave plays the role in comedy that Socrates plays in Plato's dramatized dialogues. While the former directs a plot, the latter steers a dialectical argument. Both the slave and Socrates appear, perhaps deliberately and ironically, as somewhat simplistic, as "fools." However, we quickly discover a powerful and sophisticated mind behind each of their foolish and ironic guises. Hence, both the slave and Socrates are dialecticians: the slave is a practical thinker, the one who leads us through the labyrinth of a plot; Socrates guides us through the maze of an argument, even if often toward a negative outcome. For their part, both selflessly promote the happiness of others: the slave directs other characters toward a desired ending; Socrates steers his interlocutors to freedom of and in thought. And, importantly, both liberate themselves by helping others: the slave's deeds often win him the highest gift, that of freedom; Socrates's knowledge of his own apparent ignorance frees him from the bind of fixed knowledge, allowing him to ever strive toward discovering how and what things are.

In comedy, only a slave is capable of transgressing social differences and driving action toward justice and equality. Only the mastermind of comedy can show that such distinctions are matters of convention and have nothing to do with the truly comic and rational human condition. The slave is the master of the comedy of philosophy, the comedy of life; she is the master dialectician and the architect of its plot. On the other hand, the master is the slave of comedy, for he must follow the unfolding of comic action and philosophical argumentation that keeps him in tow. Comedy and philosophy, then, restore social and dialectical justice. We might say that the justice of comedy consists in the recovery of human equality and dignity, of the well-being and freedom that is achieved in and as the end of (often difficult) action and deliberation with others. Comedy can be taken as a dramatic action that unfolds through a plot, which intends to resolve a complication through a mutually shared performance where one of the characters serves as a mastermind, or "philosopher," who moves action toward a resolution of the conflict and the fulfillment of the aspirations of all the participants. Which is just to say, comedy can be taken seriously.

Acknowledgments

I want to thank Rainer Forst, Manfred Frank, Saulius Geniusas, Burke Gerstenschlager, Agnes Heller, Michael Iampolski, Joseph Lemelin, Andreas Kalyvas, Paul Kottman, Duane Lacey, Mark Roche, Anna Strelis, Anastasiya Nikulina, Alex Nikulin, and Elena Nikulina for their comic comments and sagacious interventions that have been enormously helpful and encouraging. The generous support of the Kassel-Stiftung and the Forschungskolleg in Bad Homburg has been indispensable in writing this book.

PART I

History of Comedy

CHAPTER 1

The Good, the Bad, and the Ugly: On the Ancient Origins of Comedy

In antiquity, comedy was one genre of *drama*.

As drama, comedy was an activity shared with other people through action and dialogue. Comedy was thus communal, and its meaning was established in the interaction of both actors and spectators.

As a genre, comedy presupposed a set of explicit and implicit rules. Regardless of whether these rules were pure conventions or arose from common human concerns, they governed the comic action according to its purpose. So, let me begin by attempting to clarify these rules, as well as the structure, purpose, and action of comedy, in order to then trace their philosophical implications.

It is always difficult to look (back) into the origin of any form of action. After all, such an origin is invariably given to us through a narrative, which is always an interpretation that, though it tries to grasp a phenomenon in its entirety, inevitably has to omit much.[1] Let us, then, start with the word itself: *comedy*. Even if etymological explanations almost always miss the point of origin, seeking the "original" meaning of a word rather than the reason behind the original people's activity, they can nonetheless be somewhat helpful.

According to Aristotle's *Poetics*, the best-known "archeological" text on early comedy, the word *comedy* comes either from the Doric Peloponnesian word for *village (kōmē)*[2] or from the word for *merrymaking (kōmos)*.[3]

The rural *kōmē* reveals a communal activity in which peasants sing songs that mock their fellow citizens for wrongdoings—a spontaneous dialogical exchange within a critical, reflective community. For example, at the feast of Dionysus in Attica, peasants came down to the city and lampooned wealthy burghers who had somehow provoked their grudge.[4] This activity brought rivalry down from the level of war and legal action to the level of carnival, where justice was accomplished without bloodshed and without much resentment.[5] Such open critique was closely connected to democracy, to the ideal of social equality that promoted critical free speech (*parrhēsia*)—something which became risky in the face of a tyrant.[6] At any rate, critical lampooning and personal attack, or even abuse, eventually became major features in the Old Comedy of Aristophanes and other playwrights.[7]

The term *kōmos* appears to be related to *kōmē*.[8] A *kōmos* was traditionally a revel, celebrated in many cities and often accompanied by "a festival of Dionysus in which a phallus was carried in procession" (*phallēphoria*) and by the singing of phallic songs (*ta phallika*).[9] This erotic action would continue up to the moment of complete physical exhaustion and drunken forgetfulness. Such an "ending" is itself still an affirmation and renewal of life against social conventions and, most importantly, against death. However, for philosophy, finding the origin of comedy in a banquet and a procession of throngs of drunken people (singing obscenities and ultimately collapsing into drunken forgetfulness) already seems suspicious, bawdy, and indecent.[10] The outright celebration of life, love, and sexuality, the affirmation of "natality," and the presence of the uncontrollable Dionysian drive make the revel a conspicuous activity. Yet, while the comic revel always has a somewhat indecent taste, it is the taste of good life and of the suspension of one's mortality. Therefore, displaced (or perhaps properly placed) into a ritualistic carnivalesque setting, the revel was perfectly acceptable and welcomed by the participants. It was subsequently taken over and satirically imitated in Old Comedy.

Because comedy allowed people to speak their minds freely in the form of bitter mockery, Aristotle sought the origin of comedy in the *iambus*, which, together with the *elegy*, was one of two major forms of archaic poetry.[11] According to Aristotle's account, lampoons or "blameful songs" (*psogoys*) gave rise to iambus, which in turn gave rise to comedy (as epic did to tragedy).[12] At the very heart of iambic poetry one found agonistic verbal battles, personal attacks, and scoffs, all of which included allusions to the favored topics of eating, drinking, and, quite explicitly, sexuality. Indeed, the iambus was a celebration of life in all its physically explicit forms.[13] These features were later refined and incorporated into Old Comedy.

While the iambus was originally used for derisive ribaldry, it also had the capacity to hearten people (and even gods) by seemingly indecent sarcasm, pungent gestures, and acrimonious acts. As a case in point, the Homeric hymn to Demeter personifies the practice of jesting in the figure of Iambe, a maiden of the king Keleos.[14] Demeter comes to the house of Keleos looking for her abducted daughter: "She greeted no one with word or movement, but sat there unsmiling, tasting neither food nor drink, pining for her deep-girt daughter, until at last dutiful Iambe with ribaldry and many a jest diverted the holy lady so that she smiled and laughed and became benevolent—Iambe who ever since has found favor with her moods."[15] Going against social conventions, such theatrical acts of the iambus are meant to restore a person to the fullness and joy of life, lost for a while due to infelicitous and dire circumstances.

At the same time, the iambus was attractive to dramatists thanks to its conversational character and colloquial simplicity.[16] For this reason, iambus can be used in dialogues and is suitable for the depiction of dramatic interaction.

Beyond these etymological origins, we can also trace the birth of comedy historically—by names and textual narrative. As a dramatic and literary genre, the birth of comedy was associated with Sicily.[17] The sixth- through fifth-century BCE Sicilian dramatist Epicharmus was one of the first writers to invent comic plot (*mythos*), both of a commonplace and of a mythological character.[18] Importantly, the tradition marks him as a prolific writer of some forty works—preserved only in a few fragments—*and* a Pythagorean philosopher—which establishes an early connection between philosophy and comedy.[19] Plato mentioned Epicharmus as well, naming him as the founder of comedy (with Homer as the founder of tragedy) and noting that he agreed with the philosophical position also held by Protagoras, Heraclitus, and Empedocles—namely that nothing ever is or exists but always comes to be.[20]

The association between the origins of comedy and Sicily continues with two later related genres: *mime*, which displays short scenes from everyday life in the form of monologue or dialogue; and *flyax*, which presents equally brief dramatic pieces, mostly parodying myths.

Although not much is preserved of *flyax*, aside from some vase depictions, we have a long tradition of mimes. The most famous writer of mimes was the fifth-century BCE Sicilian Sophron.[21] Sophron wrote in prose, and thus his mimes should count as early comic literature. Here, again, we find a trace of the early connection between philosophy and comedy: the later tradition says that Plato admired Sophron. While he never mentions Sophron by name, Plato, in order to perfect the art of the imitation of characters—an important skill for every writer of dialogues, whether in comedy or philosophy—is said to have imitated Sophron's (jester) mimes.[22]

Philosophy, Tragedy, and Comedy

It is easier to say *when* philosophy arose than *why*. Before philosophy became a scholarly enterprise with Aristotle, it was practiced by Plato as a dialectical, literary, and written work and by Socrates as an oral, dialogical conversation. Through these two figures, we can see that, from the very beginning, philosophy found comedy daunting—not only personally, in the figure of the philosopher, but also topically, in its form and content.

The philosopher typically appeared as a comic figure and as an object of ridicule—"the jest not only of Thracian handmaids but of the general herd, tumbling into wells and every sort of disaster through his inexperience."[23] Socrates, for instance, was famously lampooned in Aristophanes's *Clouds*.[24] Topically, philosophy seemed well aware of its uncomfortable proximity to comedy, both as a genre and by virtue of its problematics.

Indeed, one of the central arguments of this book is that philosophy's proximity to comedy is a blessing for philosophy. However, since philosophy has often wanted to be purely rational—to be an *a priori* thinking about the nonchanging within the changing—philosophy has tended to perceive any association with comedy as a burden and an embarrassment. Hence, philosophy generally tries to detach itself from such a derisive and indecent activity and to be taken in earnest—by others but most importantly by itself. As a result of this discomfort, as early as Plato, philosophy launched various attacks on comedy.

What were these attacks?

Philosophy attacked comedy for the same reason that it attacked poetry in general. The grouchy Heraclitus, to pick an extreme instance, suggested that Homer and Archilochus should be banned from competitions and flagellated—apparently, as two major representatives of poetic lying in heroic and iambic poetry.[25] By comparison, Plato's well-known attacks on poets seem mild. For Plato, philosophy had the task of clarifying (the meaning of) being, whereas poetry was seen only as an imitation (*mimēsis*) of becoming and thus as a betrayal of "the true" (*to alēthes*).[26] Since comedy belonged to poetry, it, too, was seen as *imitative*. Worse, comedy concerned itself with the funny and the ridiculous and hence was unable to contribute to the improvement of public morals.[27] No doubt, Plato was aware of his famous predecessor, Plato the Comic,[28] and it may be that Plato the Philosopher wanted to dissociate himself from his namesake in his own work and genre. As imitative poetry, comedy can be dangerous to a serious political constitution and hence has no place in it. Indeed, comedy reproduces and imitates "base" human actions that can ridicule, and thus become critical, of the sublimely serious foundations of a political order. And yet an utter seriousness entailing the loss of a sense of the comic is itself pathetic. Though, in Plato's defense, and against the seriousness of the philological interpretations of his works that arise later in the Romantic period, one could argue that many of his dialogues are subtly comic, both in form and content.

Moreover, for Plato, dramatic poetry, and comedy in particular, represented an unwelcome mixture of pain (*lypē*) and pleasure (*hēdonē*), or of fear and love.[29] The presence of these two opposite feelings does not lead to the realization of law (*nomos*) and (calculating) reason (*logos*) but rather prevents it.[30] Hence, while comedy suited teenagers, foreigners, and slaves,[31] according to Plato, it was improper for serious adults and responsible citizens. And yet, in its psychological effect, comedy, like tragedy, could affect purification or catharsis in its spectators.[32] Comic purification arises from the impure and improper mixture of pain and pleasure. According to the sixteenth-century Italian theorist Giraldi, "Just as tragedy purges men's minds, through terror and pity, and induces men to abstain from acting wickedly, so comedy, by means of laughter and jokes, calls men to an honest private life."[33] On Northrop Frye's account, tailored to modern psychological perception, "just as there is a catharsis of pity and fear in tragedy, so there is a catharsis of the corresponding comic emotions, which are sympathy and ridicule."[34] To use Aldous Huxley's fortunate typo, comedy is thus always "vomedy."[35] Comic catharsis is ridiculous, because it purifies both soul and body; it is both "high" and "low"; thus, it corresponds to the initial meaning of catharsis as a purification of stomach, of the human inner. However, unlike tragic catharsis, which apparently leads to the restoration of the abandoned balance in the soul's passion, comic catharsis leads to the renewal of the soul's vital function and to the enjoyment of life in its various exuberant manifestations.[36] This comic joy of life is celebrated and typically represented in the wedding feast at the end of a play, as in Aristophanes's *Peace* and *Birds*.

In his *Poetics*, Aristotle, too, listed comedy, together with tragedy (both epic and dithyramb), as a way of imitation.[37] Which is to say, comedy is just one of many different ways of imitation. In this context, comedy was associated with dithyramb (which was connected with the cult of Dionysus and broadly related to iambus), just as tragedy was associated with epic. At this point, Aristotle followed the dichotomous distinction of viewing opposites as contraries: applying this simplistic division to poetry, he took it either to imitate the good and earnest (*spoydaios*)—or the bad and worthless (*phaylos*).[38] In Aristotle's view, tragedy was an imitation of the best people, whereas comedy imitated the worst.[39] Comedy presents the funny and ludicrous, which generically belong to the base and ugly.[40] And Aristotle saw the funny itself as a mistake, though a pardonable one, insofar as it did not cause pain or inflict any harm.[41]

Without knowledge of the ridiculous—said these ancient philosophers—one cannot come to know the serious. Without understanding the bad, one cannot understand the good.[42] Consider the final scene of Plato's *Symposium*: when all other participants are drunk and sleeping, only Socrates, Agathon,[43] and Aristophanes remain sober. The *Symposium*, itself a comic event, ends with a dialogue between a philosopher, a tragedian, and a comedian. Over the course of their conversation, Aristophanes (who personifies comedy) is the first to fall asleep, followed by Agathon (who personifies tragedy). Only

Socrates (the philosopher of the bunch) remains awake, never becoming weary or drunk.[44] What could better illustrate how the subordination of comedy to tragedy parallels that of tragedy to philosophy, which alone is beyond sensual pains and pleasures and which stands soberly awake in the realm of the rational?

Ever since philosophy began thinking about drama, it has understood comedy in opposition to tragedy. Comedy is seen as presenting and showing the negative, the unreal, the improper—as the subordinate "other" of tragedy—and hence is not considered on its own grounds. Remember, too, how Socrates apparently made his interlocutors recognize that one and the same writer should be able to write both tragedies and comedies and that a tragic poet is also a comic poet. Or that Aristotle intended to dedicate the second book of his *Poetics* to comedy.[45] This way of considering comedy as the other of tragedy persists well into modernity and is a distinct feature in the Romantic treatment of comedy. Indeed, this kind of oppositional thinking plays an important role in the place comedy came to have in our understanding.

At the same time, one of Aristotle's major criticisms of Plato was his critique of unmediated opposites. For Aristotle, the primary law of thinking and being was the law of noncontradiction, according to which "the same cannot at the same time be and not be in relation to the same and in the same respect."[46] Aristotle further distinguished between *contrary* and *contradictory* opposites, which are those that allow and do not allow for mediation.[47] Considering opposites—such as good and bad—without mediation is impossible, because it would destroy being and thinking. Aristotle therefore criticized Plato for taking opposites to interact without mediation.[48] In his own philosophy, Aristotle looked for a neutral third (e.g., *Phys.* A 7), a substrate that would mediate contradictory opposites and thus make them contraries.

And yet, when it comes to drama, the situation appears to be different. It is Plato who seemed to have presented philosophy as the highest dramatic art of dialectic. Rather than mediating between tragedy and comedy, philosophy goes beyond both. For Plato, paradoxically, philosophy itself became a formal imitation of the imitative art of drama. Aristotle, then, was the one—his own critique of Plato notwithstanding—who took comedy to stand in unmediated opposition to tragedy, as its dramatic contradictory. Remarkably, Aristotle seems not to have followed his own remarks in the *Poetics* about three kinds of painters: those depicting the best people (Polygnotus), those depicting the worst (Pauson), and those depicting people who are like ourselves (Dionysius), that is, ordinary people.[49] Drama's depiction of human—not divine—ordinariness escaped Aristotle's own attention. Falling into the pattern that he himself criticized in Plato, Aristotle drew a dichotomous distinction within drama, missing Sergio Leone's later, more subtly ironic division of characters into the good, the bad, and the "ugly." At any rate, this "third" type of drama—which mediates between the opposites of the good (tragedy) and the bad (Old Comedy), making them "contrary" rather than "contradictory"—seems barely to have been glimpsed by Aristotle, taking root only after his time.

Following the historical development of the birth of comedy, we stumble upon a creative tension and mediated opposition between Old Comedy and New Comedy (Nea) and then the Nea's later transformations. Here, the important thing to bear in mind is the conventional division of Attic comedy into Old Comedy, of which the most famous representatives are Cratinus, Eupolis and Aristophanes;[50] Middle Comedy, of which we know only fragments and play titles; and New Comedy, of Philemon, Menander, and Apollodorus, which coincides with the end of classical antiquity and the worldwide spread of Greek culture.[51]

First, one last word on Attic comedy itself: Attic comedy existed for a long time as an improvised action.[52] Appearing after tragedy (sometime after the Persian Wars), Attic comedy was eventually written, institutionalized, and included in the state festivals and competitions associated with the cult of Dionysus.[53] From early on, ancient Attic comedy apparently used mythological stories to produce parodies of contemporary events. It thus applied the *mythos* as an elaborate plot, in which everything converges in the end, and a narrative, whose heroes are substitutions for familiar mythological creatures.[54] An ordered structure of narrative based on *logos* and *mythos* is thus present in comedy from its very beginning, although, except for the comedies of Aristophanes, we have only fragments and titles of the plays of the earlier comedy.

Some Comic Structures and Definitions

Ancient thinkers considered drama to be reflective of human activity in all its discernible structural components.[55] Such an analysis generically belonged to *logical* thinking. To put it as logicians would, comedy was seen as aiming to discern a possibly complete system of constituents in their mutual relations and interactions. Now, once philosophy began, with Plato, to take the form of a written dialectical enterprise, it borrowed its form from drama, and in particular, as I will argue in what follows, from comedy. However, once philosophy became a systematic enterprise, with Aristotle, it imposed its categories of logical philosophical analysis onto drama. And, soon after Aristotle, philosophy internalized and appropriated these categories.

In his *Poetics*, Aristotle famously identified six qualitative constituents of drama (in tragedy but apparently equally discernible in comedy). These are plot (*mythos*), characters (*ēthē*), diction (*lexis*), thought (*dianoia*), spectacle (*opsis*), and melody (*melos* or *melopoiia*).[56] One might wonder why Aristotle chose these six aspects, but he neither provides a systematic deduction of them from certain principles nor explains their mutual dependence. However, Aristotle is exempt from providing such explanations, as he follows his own program of "distinguishing the names," where each notion or phenomenon is considered according to the ways it is *said*, or used in language. Correspondingly, distinctions helpful for a comprehensive consideration of a phenomenon are provided by looking carefully into its constituents, without a guarantee of their fullness or redundancy.

In other words, these categorical analytic distinctions in drama are neither deductive nor reductive. That is to say, they are not deduced from a single principle according to a set of rules and procedures, nor are they reduced to one or several foundational principles that would explain the functioning of drama. The constituents are rather pragmatic, as they are *descriptive* of the existing activity of human interaction (a "sun" light) that is reflected in drama (a "moon" light). However, the very completeness of the list of enumerated "parts," which are the ways in which a phenomenon—drama—can be *spoken about*, is never guaranteed within the enumeration itself. It is always left open, provisional, and, in principle, subject to revision and change. In brief, any classification is always only *a* classification.

Furthermore, as a vulgar activity and a bawdy spectacle,[57] comedy existed and developed in obscurity for a long time, hidden from a watchful philosophical eye. Thus, not even Aristotle could establish the names of those who made significant innovations in comedy.[58]

Nonetheless, we are still (thankfully) able to discuss some of the key aspects of the genre of comedy in its early stages. The stable structural features of Old Comedy, as Michael Silk presents them in his in-depth discussion of Aristophanes's comedy,[59] are

> a spoken introductory scene ("prologue"), the chorus' entrance song (*parodos*), a formal debate (*agōn*), a sequence in the form of a direct address by the chorus to the audience (the parabasis or "approach"), and a concluding scene ("exodos") which often contains or promises a *kōmos* (the "party," from which the name of "comedy" is itself derived). There may be additional unclassifiable scenes ("episodes") and songs, especially in the later part of the play . . . The agōn and parabasis tend to have elaborate structures of their own.[60]

To these, one might also add the actor's rich and exaggerated garments, as well as the character of *bōmolokhos* (a "jester by the altar," usually a simpleton or peasant), who later became a defining figure in comedy.

The chorus is preserved from the very early forms of drama. Some scholars have argued that dramatically staged wedding and funeral songs were performed by two choruses that sang one after the other.[61] Apparently, the chorus was so important for drama that its introduction is mentioned as a historical event in the Greek chronological table, the Marmor Parium.[62] The chorus was originally all-male. It was present in tragedy from its inception and important in the satyr play. The chorus grew in size and became more elaborate in comedy, where it is often represented by animals.[63] Yet the role of the chorus diminishes already in the fifth-century tragedian Euripides, and in Menander it practically disappears.[64] In New Comedy the chorus is present only in a nontextual way (absent in the author's text), in the *entr'actes* and as a parody of the classical chorus. The disappearance of the chorus signifies the establishing of a personality that is much less dependent on the community, as I will explain in the following section.

In the exodus, the chorus both sang and danced, and the full choral parabasis (sometimes two in a play) included seven parts. Some of them were paired and metrically corresponded to each other: the ode (*ōidē*), a song of the semichorus, was answered by the antode (*antōidē*); and the *epirrhēma*, a speech of the coryphaeus, leader of the semichorus, was answered by the *antepirrhēma*. Songs alternated with speeches: an ode was answered by an *epirrhēma* that was answered by an antode, in turn answered by an *epirrhēma*, thus forming a sort of impersonal dialogue of carefully calculated components.[65] Moreover, this structural part of the parabasis presupposed a dialogical interaction between the spectators, persons (leaders of semichoruses), and two parts of the chorus.

Interestingly, the Aristotelian analysis of comedy pays most attention to the structure of the action. This accords with Aristotle's claim that plot takes precedence over action: the presented acts and plot (*ta pragmata kai mythos*) are the end (*telos*) of drama—and the end defines the beginning, as well as the very being, of human action. Thus, for Aristotle, drama was impossible without action and plot, but it could proceed without properly portrayed characters.[66]

Indeed, in ancient drama, plot was presented through action rather than by a narrative assigned to a hero. This made the comic prologue very important, though it appears unusual to the modern literary consciousness. The comic prologue in Old Comedy formulated the story and explained the plot—before the action had even begun. Further, in New Comedy, the prologue often—though not always—provided the author's response to his critics by addressing the audience.[67] This is totally unthinkable in the modern drama or novel, where the spectator or reader should be unaware of the ending, lest she be disappointed, lose interest, or simply refrain from watching or reading the piece. Thus, the comic prologue announces and anticipates—in the beginning—the end as the purpose of action.

Comedy, Old and New

In the commonly accepted view, the decline of Old Comedy and the later development of New Comedy are linked with the decline of Athenian democratic institutions and the loss of political freedom. Hence, the great "high mimetic" Old Comedy loses its power of political and religious criticism, as well as its reflective capacity, and degenerates into "low mimetic" New Comedy, concentrated on the consideration of everydayness and the banal subjects of love and marriage.[68]

Contrary to this disparaging view of New Comedy as secondary to sublime Old Comedy and thus as only a mannered, down-to-earth, and commonplace expression of urban (bourgeois) sensibility, I want to argue that New Comedy inherits much from both late tragedy and Old Comedy, refining its characters and perfecting the plot. I also intend to show that the view of the supposed decline of comedy after Aristophanes is a Romantic distortion of both the historical significance and philosophical meaning of New Comedy, which represents a much more sophisticated and *modern* kind of drama.

Among the defining features of Old (Aristophanic) Comedy, we find a critical reflection on social and political matters in the form of personal attacks on concrete people (*Clouds, Thesmophoriazusae*) or on specific gods (*Birds, Frogs*). In doing so, both the comedian and the public exercise an impressive freedom of judgment in speech and action, often accompanied by crude invectives and obscene jokes and moving in a well-structured plot (*mythos*). Yet, in Aristophanes, such attacks are more satirical than comic, for human characters (such as Aeschylus, Euripides, Agathon) are deliberately caricatured and exaggerated, *not* portrayed as true to life.

Old Comedy is often associated with the peak of the development of democratic institutions in Athens. However, Aristophanes's political sympathies were not on the side of democracy, rather idealizing traditional aristocratic values.[69] He viewed urban life, with its tendency toward modernization, as a source of moral and political corruption. The political mood of his comedies was best captured by Corrigan:

> In each of his plays, Aristophanes is attacking the manifestations of political, social, and moral corruption which he believed were the direct result of the Athenians' shift away from an agricultural to an artisan and mercantile economy, their adoption of a more imperialist "foreign policy," and their willingness to accept the validity of new forms of thought and art. All his life, Aristophanes

shared the attitudes of the rapidly disappearing landed aristocracy, whose religion, morality, ideals, and patterns of social organization were based upon an agricultural economy and a closed, heroic view of society. He resisted all that was modern.[70]

Aristophanes "refused to give up what was already lost. Instead of welcoming the new, he mourned the loss of the old . . . The traditional code is never the *only* morality; there is always the possibility of another sanction."[71] This view is further supported by the depiction of the Athenian impersonated in the decrepit, grouchy Demos in Aristophanes's *Equites*.

However, we should keep in mind two important factors: First, comedy is not conservative in nature. On the contrary, comedy is the place for providing social and political criticism of oppressive institutions and corrupt practices. And second, democracy in the classical age was radically different from modern liberal democracy. Athenian democracy was based on the imperialist hegemony of Athens over its allies, and political rights were granted only to a minority of the inhabitants of Athens: women, metics, and slaves did not participate in the political process.

The *querelle des anciens et des modernes* is a popular genre of philosophical and historical reflection in modernity. It occurs when *we*, who now understand ourselves as moderns, oppose ourselves—and thus negatively establish our identity—vis-à-vis those whom we consider ancients. This opposition has occurred many times: in the late middle ages (where the "moderns" are the nominalists), in early modernity (with modern science, philosophy, and historiography), and in the modernism of the twentieth century (from Martin Heidegger to Hannah Arendt). Yet this opposition was also known in antiquity among the sophistically trained and enlightened youth, who became especially self-conscious in the rejection and emendation of the "ancients" in the generation following Aristotle. This happened not only in philosophy, where Stoicism critically appropriated previous philosophical achievements,[72] but also in drama. With the advent of "new" comedy, much changed in the scenic and dramatic art. In particular, Philemon, Apollodorus, and especially Menander,[73] all known in later Roman comedy, forever changed the shape of dramatic consciousness.[74] The new comedians are true "moderns." In this sense, the "quarrel between ancients and moderns" is really between Aristophanes and Menander.

However, when looking for a "modern" identity today, we do not want to recognize our affinity with the ancient moderns of New Comedy, such as Menander. We moderns, for whom the desire to be modern is epitomized by the Romantics, prefer Aristophanes and Old Comedy. Our preference lies in the fact that they are "ancient" and can thus conveniently constitute our "other." In contrast, New Comedy is viewed as too modern, or as too closely resembling ourselves, and to be associated with it could lead to a profound identity crisis. Consequently, New Comedy goes largely unnoticed in its originality.

Among the relatively few modern critics who appreciate Menander is George Meredith, but this is mostly because he recognizes the exceptional importance of New Comedy for the development of modern European comedy.[75] Yet many ancient writers, including Virgil and Quintilian, highly praise Menander. Some, such as Plutarch, even acknowledge Menander's unconditional superiority over Aristophanes.[76] Menander is so admired in later antiquity that he becomes proverbial: "O Menander and life! Which of you is imitating which?"[77]

Unremarkably, however, previous critics could not properly appreciate Menander: little of his corpus remains extant. From more than one hundred comedies, we have only one (almost) fully preserved play, the *Dyskolos*; beyond that, there remain only a dozen that can be read and understood well,[78] along with a number of fabulae and fragments from unidentified plays. Finally, reliable translations and editions of Menander's extant corpus are only very recent.[79]

Despite the near obscurity of Menander's comedies, they play an important role in the development of the genre. It is also crucial to our understanding of the relationship between comedy and philosophy that we look closely at the changes introduced in comedy with the Nea. Thus, we should be aware that Menander, who received an excellent education in Athens, knew Aristotle's famous analysis of drama, the *Poetics*, the first "theory" of literature based on a remarkable knowledge of the poetic sources.[80] Aristotle's *Poetics* is both descriptive of the existing drama and prescriptive in its evaluations and suggestions of what the dramatic constituents should be. Yet Aristotle is aware he is a philosopher and not a playwright. In Menander, we see a reversal of the relationship between literary "theory" and "practice": he clearly pays attention to Aristotle's instructions when constructing the plot, depicting the characters, and implementing other elements of drama, appropriated to the new tasks of "new" comedy.[81]

As mentioned earlier, one of the major innovations of the Nea is the deliberate rejection of the chorus. This is a revolutionary move: the disappearance of the chorus means that the initially monodic communal action, which was counterbalanced by one actor in tragedy, two in Aeschylus, and three in Sophocles, becomes a polyphonic dialogical action, where each character casts off his or her mask and becomes a person capable of defining, and not just following, the action of the plot. In other words, the chorus becomes substituted by a plurality of unique individuals, not reducible to each other or the task they are performing. For this reason, the "heavy" stock characters become more subtly nuanced and humane. The personal caricature, first practiced by iambic poets, cedes to a much more probable and sympathetic depiction of characters.[82] Character types yield to unique individuals, gods to humans, and chorus participants who are virtually indistinguishable among themselves to finely sculpted personalities.

Thus, with New Comedy, the characters and actors portray recognizable and humane people, capable of honesty, kindness, and generosity, with whom the spectators can identify or from whom they can dissociate themselves. Instead of Old Comedy's toying with vulgarity (*aiskhrologia*), New Comedy uses hint and conjecture (*hyponoia*).[83] Correspondingly, in comic language vulgarity gives way to *decorum*. The language is often tailored to individuals in such a way as to portray their "distinctive modes and habits of speech."[84]

In this respect, Plato's dramatic portrayal of Socrates falls between Old and New Comedy. On the one hand, Socrates is a "heavy" and idiosyncratic character, especially in earlier dialogues, almost a parody of the thinker, the epitome of a dialectician overpowering all other characters in philosophical debate. On the other hand, in some later dialogues, such as the *Phaedo* and *Symposium*, Socrates is more refined in his personal features and can be glimpsed into—although never fully seen—as a person.

Out with the chorus goes the parabasis, the main choral event of Old Comedy.[85] The role of the chorus in general is reduced to a comic scene with a posse of inebriated young men, which was parodied by Plato in the *Symposium*, when drunken Alcibiades enters the scene of the banquet with a gang of friends.[86] The dialogue ends with the arrival of yet another "chorus" of drunken young people.[87] In Menander, the chorus was residually reduced to choral scenes between the acts, thus separating the piece into five acts.[88] It is "a conventional chorus of tipsy revelers, characterized . . . as Pan-worshipers, to perform the *entr'actes*."[89]

Once the parabasis is abandoned, the course of comedy is drastically and forever changed. Mythological and fantastic stories yield to everyday ones. The plot, relatively simple and straightforward in Aristophanes (e.g., in the *Clouds*), became more sophisticated and refined, more subtle and well constructed.

Euripides and Menander

When the "new" rebel against the "old," they usually do so by reproducing, although in a new and "sublated" form, some of the "original" features of those against whom they are revolting. Old Comedy was already seriously engaged not only in the portrayal of tragic playwrights but also in the appropriation of its techniques of characterization and plot building.[90] An "originary" source for the poetics of New Comedy appears to be the later tragedy of Euripides, a "philosopher of the scene."[91] Indeed, the affinity between Euripides and Menander was already stressed in antiquity.[92]

The influence of Euripides on the Nea can be seen in various features of New Comedy. To begin with, the sublime and mostly mythological stories of tragedy and the fantastic stories of Old Comedy were reproduced in New Comedy, though "downplayed," now based on events from everyday life.[93] Already in Euripides, we often come across scenes that can be read as deliberately "lowered." For example, a dispute between Medea and Jason resembles a quarrel between husband and wife.[94] Now, as in Euripides, the plot in Menander is well conceived and tightly constructed, presupposing a complicated intrigue. However, while Menander adopted and repeatedly used dramatic scenes from previous tragedy, he "lightened" them.[95] Such "secularized" familiar scenes presented a useful repertoire that can be recycled.[96] Since such scenes were already known to the public, they could be subtly and comically alluded to and easily played with. The appropriation and "recycling" of familiar tragic and—by that time—comic scenes became usual procedure, through contamination, in Roman comedy.

The influence of Euripides on the Nea is further revealed in Menander's use of *sententiae* (or maxims), as well as in the tendency against vulgarity in drama, not only in plot but also language, which in Euripides already becomes simpler and closer to life.[97] Further, in Euripides, we find a number of comic figures—precursors of the comic character of the slave or servant—that easily migrate into New Comedy, such as the drunkard, Heracles, in the *Alcestis*, and the reveller, Silenus, in the satyr play, *Cyclops*. Some scenes in Euripides can be easily included in a comedy, such as the exchange between Orestes and a Phrygian.[98] Interestingly, the cult of Dionysus that gives rise to comedy is depicted in the *Cyclops* and the *Bacchae*—although with a tragic death as the ending. Further, Euripides pays close attention to the subtle psychological portrayal of characters, especially when they are afflicted by passion and love. As the role of character increases in his plays, the role of the chorus diminishes. Originally a counterbalance to heroes, the chorus becomes a part of the integral action and thus practically equals a character in the play.[99] Thus, in principle, Euripides's tragedies can be staged *without* a chorus, similarly to the comedies of Menander, where, as said, the chorus is an atavism and plays only a perfunctory role.

Finally, the ending is important: as in New Comedy, some of Euripides's plays, such as the *Alcestis, Ion, Iphigenia in Tauris*, and *Helen*, already have *good endings*. However, New Comedy does not follow Euripides in his use of a *deus ex machina*, who, once the major collisions are portrayed, ends the play abruptly by resolving the tension and conflict. Such a sudden resolution may be comic, though it tends not to be,[100] and it never strictly follows from the plot, actions, and speeches of the heroes. The vestige of such an "unjustified" resolution is, nonetheless, preserved in the occasional works of comic fate.

Roman Comedy: Plautus and Terence

As a genre, comedy continues its development when the existing Greek New Comedy is picked up in Latin plays. This occurred with Rome's accession to a world power, when the world had already become cosmopolitan and, to a great extent, multicultural. The language of culture was Greek, so it had to be appropriated, together with its literature and drama. This appropriation in Roman comedy began in the works of Titus Maccius Plautus (254–184 BCE), who was born one generation after Menander, and came to fruition in Publius Terentius Afer, "Terence" (195 or 185 to 159 BCE), born around the time of Plautus's death. Many features of Greek New Comedy survive in Roman comedy. We see identifiable ("true-to-life") characters who are both typical and individual, sometimes grotesque but more often humane. The importance of love and lovers is maintained, as well as of the character of the slave. Deliberately simple yet refined language that avoids profanity and vulgarity and exemplifies propriety, so admired by the Roman philosopher Marcus Tullius Cicero, keeps its place. Further, seemingly buffoonish yet subtle jokes and the *quid pro quo* bewilderment that steers the development of action remain. We also see the diminution of the role of the chorus, which is matched by the increase of the role of the character's song or *canticum*. Finally, Roman comedy conserves the everydayness of the depicted situations, the organization of speech in dialogue that discloses a character and develops the plot, and a well-constructed and thought-through plot.

New comic characters, especially in Terence, were far removed from grotesque vulgarity and tried carefully to preserve *decorum*, the proper and dignified ways of speaking and behaving. Through this, the actors were able to appear not as mere masks but as subtly modeled and true-to-life personages. In New Comedy, the characters were not public figures but primarily family members. Frail and mundane, they were humane, often ready to help and be helped by others in a disinterested and self-sacrificial way.[101]

Both Plautus and Terence themselves were of humble origin. Moreover, for the Roman dramatic culture, Terence, to use Yirmiyahu Yovel's expression, was "the other within," since he was born a Carthaginian ("Afer") and a slave yet became Rome's greatest playwright. The "otherness" of a comic playwright allows him to keep a critical distance from the depicted culture, making observations and providing a diagnosis that becomes evident to everyone, though only *after* it has been made in comedy. The possibility of obtaining such reflective distance often comes from a playwright's belonging simultaneously to different cultures, without fully identifying with any one. For example, we note both the oppressed culture of memory and the dominating culture of imperialism in Terence (Carthaginian and Roman), Gogol (Ukrainian and Russian), Tom Stoppard (Czech and English), and Woody Allen (Jewish and American).

Although the social status of the writer in Rome was rather low (unlike in Greece and later in France), both Plautus and Terence were much appreciated by their respective contemporaries. It is no wonder that of Plautus's approximately 130 plays 21 survive and all six plays by Terence, who died young, have been preserved.[102] "After the death of Plautus," says the ancient Roman scholar Varro, "comedy mourned, the stage was deserted, and laughter, sport, jest, and countless numbers [*numeri innumeri*] all shed tears of sorrow."[103] However, "mourning comedy" appears to be an oxymoron, just as *numeri innumeri*. Yet these oxymorons appear to be intentionally comic: pragmatically self-contradictory, they suspend themselves and assert their opposites. For, in comedy, mourning is surmounted by the joy of life's going on, and the stiffness of the countable and definitive is suspended and turned into its opposite by the character's fooling around for the sake of the affirmation of life.

Although Roman comedy follows in the footsteps of the Greek Nea, "Attic salt" is seasoned with "Italian vinegar."[104] The Greek comic characters and plots were widely used, liberally fused, and continually recycled, yet they were set within the context of Roman moral and political life. More often than in Greek New Comedy, Terence, and especially Plautus, changed meter, which allowed them to make the play engaging and communicate subtle nuances of the mood and action.[105] Roman comedy also develops under the influence of various local comic, often folk, traditions.[106] In fact, Plautus's own *nomen*, *Maccius*, probably comes from the name of *Maccus*, a farcical jester in Atellana, whom he might have played as an actor. However, some of the later philhellenists—namely the Roman Romantics—considered the original Greek comedies superior to their later imitations, which is why Caesar addressed Terence "o dimidiate Menander" ("half-Menander").[107]

New and Modern Comedy

Finally, New Comedy exerted a major influence on modern comedy, both in the structure of the plot and the set of characters. Plautus and Terence spoke the European *lingua franca*, which allowed their works to be preserved, transmitted, closely read, and creatively reinterpreted, through the Middle Ages and into the Renaissance and modernity. They made a distinct impact on the Renaissance Italian theater (particularly in the *commedia erudita*), on Machiavelli's *La Mandragola*, on Shakespeare, Ben Jonson, Molière, on the Restoration comedy of Wycherley, Etherege, and Aphra Behn,[108] and on Fonvizin, all the way up to the contemporary existential comedy of Beckett. This influence has been discussed in detail in contemporary scholarship.[109] For my purpose, a few examples will suffice.

Shakespeare named two characters in *The Taming of the Shrew* after those in Plautus's *Mostellaria*: Grumio (the good country slave) and Tranio (the bad town slave). Ben Jonson's Cordatus, in the introduction to *Every Man Out of His Humour* (1599), provides a brief yet meaningful account of the development of "Comoedia" from Susarion and Epicharmus, through Old Comedy, up to New Comedy, noting with approval that comedy

> chang'd since, in Menander, Philemon, Cecilius, Plautus, and the rest; who haue vtterly excluded the Chorus, altered the property of the persons, their names, and natures, and augmented it with all liberty, according to the elegancie and disposition of those times wherein, they wrote. I see not then, but we should enjoy the same licence, or free power, to illustrate and heighten our inuention as they did; and not to bee tyed to those strict and regular formes, which the nicenesse of a few (who are nothing but forme) would thrust vpon vs.[110]

Clearly, Jonson identifies his methods of composition with those of the Nea, even when trying to overcome them. And Molière, while studying at the Collège de Clermont, attended and might even have performed in the Latin plays of Plautus and Terence, which he knew well. Terence is explicitly mentioned by Molière as a great poet, along with Horace, Virgil, and Catullus.[111] Not surprisingly, Molière's Harpagon in *The Miser* (*L'avare*) follows Menander's Knemon in the *Dyskolos*, which itself follows Plautus.[112] Among French philosophers and literary theorists, Denis Diderot was a great admirer of Terence. The perception of a profound affinity of modern comedy with New Comedy, which is itself "modern" vis-à-vis Old Comedy, is summarized by Charles Augustin Sainte-Beuve when he exclaims, "For the love of me love Terence."[113]

Modern comedy thus remains New because of the continual historical transmission and constant rethinking of the tradition, which keeps comedy alive and, to use Agnes Heller's word, makes it "immortal"—always psychologically engaging and never philosophically outdated.

Reflections on Comedy

One can write a literary work; one can reflect on a written literary work; and one can write a literary work that reflects on another literary work, on itself, or on literary work in general. Aristophanes already reflected on drama—on tragedy by means of comedy—in the final part of the *Frogs*, through a parody of an agon between Aeschylus and Euripides. By doing so, Aristophanes both *discussed* the norms of a dramatic work, its parts (e.g., the prologue), and its language and also *illustrated* its use. Plato, in turn, when occasionally discussing poetry and drama, provided a philosophical analysis by using dialectical reasoning that often seems inconclusive. Yet Plato's discussion is itself an impressive literary work written in the form of a dramatic theatrical dialogue that can also be presented onstage. And when Aristotle wrote his *Poetics*, he did so explicitly *not* as a literary work but as a modern scholarly work that reflected on the structure of a dramatic piece and the arrangement of its parts.

While making such maneuvers, one reflects on what has been done already or, in rare cases, on what is being done at the moment. For the most part, the owl of Minerva flies at dusk. Philosophical thinking comes late—perhaps too late—after the thought has already happened. The great tradition of Greek tragedy is already there when Plato and especially Aristotle provide its systematic explanation and dissection. However, when New Comedy finds its completion in Terence, it takes a while to give an explication of its action, meaning, and constituents. Cicero, who quotes Terence about seventy times in his works and occasionally speaks about comedy, does not dedicate a single special treatise to comedy. Neither does Horace, who introduces the *res comica* in his *Ars poetica*[114] and yet provides only general prescripts of the kind "you must note the manners [*mores*] of each age, and give a befitting tone [*decor*] to shifting natures and their years," taken seriously by later playwrights, including Molière.[115]

The Nea did not have an Aristotle to explain its own philosophical significance. Not until the mid-fourth century CE did Aelius Donatus compose a most prominent Latin commentary on Terence, the yardstick of comic art.[116] The commentary contains references to Livius Andronicus, Cicero, and Horace and discusses five of the six Terentian comedies.[117] Following the pattern of Aristotle's distinctions, Evanthius (in a preserved excerpt from *De comoedia*) defined various constituents of comedy. These are mostly in reference to Terence and Plautus but also some other Latin comic writers.[118] Evanthius introduced the famous and later much used distinction of the four parts of comedy—*prologue, protasis, epitasis,* and *catastrophe*—which describes the structure and development of comic plot and which I will discuss below. According to Evanthius,

> comedy is a fable[119] involving diverse arrangements of civic and private concerns, in which one learns what is useful in life and what on the contrary is to be avoided. The Greeks define it in this way: "Comedy is a harmful arrangement

of private and civil deeds." Cicero says that comedy is an imitation of life, a mirror of custom, an image of truth.[120]

The ancient tradition thus sees comedy as popular and down-to-earth, meant to depict the daily life of ordinary people represented by plausible characters and through them to show that which is useful and that which is to be avoided.

CHAPTER 2

The Moderns: The Romantic Loss of Comedy

"Italian Theory"

Of all the authors of New Comedy, Menander was probably still known in the Middle Ages. However, unlike Aristophanes's comedies, his works did not survive the medieval era, since they were perceived as frivolous and, hence, out of line with the current morality. Plautus, Terence, and Saint Jerome's teacher, Donatus, were read, owing to the interest in Latin literature in the Middle Ages.[1] Nonetheless, ancient comedy had a limited impact on medieval comedy in general, which had a great variety of forms.[2]

The real revival of comedy would have to wait for the Renaissance, with regard not only to the production of comedy but also to a systematic reflection on poetics in which the discussion of comedy played a major role. Sixteenth-century Italian poetics scholarship is a whole world of its own still in need of rediscovery and proper appreciation. Among the studies on this exceptionally rich tradition, two stand out: Bernard Weinberg's fundamental work and Marvin T. Herrick's book, which remains a classic.[3]

The so-called "Italian Theory" of the sixteenth century began with numerous commentaries on Aristotle's *Poetics* and *Rhetoric* and Horace's *Ars poetica*.[4] Scholars often found intermingling theory between these two thinkers. Others were important constituents of the debate: the discussions of Cicero and Quintilian, the commentaries of Donatus and Honoratus on Terence, and the writings of numerous Latin rhetoricians and grammarians of the second through fourth century CE.[5] This debate included philological and textual disputations and aimed to establish rhetorical and grammatical figures. Interestingly, however, it also turned to systematic philosophical interpretation.[6] Italian scholars developed an increasingly elaborate discussion of new genres and sophisticated poetic theory, which itself arose within the "quarrel between ancients and moderns."

Renaissance and early modern scholarship did not simply remain within their own spheres—they also affected contemporary poetry and drama.[7] Commentators writing about Aristotle, Horace, Donatus, and various aspects of poetic art reveal an impressive revival of interest in poetic theory—including a discussion of comedy.[8] Every *homme de lettres* of the sixteenth century, it seems, either wrote poetry or wrote about poetry. Comedy studiously followed the precepts of Terence and Donatus regarding the key elements of the work: the poetic style, the work's sententiousness, the didactic and moral message it contained, its structure, and the classical unity of form were all of interest.

And yet, despite the revered attention it was receiving, comedy soon found itself under attack by zealous religious militants who considered theater—and comedy in particular—sinful, profane, and immoral. In *A Refutation of the Apology of Actors* (1615), a certain I. G. (apparently, a Puritan clergyman, one John Green) keenly enumerated the vices promoted by comedy: "love, lust, lechery, bawdry, scortation, adultery, uncleanness, pollution, wantonness, chambering, courting, jeating, mocking, flouting, foolery, venery, drabbery, knavery, cozenage, cheating, hypocrisy, flattery, and the like."[9] Strictly speaking, these accusations were, of course, true. Yet, if comedy is at all didactic, then, among other things, it teaches—not by preaching but by showing—that what is meant should not necessarily coincide with what is said. In other words, from Greek philosophy we gain a healthy, but not excessive, dose of subversive and liberating Socratic irony, which teaches us to properly appreciate comedy. Consequently, versed in philosophically minded poetic theory, modern comedy was capable of defending itself against overzealous religious criticism, which was itself comic and entertaining in its viciousness. Comedy did so *both* artistically and philosophically *within* comedy.[10]

One can thus tell a history of poetics.[11] Importantly, however, the Renaissance debate about poetics and drama—modern, on its own account—was set within the horizon of philosophical thinking of a very distinct kind: the thinking of Aristotle, with all its logical systematic distinctions, was reproduced and developed by Renaissance commentators.[12] And yet this tradition of philosophical deliberation about the fictional, about literature and drama, was itself *both* historical and systematic. It remains such until our own day, even in efforts to overcome this tradition, as such attempts are only meaningful vis-à-vis the distinctions they are meant to overthrow. Writing about it here, I am inevitably reproducing this tradition myself.

In the Italian discussions, commentators reappropriated the ancient philosophical and philological tradition of thinking about comedy in such a way that influenced a new comedy—as Menander had done through Aristotle's *Poetics*. Through this, they assured that comedy lived on within a tradition.

Yet, in the case of the Renaissance, comedy as a genre was simply identified with New Comedy. Admiration for Plautus and, especially, Terence was universal. Thus, Francesco Robortello unambiguously accepted Plutarch's elevation of New Comedy over and above Old Comedy's buffoonery and slander.[13] Similarly, Antonio Sebastiano Minturno, in his dialogue "The Art of Comedy," said that New Comedy "didn't bite the living people like the first [kind of Old Comedy, in Aristophanes], nor did it make fun of the ancient poets like the second [Cratinus, Antiphanes, Plato the Comic], but, having eliminated the chorus completely, without criticizing others, by introducing imaginary characters, and representing things and habits of private citizens, it amended life."[14]

Comedy was thus praised as capable of amending life for ordinary people without humiliating them. It could show them the best of life without becoming too serious, didactic, or moralistic.[15] Since the sixteenth-century theorists mostly followed Aristotle, they accepted his definition of genre by its purpose, which, in the case of comedy, was the *imitation* of the characters of *common people* and their actions in *ordinary situations*. For Lucio Olimpio Giraldi, "Terence's intention was to show the ugliness of foul things so that men would abstain from them, not so that they would follow them; and to propose to them the praiseworthy and virtuous and honest ones so that they might embrace them and adorn themselves with them."[16] Comedy depicted, according to Minturno, "not heroic, not illustrious or great [as in tragedy]; but low, humble, sometimes mediocre."[17] This allowed, in Riccoboni's words, for "a secure understanding [*complexio*] of private and civil affairs."[18] And yet, as we know, for Plato, imitation was always removed from being and truth, and thus it either had to be altogether avoided or at least overcome. When Aristotle spoke about imitation in his *Poetics*, however, he did not specify what he meant by the term.[19] Therefore, commentators needed to clarify what kind of imitation comedy represented. For Minturno,

although Cicero defines [comedy] for us as an imitation of reality, mirror of custom, image of truth; we could nevertheless say, according to Aristotle's opinion, that comedy is nothing but imitation of some festive event and of some comic aspect of civil life, or of domestic and private life, represented in the theater by a complete and perfect subject of appreciable magnitude; this is achieved not simply by narration but by introducing characters of humble and mean life, equal to others in actions and thought, and apt to correct human life with harmonious and pleasant sayings, not deprived of songs, dances, and props; and in such a way that each part of the comedy be well constructed and appropriate.[20]

Comedy was thus an imitation of things, characters, and actions both good and bad in their ordinariness or "lowliness." But in imitating life and what is alive, comedy revealed a profoundly humane and democratic character by portraying the humanly, morally, and politically important in the seemingly ordinary and even mediocre. This revealed comedy's goodness, which was best seen in its purpose, which, *qua telos*, shows itself at the very end—in Minturno's words—as "a pleasing and gay ending."[21] As in Aristotle, comedy in the Renaissance was commonly opposed to tragedy. Tragedy has a good beginning but a bad ending, so that we do not desire the kind of life it shows. With comedy, it is exactly the opposite: A troublesome beginning yields a good ending, which represents the desired life possible for all.

Romantic Digression

If Renaissance comedy and poetic theory represented a continuity with ancient tradition, then Romanticism constituted a break. A great interest in antiquity, rediscovered in the eighteenth-century German art historian Johann Winckelmann's time, was still a part of the ongoing *querelle* in the attempt to understand—or construct—oneself as modern. One seeks to be a unique yet culturally and historically shaped *self* in the face of the other who, if not given, has to be (re)invented. It is within this effort of cultural self-reevaluation and understanding that the German Romantic and post-Romantic infatuation with antiquity, and particularly with tragedy, must be located. It can be seen in thinkers as different as G. W. F. Hegel, Wilhelm Dilthey, and Martin Heidegger, all for whom the discussion of antiquity is framed in terms of thinking about—and overcoming—the logical and historical inevitability of the modern self.[22]

However, when the Romantics spoke about "antiquity," they primarily had in mind *Greek* culture, from the archaic times of Homer through the conquest of Alexander, reaching its peak in the classical epoch, which was deemed the climax and epitome of the whole of antiquity and thus fit the position of the cultural "other" of modernity. Nobody else deserved this: Hellenism was already in decline, and the Romans were considered only epigones and imitators of classical Greek antiquity. All other known cultures and epochs were shifted elsewhere, mostly to the shoulder of the highway of modernity's development. However, a new philosophy of history, most notably in Hegel, found a decent—though not central—place for every culture: they were considered preliminary to modern culture and, therefore, deserving of little attention. The exception is the cultural and historical other needed for the construction of the modern self, that is, classical Greek culture, which alone had to be engaged with seriously.

This need for an ancient other explains why the Romantics had an uneasy attitude toward the Romans, who were too inexcusably modern and very much like "ourselves." Due to their similarity, the Romans, including the great and highly original Neoplatonic thinkers, had to be suppressed and mostly disregarded. They were not regarded as original but rather as secondary to and imitative of the Greeks. In the Romantic view, a historical and aesthetic reconstruction had to explain and justify the purposefully achieved terminal greatness of the (German) moderns. Consequently, Hegel begrudgingly gave the Roman world a place in his philosophy of history—but only as a step toward "us moderns."

It is worth pausing to justify Hegel's acceptance into the Romantic pantheon, as he can legitimately be considered a transitional figure from the Enlightenment to Romanticism. Indeed, together with Hans-Georg Gadamer, one might take modernity as defined by two types of thinking.[23] One is the Enlightenment, in which all historical and cultural occurrences were viewed from the panoptical point of view of a universal Reason that comes to its full reflective historical self-realization, vis-à-vis its other, as a necessary result of historical development. This is an embodiment of a strongly historiographic program, which intended to consider any phenomenon from an already accepted point of view and within a preconceived interpretative theoretical frame. On this account, any "fact" was selected only if it fit in; otherwise, it was ignored. The other pole is Romanticism, which, on the contrary, suspended generalizing claims as abstractions and emphasized the uniqueness of each cultural phenomenon and person as equal and comparable with, but not deducible from, other epochs and individuals. If this is the case, then Hegel clearly exemplified the features of both the Enlightenment and the Romantic approaches. On the one hand, he embodied the Enlightenment agenda by explaining the rise of modern self, culture, state, institutions, art, religion, science, and philosophy within a totalizing development of spirit. This inevitably ends in an absolute (knowledge or idea) that teleologically fulfills and redeems the sufferings of humankind. On the other hand, Hegel was also close to the Romantics, insofar as he tried to be genuinely perceptive of historical differences, particularly in the discussion of aesthetic phenomena, which, although always subsumed under a general interpretative scheme, are to be understood from within their own makeup.

Hegel's Unfulfilled Comedy

Among philosophical theories of tragedy today, the most discussed are those of Aristotle and Hegel. However, neither thinker said much about comedy: Aristotle promised a book that we do not have, and Hegel was brief on the subject, providing rather different interpretations of comedy in his *Phenomenology of Spirit* (1807) and *Lectures on Aesthetics* (1820–1828, published

1835), which is the work of Hegel and Hotho. Comedy thus remains largely "unwritten" by philosophers, a desired topic that they hope and promise to elaborate yet never properly come to. There is something in comedy that irritates philosophy, something that seems to escape a philosophical grasp.

This irritation and bewilderment were seen in Hegel's treatment of comedy. For Hegel, every phenomenon or term, be it logical, historical, or aesthetic, had to be considered within a preconceived and therefore biased philosophical agenda. This meant that it had to be inscribed into a system—preferably, triadic and dialectically organized. For Hegel, as for the other Romantics, ancient Greek art was the paradigm of artificial, man-made beauty, an ancient "wonder" that still inspired awe in the moderns and called for an explanation. Thus, the *Phenomenology* traced the (self-)transformation of consciousness, moving through the shapes of self-consciousness, reason, and spirit, and finally arriving by way of religion at "absolute knowledge," which was apparently gained in Hegel's very *Phenomenology* as a redemptive teleological act of the history of human spirit.[24] There, the discussion of art was confined mostly to classical Greek art considered within, and in reference to, religion. Art was thus not fully autonomous for Hegel but an expression of something else—of religion, which itself was only a necessary stage in the progressive march of spirit. Greek art was proclaimed to be "artistic religion," mediating between the religion of nature (in Persia, India, and Egypt) and the "absolute religion" of revelation in Christianity. Greek art was further divided into three categories: the abstract, which was embodied in statue, hymn, and cult; the living, which was seen in the mysteries of Ceres (curiously enough, a Roman goddess) and Bacchus, in bread and wine (which apparently prefigured Holy Communion), and in the beautiful athlete; and the spiritual, which embraced epic, tragedy, and comedy. Greek art for Hegel thus found its end and completion in comedy.[25]

In the later *Aesthetics*, or the *Lectures on Fine Art*, Hegel still considered art a realization of the idea of artistic beauty, which in its development was not fully autonomous but became meaningful only in reference to various historical forms of religion. The end of this movement, rigidly and schematically distributed into triads, was achieved in a fully developed subjectivity, which happened precisely in Romanticism. Part III of the *Aesthetics* presented the equally triadically organized system of individual arts, which embraced architecture, sculpture, and the Romantic arts. The latter were divided into painting, music, and poetry; poetry was further distinguished into epic, lyric (absent in the *Phenomenology*), and dramatic poetry;[26] and dramatic poetry was made up of tragedy, comedy, and (mostly modern) drama. There, comedy was not the completion of the arts but its penultimate step. Yet drama, as Hegel himself recognized, was clearly defined.[27] At the same time, the voluminous lectures on aesthetics ended with a rather passing reference to comedy: "[T]he modern world has developed a type of comedy which is truly comical and truly poetic . . . As a brilliant example of this sort of thing I will name Shakespeare once again, in conclusion, but without going into detail."[28] Ironically, referring to Shakespeare, Hegel failed to recognize in him the disguised New Comedy of Menander and Terence.

Comedy thus stood at the end of Greek art and almost at the end of drama, the highest form of the Romantic art. However, Greek comedy for Hegel ended (historically and teleologically) with Old Comedy, with Aristophanes, who is "the comic author par excellence."[29] We find exactly the same attitude in all the Romantics, for whom Greek comedy reached its dramatic and philosophical climax in Old Comedy, particularly in Aristophanes. Thus, Søren Kierkegaard, Hegel's obstinate critic, found the portrayal of Socrates in Aristophanes's *Clouds* even more convincing and precise than in Plato's dialogues.[30] The first philosophical critics of comedy, Plato and Aristotle, did not know New Comedy *yet*, whereas the properly modern philosophical critics of comedy, the Romantics, did not know New Comedy *already*, or rather chose not to know it, since it did not fit their system of arts and the construction of the other.

Hegel practically disregarded New Comedy, as it did not suit his interpretative historical scheme of the development of spirit, religion, and art. New Comedy was too new and dangerously close to Roman comedy. This made New Comedy almost invisible and negligible for the moderns. For this reason, Hegel did not recognize it in its uniqueness in his discussion of the *new* drama.

Consequently, Hegel, who knew ancient literature fairly well, *never* mentioned Menander in any of his works. However, he cannot be reproached for this, as Menander was not yet properly published in his time, being known only through a few fragments. On the other hand, Plautus and Terence *were* known, but only *too well*: they were school authors whom one read when learning Latin. Their comedy seemed too much like "ours" and was considered merely a "comedy of manners," lacking the puns and colorfulness of the great cultural characters like Socrates and Euripides. *The* comic playwright, Aristophanes, was referred to several dozen times in Hegel's whole corpus; Plautus was mentioned only three times in the lectures on aesthetics and once in an earlier work. Hegel mentioned Terence only twice in his lectures on aesthetics, merely to note in passing that Plautus and Terence imitate the Greeks.[31]

Hegel's discussion of comedy accepted the familiar Aristotelian opposition between tragedy and comedy,[32] in which tragedy corresponded to the sublime and comedy to the vulgar. Even the German term for comedy, *Lustspiel* ("lust-play"), offended a cultivated ear. By contrast, the characters in tragedy were predominantly aristocrats, because, for Hegel, "the perfect freedom of will and production . . . is realized in the idea of royalty." Comedy, on the contrary, depicted the "lower classes," who were not free, in every way dependent upon circumstances, authority, and their social and political position. Comedy was for those who did not—and could not—determine themselves in their actions and thus lacked self-reliance. In other words, tragedy was for aristocrats, whereas comedy was for plebs:

> [I]n comedy, individuals have the right to spread [*aufzuspreizen*] themselves however they wish and can. In their willing and fancying and in their idea of themselves, they may claim an independence [*Selbstständigkeit*] which is immediately annihilated by themselves and by their inner and outer dependence [*Abhängigkeit*]. But, above all, this assumed self-reliance [*Beruhen auf sich*] founders on external conditions and the distorted attitude of individuals to them. The power of these conditions is on a totally different level for the lower classes from what it is for rulers and princes.[33]

In this respect, Hegel continued the conservative and antidemocratic Aristophanic tradition. We could ask to which of these classes Hegel, a bourgeois at the royal service, imagined himself to belong.[34] Of course, any genre for Hegel was historically conditioned as a necessary stage in the progression of spirit and hence at a certain point should be inevitably overcome. And yet Hegel seemed to yearn for the heroic, the noble, and the sublime.

The lesson we learn here is that comedy shows the base and vulgar, the null and odd, the not-worthy-in-itself. In this respect comedy differs from irony, which targets the bad: "[T]he comic must be restricted to showing that what destroys itself is something inherently null [*ein an sich selbst Nichtiges*], a false and contradictory phenomenon [appearance, *Erscheinung*], a whim, e.g., an oddity, a particular caprice in comparison with a mighty passion, or even a *supposedly* tenable principle and firm maxim."[35] However, in ancient literature, the denunciation of vices was the prerogative of satire, rather than of irony.

Unsurprisingly, in discussing tragedy, comedy, and drama in the *Aesthetics*, Hegel recognized in antiquity a third dramatic genre that was not clearly defined, which he needed for systematic reasons, precisely *qua* the *third*. Yet in antiquity, this third genre was identified, on the one hand, with the satyric drama[36] and, on the other, with tragicomedy.[37] According to Hegel, most modern plays were of this kind: "What they aim at producing is not a genuinely poetic emotion but only one that people ordinarily feel, or else they seek to reform the public or merely to entertain it."[38] However, satyric drama, as in the satyr play, differed from Greek comedy and, contrary to Hegel's claim, was *not* imitated in Roman comedy. Moreover, this third type of drama came in Hegel's lectures on aesthetics *after* the discussion of tragedy and comedy, though he claimed it was *intermediate*, "in the center" between them.

Comedy, for Hegel, was thus a poetic and dramatic enterprise whose meaning was established in a reconstruction of the development of religion. Particularly, the reconstruction dealt with artistic religion, where the spirit realized itself as self-consciousness (in the *Phenomenology*) or subjectivity (in the *Aesthetics*). The theme of tragedy was the divine, and yet subjectivity was comic: as reflective self-consciousness, it both produced a comedy and depicted itself in comedy. Self-consciousness is the self that "takes off the mask" and dares to become self-reliable as "the individual consciousness in the certainty of itself that exhibits itself as this absolute power."[39] For Hegel, this inevitably led to the destruction of the traditional gods: since individual self-consciousness trusted itself, it did not need the gods as independent and defining powers in the world. Hence, the gods became only imaginary, the product of the independent and self-certain artistic self-consciousness. Consequently, fate, which reigned over both humans and gods in epics, and over humans in tragedy, became internalized in comedy. And because self-consciousness was independent, it now assumed the role of fate as the fate of the gods.[40] However, since self-consciousness could freely imagine and construct anything, any character or plot, the gods became *anything*, "simple thoughts" devoid of any particular content, Aristophanes's "clouds." Comic self-consciousness, then, was a force that defined, and into which disappeared and dissolved, both nature and gods. For Hegel, however, the self-determination of comic consciousness was still arbitrary and insufficient for the ultimately grounded self-reflective knowledge: self-consciousness still needed to move from in-itself to for-itself, to become fully self-accountable and reflective, in order to reach the end of its journey. To that end, one needed to "overcome" or "sublate" the vulgarity of the comic through the nobility of suffering and resurrection in the revealed religion. Hegel was thus unwilling and unable to accept comedy on its own grounds: it was only a step, a brick, a moment within the project called "antiquity," our constructed cultural and historical other, which reflected and negatively defined us within the project called "modernity."

Since the individual self is capable of producing (that is, imagining) comic characters—among whom are also the gods, as well as the situations into which they become entangled—this self is a *negative force* (*die negative Kraft*). In its negativity, the self is capable of destroying even the gods.[41] This self coincides with the person (*Person*), who is also a mask in comedy and can represent anyone at will. In this sense, the comic self takes off its mask but only because its face is indistinguishable from the mask: it can assume any face at will.

And yet such a demiurgic self or subjectivity is also *contingent*, insofar as it is subjected both to external contingency (*Zufälligkeit*) and *its own* willing and actions (*Wollen und Handeln*).[42] For Hegel, this was only a negative determination, precisely because this comic subjectivity could be anything or take on any role. This self, therefore, determined the gods as pure abstractions but did not really determine itself. For it still did not realize the *noncontingency* at play—in the coincidence of the "necessity" of the development of the spirit with real freedom—where "what should be" would finally be reconciled with "what is." Fate itself, then, became a mere arbitrary abstraction and was effectively extinguished with the end of Greek art in comedy—that is, again, in Aristophanes.

Since such a comic self determines itself in its willing and actions, it is a *free* self, free from the *fear* of death and fate. Such freedom, however, is only negative and arbitrary and thus is not the rationally achieved and morally deserved freedom of autonomy. In comic freedom, artistic self-consciousness becomes *happy* consciousness. Yet Hegel was not happy with this happiness. For him, the comic consciousness was the opposite of the unhappy consciousness (*das unglückliche Bewußtsein*) of the death of gods and God.[43] Hegel was troubled by the foolishness of comic happiness, because it was not "deserved," not obtained by suffering, by death and resurrection, by an impossible overcoming of the split between the "ought" of the law and the "is" of its violation in the arbitrariness of will. Historically speaking, Hegel wanted the imagined Greek other to be subjected, negated by, and reconciled in the Lutheran self. As Reiner Schürmann has argued, the modern self, or "ego," was born only through a free transgression of established moral and historical—"divine"— norms.[44] The modern self was inevitably split within itself and had to suffer through the unhappy consciousness. Thus, it needed its other, which the modern self found (or thought it found) in the constructed other of ancient Greece. This modern self put all its hope into surmounting the split between the "ought" and the "is." This is an act in which the self overcomes its finitude both by acting morally and also suspending morality, as it awaits the divine assistance of the historically and artistically self-revealing spirit.[45] Hegel wanted the final act of his own philosophical drama to be the epic battle in which the human finite self would finally overcome the tragedy of the death of God and embody the divine comedy of the ultimate liberation.

Hegel applied his dialectic to various areas of his philosophy, including aesthetics, which not only entailed a triadic (thesis-antithesis-synthesis) division of the subject matter but also presupposed a constant search for contradiction as a defining moment of each phenomenon. In particular, the individual self was comic for Hegel—not only because it was capable of contriving a comedy by extending the action into the realm of the imaginary and by manipulating gods and characters but also because it *itself* was inherently contradictory and thus incapable of reconciling the order of the ideal with that of crude reality.

Thus, for Hegel, the comic as such was embodied in the comic character, the paradigmatic example of which was Don Quixote, who personified "the comic contradiction between an intelligible [*verständigen*] self-ordered world and an isolated mind which proposes to create this order and stability solely by himself and by chivalry, whereby it could only be overturned."[46] Yet, because comedy always rests on contingency, it inevitably implies "contradictory contrasts both between aims in themselves and also between their objects and the accidents of character and external circumstances."[47] Moreover, since comic characters are intrinsically contradictory, they cannot *accomplish anything*.[48] Comedy, then, cannot really resolve any conflict by itself.

And yet a major problem surfaces with Hegel's interpretation of comedy: he repeatedly stressed the centrality of the self-conscious self, or subjectivity, in the constitution of comedy—as its author, spectator, and inherently contradictory actor. Consequently, comedy was always judged from a point of view of the *subject* on both its historical and logical journey to full realization, reflective clarification, and ultimate justification. Comedy was the victory of subjectivity (*Subjektivität*) in its infinite assurance, confidence, or reliability (*Sicherheit*).[49] Subjectivity is comic insofar as it "makes its own actions contradictory and so brings them to nothing, while remaining tranquil and self-assured in the process."[50] Such self-assuredness is comic precisely because it is based on the irresolvable contradiction between the ideal ends and their inevitable absence from the contingency of comic circumstances and characters.

Hegel's emphasis on subjectivity explains why he paid practically no attention to the *structure* of comedy, its plot and development toward a resolution of the conflict. Besides, since the opposition of comedy to tragedy was crucial for Hegel's reconstruction of art, he maintained that "comedy has for its basis [foundation, *Grundlage*] and starting-point what tragedy may end with, namely an absolutely reconciled and cheerful heart."[51] Yet, in this case, it is unclear why Hegel ended his own lectures with a "reconciled and cheerful heart" and a reference to comedy. Despite his repeated claim that comedy necessarily comes after tragedy, Hegel seemed to want to stay with the sublime tragic reconciliation of the royal tragedy rather than sink into the coarseness of comedy. No wonder that at the very end of his *Aesthetics* Hegel complains that, standing at the very peak of the development of art, comedy leads to art's complete disintegration.[52] Tragically for Hegel, comedy buries art, so the end of the long philosophical story of art is not comedy but the mourning of the end of art in its comic self-destruction. Yet even a perfunctory glance at New Comedy shows that Hegel was wrong in claiming that comedy starts with reconciliation and ends in havoc—for comedy works exactly the other way around, always resolving the conflict at the end *as* its end. Hegel intended to follow his firmly established scheme of comedy: comic subjectivity, the overlord and fate of the divine, moves within contingency and ends in a liberating yet vulgar happy consciousness that still needs to be overcome in the freedom of a final *apokatastasis*.

However, comedy, by building its plot after a philosophical argument (and also by entrusting the motion of such a plot to the model comic character: not Don Quixote but Sancho Panza), can, and does, come to a resolution of a seemingly insurmountable conflict.[53] Yet Hegel did not want a definitive resolution within a particular dramatic genre: Hegel wanted resolution within the grand drama of his own philosophy, which he weaved in such a way as not to miss any single category, term, or genre and in which he found a deserving place for each possible constituent. Unfortunately, Hegel remained unaware that his effort was comic and that he himself was a comic character. Curiously enough, while Hegel's philosophy is comic in his own sense, it is also comic in the sense of the Nea: if one considers Hegel's ultimate reconciliatory effort a failure, then it is comic in Hegel's sense; if a success, then in the sense of New Comedy. But there is a kind of comedy capable of ultimately rational resolution within itself: it is Greek *and* Roman New Comedy, although Hegel remains unable to fit it within his interpretative scheme.

Freedom from Restraint: Romantic Literary Criticism

In 1808, August Wilhelm Schlegel delivered 30 lectures on dramatic art and literature in Vienna, which are perhaps among the defining texts of modern literary criticism and still represent comparative literature at its best.[54] Schlegel's knowledge of ancient and modern literature was most impressive (even better than Hegel's), and his approach to the analysis of literary texts in their history and structure was exemplary in Romanticism. Consequently, Schlegel's treatments of comedy—four of his lectures were dedicated to ancient comedy—are particularly instructive.[55]

In his attempt to understand comedy, Schlegel accepted three historically established oppositions.

(1) First, Schlegel assumed the opposition of comedy to tragedy as its complementary genre.[56] As previously mentioned, this tradition goes back to Aristotle and continues uninterruptedly into modernity.[57] Similarly to Hegel, Schlegel took ancient comedy to be paradigmatically represented in Aristophanes's Old Comedy, which, however, was "a complete parody of the tragic form."[58] The ideal of the sublime and uplifting—*serious*—drama was realized in tragedy—primarily, in Aeschylus and Sophocles. In this line of thinking, tragedy is "the highest earnestness of poetry; Comedy altogether is

sportive."[59] Tragedy is mournful, comedy mirthful. The very etymology of the two genres suggests such an understanding: *Trauerspiel* ("sorrow-play") versus *Lustspiel* ("lust-play"). Tragedy shows the "dignified, noble, and grand in human nature" and thus corresponds to "a monarchy without despotism." Comedy, on the contrary, corresponds to democracy and shows "a dependence on the animal part of human nature."[60] Schlegel wrote further that tragedy "delights in harmonious unity," while "comedy flourishes in a chaotic exuberance,"[61] and that tragedy, "by painful emotions, elevates us to the most dignified views of humanity," while "comedy, on the other hand, by its jocose and depreciatory view of all things, calls forth the most petulant hilarity."[62] Comedy, therefore, is unruly and as such exhibits "the apparent want of aim, and freedom from all restraint in the exercise of the mental powers."[63]

The main driving force of comedy thus understood is wit as caprice or arbitrariness (*Willkür*). Wit indulges in freedom uninhibited by any considerations of objective necessity or self-imposed rules (such as the "three unities" of action, time, and space), which governed later classicist French comedy.[64] The comic poet, then, could arbitrarily devise any character or action.[65] Only a proper balance in the development of *both* characters and plot had to be respected by the author, in order to avoid the one-sidedness of either the play of characters or the play of intrigue.[66] The joyous anarchic freedom of comedy implies licentiousness in the intercourse between the sexes, which, for Schlegel, was all about either the passion of sensual enjoyment or the duty of marriage, neither of which for him knew modern "gallantry."[67] Schlegel was afraid of explicit sexuality and was "disgusted with the unveiled sensuality of the love intrigues of the Greek Comedy," because apparently such sensuality overstepped the limits that "have been fixed by nature herself to sensual excess."[68] Comedy had to achieve "the unity and harmonious blending of the sensual with the mental."[69] Rational understanding (*Verstand*) alone was capable of checking the uncontrolled impulses and keeping humans from indulging in libertine pleasures. In this respect,

> comedy bears a very near affinity to Fable: in the Fable [*die Fabel*] we have animals endowed with reason, and in Comedy we have men serving their animal propensities with their understanding. By animal propensities I mean sensuality, or, in a still more general sense, self-love [*Selbstliebe*]. As heroism and self-sacrifice raise the character to a tragic elevation [*adelt*], so the true comic personages are complete egotists [*ausgemachte Egoisten*]. This must, however, be understood with due limitation: we do not mean that Comedy never portrays the social instincts, only that it invariably represents them as originating in the natural endeavour after our own happiness [*aus dem natürlichen Streben nach unserm eignen Glück*].[70]

The unrestrained freedom of comedy ultimately means that comedy is not concerned with morality as "the call of duty." Nonetheless, in comedy morality is not violated but rather suspended. Schlegel applied the terms of Kantian ethics to describe this situation: the moral apophthegms of comedy are the "maxims of experience," yet we do *not* gain the knowledge of our duty (*Pflichten*) from experience, which can only give us knowledge of the "profitable or detrimental." As Schlegel stated, "The instruction of Comedy [*die Belehrung des Lustspiels*] does not turn on the dignity of the object proposed [*die Würdigkeit der Zwecke*] but on the sufficiency of the means [*die Tauglichkeit der Mittel*] employed. It is . . . the doctrine of prudence [*Klugheitslehre*]; the morality of consequences and not of motives [*die Moral des Erfolgs und nicht die der Triebfedern*]."[71] Comedy, for Schlegel, must only keep the spectators "in a mirthful tone of mind" and hence "aloof from any moral considerations and appreciation of its personages."[72] Morality is thus alien to comedy, which is why many modern critics, including Jean-Jacques Rousseau, reproached comedy for being immoral.[73]

Certainly, Schlegel's was a moralistic judgment and reading of comedy. Indeed, the comic poet must, according to Schlegel, be a moralist.[74] If there is any moral message in comedy, it is there only insofar as comedy "is an applied doctrine of ethics, the art of life."[75] For Schlegel, the "pure ethics" of duty is far superior to this applied ethics, which is "moral instruction" exercised through moral apophthegms and examples.[76] Modern deontological ethics was alien to the ethos of comedy, even when characters acted out of duty. The ethics of ancient comedy was teleological: it was the ethics of happiness. But what Schlegel missed is that the ethics of comedy is *not* necessarily egotistic, insofar as people make the happiness of others possible without sacrificing their own. In his approach to comedy, Schlegel clearly sided with the totalizing explanatory schemes of the Enlightenment within the "ancients-moderns" opposition rather than with the Romantic receptivity of difference. Comedy is immortal but not immoral. Always capable of looking into something more interesting than the boring moral norms and precepts of duty, it often suspends, though never violates, them. Comedy's attention lies elsewhere than in straightforward instructions in morality: its moral lessons are subtle and can be drawn only by a nonmoralistic reader and spectator who dares to plunge into the sensual pursuit of happiness rather than follow the stern prescriptions of duty notwithstanding the consequences.

(2) The second historically established opposition that Schlegel accepted was between Old and New Comedy. Schlegel followed the common view that New Comedy was "the old tamed down."[77] Unlike Hegel, Schlegel even praised Menander as "a philosophical comic writer," though only as a creator of moral and moralistic maxims.[78] And yet the Nea constituted the decline of

comedy and was therefore secondary to the Archaia—not only chronologically but also in its importance, refinement, and even language.[79] To further stress this point, Schlegel called Old Comedy *Komödie* and New Comedy *Lustspiel.*

The law adopted at the end of the Peloponnesian War, which prohibited the depiction of real people and personal attacks in theater, signified for Schlegel, as for Horace long before him, the loss of political freedom that fed Old Comedy and was paramount for its existence.[80] Consequently, comedy lost its punch, because, unlike tragedy, it was a *parody* of events that are easily recognizable and "fresh in recollection" and, as such, evoked a vivid response from the democratic public.[81]

New Comedy thus "arose out of a mere negation."[82] With it, "we descend from the Olympus of true poetry to the common earth"[83] and "into prose and reality."[84] In its very form, which was "sportive" in Old Comedy, New Comedy gained a seriousness inherited from tragedy.[85] New Comedy was "a mixture of earnestness and mirth," of tragedy and comedy.[86] The Nea was thus a *mixed* genre. And yet it was *neither* (Old) comic *nor* tragic but a genre confined to the mere "truthfulness of the represented [*Wahrscheinlichkeit des Dargestellten*]," one that gave a "portrait-like truthfulness [*die porträtmäßige Wahrheit*]" in the depiction of social and domestic life, of the morality and manners of the day.[87] We could learn something from this type of comedy: it gave us plausible pictures that only *seemed* to be true. In New Comedy, the form was still poetic, but the matter became utterly prosaic.[88] New Comedy was constructed similarly to tragedy: the Nea had a formal complication and a denouement of the plot.[89] However, instead of a sublime irrevocable truth about human existence as such, which was accessible in tragedy, New Comedy gave only convincing depictions of everyday living, which could always have been otherwise. Schlegel thus recognized that New Comedy, in a sense, was a *new* genre (which Hegel failed to do). And yet the Nea did not constitute a progression in the development of literary genres but rather the ultimate decline in ancient drama.

Schlegel thus opposed New Comedy not only to Old Comedy but also to tragedy.[90] Tragedy and the Nea shared a common earnestness, or seriousness (*Ernst*), which set them apart from Old Comedy. However, tragic seriousness came from the conflict or struggle (*Kampf*) between external finite existence (*Dasein*) and internal infinite aspirations, inclinations, or dispositions (*Anlage*).[91] Put otherwise, it is tragic that we want to be infinite, that we strive to overcome our finitude and become gods, which manifests in our facing death—yet that we cannot.

This tragic conflict is the source of all seriousness in life. It is traditionally represented as fate, or destiny (*Schicksal*). Human fate *is* tragic, because it leads a person through an inevitable conflict of opposed moral and civic obligations, which cannot be reconciled otherwise than by accepting undeserved tragic suffering and death. Death, then, is merely a dissolution, making an end or "sublation" of life (*die Aufhebung des Lebens*). For Schlegel, however, who wanted to see tragedy in the light of modern ethics of duty, fate as unconditional necessity could only be opposed and overcome by moral freedom (*die sittliche Freiheit*). This, for Schlegel, was the tragic aspect of life: we can reconcile the finitude of our existence with the infinity of our desired potential realizations, in all spheres of life, only by humbling ourselves in acting out our absolute duty (in Kantian terms). This finds no satisfaction in the achievement of any particular goal: the moral freedom of duty is its own goal and thus apparently suspends the opposition between the finite and the infinite in our *Dasein*.

The "seriousness" of New Comedy, conversely, lies in remaining within the realm of experience (*Erfahrung*). Here, sublime tragic notions are redressed according to their empirical conception (*der empirische Begriff*), that is, the way we realize them in our experience. In particular, fate is substituted by chance or contingency (*Zufall*). We face the inevitable concreteness of each situation as that which we cannot change or control, as a mere *factum brutum*. Yet we are capable of turning the contingent to our benefit by acting according to wit, purpose-oriented rationality, or calculative understanding (*verständlich . . . lenken*). In this respect, too, New Comedy was similar to fable in its morality, insofar as it was "a theory of prudence" or smart intelligence (*Klugheitslehre*). Once again, Schlegel's moralistic understanding of comedy made him consider New Comedy as a down-to-earth and essentially opportunistic enterprise drawing on the morality of consequences. As such, New Comedy for him was oriented toward situational action and was driven by the desire to achieve a concrete goal. This results in a suspiciously egotistic "empirical" human happiness rather than the actions of disinterested and sublime tragic duty.[92]

(3) The third historical opposition Schlegel inherited was that between Greek and Roman comedy. Schlegel did not hesitate in his evaluation: he recognized the influence of the Roman comedians on modern ones;[93] however, he considered Roman comedy only secondary to Greek New Comedy. Schlegel was quite condescending about the "metrical licenses" of Latin comic poets and their alleged negligence in versification, which stands in stark contrast to the utter elegance, purity, and accuracy of the Greek originals.[94] Of course, Greek New Comedy was known in Schlegel's time mostly in fragments, as were the pre-Socratics and Greek sculpture. Their imputed original beauty and perfection was only a Romantic *reconstruction* (or "retranslation," in Schlegel's words), which may not have had much to do with the lost

original, because such a reconstruction was only *imaginary* and followed the contemporary normative ideals of beauty and propriety. Latin comedies were deemed lacking in invention and were nothing more than "imitations," "borrowings," or "recasts" (a euphemism for "plagiarism") of their Greek counterparts and, as such, possessed "but little of the true poetic spirit."[95] Schlegel's verdict was categorical and ultimate and could not be appealed.

In each of Schlegel's three oppositions—tragedy versus comedy, Old versus New Comedy, and Greek versus Latin comedy—the terms of opposition are not equal: the first term is considered to be "higher" or "more valuable" than the second. Schlegel displayed the familiar set of Romantic prejudged opinions, framed as good taste. For the Romantics, the Roman was too familiar and boring—too much the "same"—unlike the exciting Greek "other." Old Comedy was fed by the political and aesthetic ideals of classical Athens, still close to the great *dramatis personae* of the Athenian world, whereas the Nea was merely a "comedy of manners." Furthermore, comedy—for plebs— was vulgar, whereas tragedy—for royalty—was noble and sublime.

Yet the modern subject is itself a Romantic construction. The modern subject is autonomous—hence lonely, always trying yet failing to reach out for the other. It is finite—"fatally" mortal, always facing its finitude in a piteous being-toward-death (*Sein zum Tode*). It is rational—and as such subdues the rational will toward what it voluntarily poses as its own duty. Finally, the modern subject is self-conscious—aware of its finitude, which is a struggle between finite existence and infinite aspirations. In other words, modern subjectivity is a *tragic* subjectivity. Comedy, however, speaks about—and *is*—an activity or praxis driven by deliberation concerning how to achieve and live a joyous and good life. This is a life shared with others and not a life served in the solitary confinement of oneself. Comedy thus evades the grasp of Romantic philosophical and literary analysis.

Modern Approaches

To a great extent, comedy still escapes the attention of philosophers, and interesting philosophical studies on comedy are few. Nonetheless, we have at our disposal several notable recent works that may be pivotal in turning philosophy toward comedy.[96]

For one, Agnes Heller wrote a remarkable book on the philosophical meaning of comedy. Therein, she discussed the multifaceted phenomenon of the comic, which appears in many different ways in thought and culture (in comic drama, novels, existential comedy, narrative prose, and visual art) and pervades all human practical—moral and political—activity. Consequently, she showed, comedy must be recognized as *heterogeneous*: no definition of comedy can stand, and ultimately it *cannot be defined* or determined. In other words, comedy is "unapproachable."[97] This is, of course, a rather astounding claim. Yet, Heller emphasized, we cannot exhaust all the embodiments and possibilities of comedy in art and life.

Other literary theorists seem to share this conclusion. Thus, Richard Keller Simon has discussed the comic across literature (Henry Fielding, William Thackeray), philosophy (Kierkegaard), and psychoanalysis (Sigmund Freud), in order to demonstrate that comic theory is "an incongruous mixture of approaches and a miscellaneous assortment of arguments."[98] Therefore, it is only when we do not take the comic seriously that we are in a position to see and appreciate all its complexities and even absurdities—and thus make comedy interesting.[99] However, this position, even if potentially engaging, is utterly skeptical, because it does not reserve the possibility of clarifying the meaning of comedy. Rather, each time we play comedy out we inevitably lose. Heller's approach, conversely, can be considered apophatic: we play comedy out in life and thought again and again, yet each time we are capable of winning a new and *different* meaning.

Theories of comedy are thus themselves quite heterogeneous. Mark Roche has proposed a fascinating interpretation of Hegel's discussion of tragedy and comedy, which he traces in drama, literature, and film. Not unlike Arnold Ruge, Roche sees the connection between comedy and immanent critique.[100] Roche follows the trajectory of the various transformations of subjectivity through tragedy, comedy, and the drama of reconciliation and comes up with an apt systematic classification of their different types. On this journey, comedy plays a major role, because, although the conflict and goals of a comedy can be trivial and its hero weak, comedy nevertheless transcends tragedy by allowing for a possibility of the "positive" within subjectivity—not by destroying it but by establishing, through the negation of the negation, proper intersubjectivity.[101]

Alenka Zupančič has attempted to grasp the elusive "illogic of comedy" through an application of Hegel's logic to what she calls the logic of "the Real," that is, human desire. The "really Real," however, can never fit within what is usually taken to be reality. Hence comedy appears as "the universal at work," defined by a constant "movement" caused by an inevitable incongruity of the reality of desire with the ways in which "realistic reality" is present and organized.[102] Because desire is the defining moment of what used to be the subject, the main attention of the book is shifted to the ways the comic hero appears to overcome human finitude within the "infinite" structures of desire and drive. The structures of comic plot and narrative, however, are largely left out of the discussion, for if they pertain to desire, they are already dissolved within the comic hero; and if they happen to belong to "common reality," then they are unavoidably missed because of their incongruence with the "Real." However, one might say that such an interpretation of comedy is just another version of the centuries-old philosophical account of the incongruence between ontological ("true being") and ontic ("deceptive appearance"). As Paul Kottman has convincingly argued in a critical reflection on Zupančič's book, if we want to tell a story of human comedy, its humanism should be narratable, that is, explainable to oneself and others.[103] In other words, comedy should be *accountable*, and even if we find ourselves to be comic characters, we should be in a position to give an account of the plot and action in which we are engaged as we keep living the comedy of life.

Anja Gerigk has presented quite a different view of comedy, which she develops through a sophisticated discussion of the "high comic" in modern literature (Heinrich von Kleist, Georg Büchner, Franz Kafka, Samuel Beckett, Thomas Bernhard) and film. Gerigk argues that comedy, or rather the comic, is "ambivalence in the form of the organization of the social."[104] The analysis of comedy understood in this way can be aptly based on Niklas Luhmann's system theory, which explains the social, and Mikhail Bakhtin's theory of carnival, which explains ambivalence. Comedy, then, is first and foremost a social phenomenon and as such needs to be studied within a system of social relations and institutions. Moreover, comedy can play a critical role as an indicator of the system's functioning and pathologies. Yet, here, comedy is understood not by its own terms but in reference to something else (i.e., social organization), which thus defines comedy and of which comedy is an epiphenomenon.

Literary scholars have equally displayed a variety of ways of understanding comedy, its various forms, and its plot, characters, and style, of which Véronique Sternberg and Andrew Stott provide helpful overviews.[105] It seems, however, that despite the fruitfulness of many of these approaches, there is something in comedy that remains unthematizable, teasingly escaping the efforts of philosophical and literary analysis at defining comedy. As Richard Keller Simon put it,

> Virtually everything that could be said about the subject has been said—every position, its counterposition, and their synthesis . . . [C]ritics have argued that comedy is a force of civilization (Meredith) and a force of nature against the repressions of civilizations (Freud, Santayana); that the comic corrects aberrant behavior (Bergson) and that the comic does not correct aberrant behavior (Smith); that comedy celebrates what is (Scott) and that it celebrates what should be (Feibleman); that it represents detachment from life (Bergson) and that it represents engagement with life (Burke); that it is an irrational attitude (Sypher), a rational attitude (Swabey), and a force both rational and irrational (Gurewitsch); that it is politically left (Feibleman) and politically right (Cook);

that it affirms freedom (Kaul, McFadden) and that it denies freedom (Girard); that it shows the victory of the individual (Torrance) and that it shows the victory of society over the individual (Bergson, Duncan); that its subject is the carnival (Santayana) and that its subject is everyday life (Kaul); that it requires self-consciousness (Burke) and that it requires a lack of self-consciousness (Mack).[106]

The apparent intangibility and indefinability of comedy even call for the assertion that "comedy is dead," which was Erich Segal's thesis.[107] Modern philosophy has established a template for solving problems in a most radical way: dismissing or killing them. Following Martin Luther, who established the pattern by speaking of "the death of God," in modernity one often talks about "the death of X," where X can be any term: author, subject, art, or comedy. Yet the notion of "the death of X" is itself an expression of the modern subject, which understands itself as fully autonomous and hence unable to accept a phenomenon as simply transmitted by the tradition. Tradition irritates the subject, for, although the subject is constantly reinterpreting tradition and even denying it an origin, the subject still does not have full control of it, because tradition is never fully and deliberately an invention. Hence, "the death of X" manifests the unwillingness of the modern subject to curb its own rational and universal legislative will. In fact, the death of anything means the "birth of the Subject," even if the subject sincerely tries to cancel or kill itself precisely in the figure of "the death of the Subject." One might say that modern attempts to overcome the limitations of the subject—as the focal point for the production of meanings about the world, about the other, and about oneself—inevitably fail. Such attempts fail because the subject is an Archimedean One that does not have a place to stand in order to overturn itself in its own thinking—and thus commit suicide. The proclaimed end of comedy is just another manifestation of the end of the supposedly all-powerful modern subject. The modern subject wants—and needs—to become God, yet it comes to an absurd ending: waiting but not encountering itself as Godot.

It is not by chance, then, that absurd or existential comedy in drama and literature lives on as a continuation of classical comedy, which is well discussed in the works of T. G. A. Nelson, András Horn (Beckett and Eugène Ionesco), and Agnes Heller (Kafka).[108]

Comedy lives on despite declarations of its terminal ending. Moreover, notwithstanding a seemingly great variety of meanings and aspects of comedy that are taken as constitutive of it, one can identify two main clusters of mutually compatible ways of describing comedy. The first revolves around the topics of incongruity, absurdity, transgression, irrationality, not-knowing, ambiguity, not-fitting, and breaking the rule. The other revolves around the themes of vitality, life-renewal, animality, sexuality, enjoyment, pleasure, and fulfillment.

To the first kind of explication of comedy belong the majority of modern theories of comedy as, in the words of Maurice Charney, "an expression of irrational, unsocialized, chaotic, and wish-fulfillment impulses."[109] Incongruity yields irony: for Charney himself, comedy is essentially ironic, that is, it manipulates with deceptive appearances, through which comic characters pretend to be something else.[110] For David Farley-Hills, the comic "arises from the incongruities between opposed ways of regarding the same ideas or images."[111] For Brian Edwards, comedy is "transactive" and implies a constant change of linguistic meaning that always slips away and cannot be firmly established.[112] For Elder Olson, the comic is based on "the unlike," on the absurd misuse of familiar tropes and figures, which results in showing the absurdity of the concern one might have.[113] For Sternberg, comedy has no plot (*sujet*) and no particular meaning, insofar as comedy does not follow any logic beyond a simple free-play.[114] For Morton Gurewitch, comedy's main interest lies in "illogic and irreverence, in disorder and disinhibition."[115] For Friedrich Georg Jünger, comedy always implies a rule that it inevitably opposes and breaks.[116] Similarly, for Umberto Eco, comedy persistently comes with the transgression of a rule that we are not concerned with defending. To our satisfaction, then, the rule is violated by "an ignoble, inferior, and repulsive (animal-like) character," to whom we feel superior.[117]

The second way of understanding comedy, as exploring and affirming life, transpires in works such as those of Robert Corrigan, for whom comedy signifies a "greed for life" and as such relieves us from problems and saves us from the pressures of everyday life.[118] For Christopher Fry, comedy is an "escape from despair."[119] Hannah Arendt, who famously stresses the "natality" of our existence, claims (following Bertolt Brecht) that comedy deals with the sufferings and calamities of humankind in a more serious and successful way than tragedy.[120] Finally, Northrop Frye, especially through his studies of Shakespearean comedy, argues that comedy "lifts us into a higher world, and separates that world from the world of the comic action itself."[121] As such, comedy is associated primarily with *spring*, *ver perpetuum*, the renewing power that allows for the triumph of life and love.

Many modern scholars stress the centrality of laughter for comedy, of which I will say more below. Comedy is often considered an action that, on the one hand, is funny through the use of jokes and, on the other, has a "happy ending."[122] In what follows, however, I will argue that comedy comes to a resolution of a conflict through a well-structured and well-conceived narrative or "argument" that must not necessarily revert to joke and laughter, though it certainly may. A comic narrative is successful if it comes to a "good ending," that is, to a justified conclusion. A good comedy ending shares the same features as laughter: superiority (to wrongdoers), relief (for managing to solve a problem and resolve a case), and ambiguity (of actions, gestures, and words—often, as the means of finding a solution). Yet the resolution of the conflict through comic action may not be funny or provoke laughter at all. This has a noteworthy psychological complement: we do not laugh in dreams, although we are often afraid in dreams—there are fearful dreams, but there are no funny dreams. If dreams are attempts at resolving problems that bug us, then dreams can be comic without being funny.

One may take a joke as a *condensed narrative*, a *sui generis* concentrated comic plot, often with deliberate omissions. In this respect, it is similar to an enthymeme. Thus, in New Comedy, gnome, sententia or aphorism often replaces jokes. In a sense, the joke is the whole story of comedy, put in a few words and presented by wit. The genre of comedy, however, presupposes a detailed development of plot in action, through the dialogue of characters. Because the narrative is extended and often quite complex, it may lose the momentous punch of the joke and thus can be considered a sort of long-winded or "sublated" joke.

Thus, we see that the contemporary approaches to comedy differ widely and mostly do not converge. As I will argue, it is not joke and laughter but rather the set of comic characters and the structure of the comic plot that become the defining features of comedy. It is comic narrative that retains the pleasure of a joke and the suddenness of the resolution of the conflict.

PART II

Logic of Comedy

CHAPTER 3

Everyone Joins the Fight:
The Dialectic of Comic Action

The logic of comedy reveals a rational enterprise meant to promote human well-being. In this chapter, I will examine comedy's own account of the ways in which this is achieved. Comedy is a well-ordered (inter)action that unfolds between a number of actors—as opposed to the isolation of a single subject. It moves through an inevitable complication to a resolution and a good ending. This resolution comes as a result of an intended common action of people who find themselves in undecided situations. As we shall see, comedy presupposes both a "dialogical" narrative and a "dialectical" solution.

Due to the efforts of the Sophists, rhetoricians, and philosophers, in antiquity it was commonly accepted—almost self-evident—that, in order to be successful, *logos* (that is, speech and reasoning) should be able to make a judgment of which it could persuade others, and thus it should be properly ordered and structured. For *logos* has an intrinsic structure that must be spelled out explicitly, through reasoning, in speech. There are immanent "logical" divisions and distinctions in *logos*. They are either already present in thinking and thus clarified through it or constructed by and produced at the moment of thinking. Either way, the implicit *logos* (the *logos endiathetos* of the Stoics) is rendered explicit (*logos prophorikos*) by our "logical" effort to clarify it.[1] Such an effort is present in various ways in the arts and sciences: in particular, our (dramatic) action reveals an implicit logical structure. To discover clearly distinguishable and identifiable structural features of objects that constitute the province of a particular discipline is a major task of theoretical and practical philosophy.[2]

As comedy is rational in its outline, it follows, inherits, and reproduces the structural features of a logical argument as developed in antiquity—in philosophical dialectical argument, rhetorical speech, and mathematical proof.

The ideal of antiquity was an educated young man well versed in literature, music, and athletics.[3] Learning was meant to establish a connection between being and knowledge (*esse—discere—scire*). Menander and his fellow comic playwrights were well educated in the tradition first established by the Greek Sophistic Enlightenment, and as young people they went through rigorous dialectical and rhetorical training. This training, just as the mathematical education of the time, was oriented toward the study and mastery of certain forms of argumentation, which grew out of the same practice of oral disputations. Unsurprisingly, the plot of New Comedy followed well-established patterns of argumentation, which found their explanation and systematization in contemporary treatises—most notably, Aristotle's *Rhetoric*. Accordingly, the work of comic writers resembled that of dialecticians, rhetoricians, and even mathematicians. First, one meticulously calculated and balanced all parts of the plot, thinking through its flow as a *sui generis* argument. Then, one animated the plot with true-to-life characters, who acted and interacted through dialogical exchange.[4]

"Dialogical" Action

In a sense, comedy *is* dialogue. As drama, comedy is an action that imitates and reproduces, but also produces and shapes, human interactions—with all their complications and complexities. As such, the action of comedy tells a story, not by *retelling* and explaining it, but by *showing*, by acting it out. Consequently, comedy evades a bird's-eye view narration of the action. Instead, the action is presented by characters who embody the story as it unfolds through their conversations. Thus, comedy is a drama composed of a series of dialogues. In fact, I argue that dialogue is central to the constitution of comedy, which, in its dramatic form, is nothing other than impersonated dialogue.

Dialogue presupposes a relatively quick exchange of rejoinders based on mutual interruptions.[5] People must act, and act quickly, in order to achieve their aspired end and keep the action from getting boring and dying. Thus, interlocutors must be able to understand each other, even through brief and seemingly casual remarks, which are often incomplete and even grammatically incorrect. Any delay is perceived as an impediment to the flow of action and provokes irritation.[6] Dialogue thus serves to keep the action rolling.

And yet drama was the first oral genre to be presented in written form.[7] While actors delivered dialogues as spoken, the author presented them as written.[8] Accordingly, comedy was conceptually oral, imitating live dialogical interaction; and yet, medially, the way it was conceived and delivered, it was first written and then oral. As oral, comedy was staged or read, either aloud in the presence of others, a common practice in antiquity, or silently with oneself and imaginary significant others, as became the habit in modernity.[9]

Hence, dialogue as found in comedy imitates live oral dialogue, though without replacing it, just as comic action imitates live action without replacing it. And yet such imitation is not a simple artistic reproduction of the live original. It also has a normative value: comic action shows human life the way it *should* and *can be*. This brings to mind Aristotle's famous distinction between historians, who show how things *were*, and poets, who show how things *might have been*.[10] In this line of thinking, comedy is not historical but poetic.

Insofar as it uses poetic, metrically organized language, comedy is imitative of spoken language—not directly but in an oblique way. Thus, comedy suspends the prosaic orality of everyday spoken language. By squeezing language into an unnatural form and state, it presents the development and rhythmic flow of dialogical action. Yet it also displays both the uniqueness and the commonality of characters. The change of poetic meter and the metric experimentation that occurs as the story develops are a kind of compromise between the oral and the written.[11]

As comic action is dialogical, it is thereby communal, for a solitary dialogue is a *contradictio in adiecto*. But communal comic action is not thereby choral. In antiquity, a chorus produced a uniformly monodic song, in which all the *choreuts* (chorus members) became mutually indistinguishable rather than uniquely defined characters. Unsurprisingly, the chorus and parabasis practically disappeared already in Menander. The author no longer needed the chorus to address the audience directly in order to make a statement. He could leave it to characters and actors to make one through action and dialogue. The author's own position, in a sense, was not as important as the dialogical action of the play—which, in fact, *was* the author's position. Parabasis, in turn, was a highly artificial dramatic device in which the chorus addressed, but was not directly answered by, the audience.[12] In comedy, conversely, every character is an individual, even if he presents a "typical" character. This character speaks not in a choral unison but contributes an independent voice, irreducible to any other or to the whole of dialogical action.[13]

Comedy as Rational and Reflective

Against the interpretations of comedy that take it as entirely undefinable, irrational, heterogeneous, and unknowable, I argue that comedy is the most *rational* of all dramatic genres. When comedy tells a story, it does so by showing its narrative through imitative action. First, this action is well organized and thought through, despite its apparent entanglement. Its structure can be rationally restored and reproduced. Second, there is an implied *judgment* about the actions, both of the acting characters and the coacting spectators, as the development of the action proceeds. This judgment is *dialogical*, insofar as it can be passed on only in a dialogical interaction with other actors and spectators. Comic judgment further implies a *process* of thinking, insofar as its meaning is established and fully clarified only at the end. Finally, such judgment is *reflective*, as the comic actors and coactors are capable of knowing not only *that* but also *why* they are involved in the comic action, although this *why* may change throughout.

Comedy often uses parody as a dramatic device. In distinction to Old Comedy, New Comedy did not practice a personal parody but rather parodied the common: a character, a situation, or even a whole genre (such as tragedy). But then comedy should be conscious both of *what* it parodies and *that* it parodies. Hence, comedy must be *reflective*. As Heller put it, comedy is always "mediated by reflection, by understanding, by work of the intellect."[14]

As reflective, comedy thinks about the limits to human possibilities. In particular, it reflects on the possibility of reaching happiness through love in—but not after—life. Thus, comedy presupposes not only thinking (practically and morally) about what is best for us but also self-reflective thinking about our situation in the comedy of life. Hence, again, comedy always implies judgment. And (free) judgment is properly possible only for reflective reason. Therefore, comedy always implies a form of thinking that itself is utterly comic—that is, judgmental, reflective, and, as such, therapeutic. Comedy saves us from death and absurdity in life, for absurdity is often disguised as boredom, but in thinking life never gets boring. Moreover, reflective thinking is not solitary but occurs together with the other, including the other of oneself. Reflective comic thinking renders both love and being, as being-with-the-other, possible and, in fact, inevitable. Let us paraphrase, and slightly alter, Hegel's claim that what is rational is actual and what is actual is rational: what is rational is comic and what is comic is rational.[15]

Comedy and Dialectic

The structural similarity between comic plot and dialectical argument—in outline, arrangement, and development—is rather striking. Dialectic is comedy philosophically disguised, and comedy is a dramatization of philosophical dialectical reasoning. Comedy is a way of resolving life conflicts so that the solution is satisfactory and commonly acceptable. Its solutions promote human well-being as being together with other people. Comedy must resolve a current conflict, just as dialectical argument must solve a current problem. Thus, neither cares much about originality of plot or argument but uses any available means to advance toward the desired end.

A dialectical philosophical argument is a proof that establishes the truth of a theoretical claim through an action of thought, which is enacted by speakers. Similarly, a comedy establishes the truth of a practical claim through its own action, which is embodied in actors.[16] In both dialectical argument and comic plot, one must not only establish *what* but also *why* something is true and just. In order to show how the conclusion is achieved, a well-calculated and understandable step-by-step movement of thought or action must be given.[17] Cleary then, comic plot reproduces the development of dialectical argument. Comedy is thus at once a realization of a practical truth and an image of a theoretical truth.[18]

In comedy, conflict always appears irresolvable in the beginning. The eventual resolution of the conflict will require not only great dramatic skill but also refined dialectical skill in the construction of the plot.

Consider when we read a story or watch a dramatic piece whose plot is not immediately clear, in which the sequence of events do not form an evident, linear, or "logical" progression.[19] Rather than simply recognize the narrative's inconsistency, we begin constructing a satisfactory, coherent interpretation, in which everything fits together and reveals a "hidden" plan. Of course, everything in fiction *is* fiction, but we always want fiction to be more than fiction, not just a random sequence of imaginary events. It should either reproduce life the way it can be or direct life as it has never been but would be livable for us. We are thus constantly at work in solving the same problem of arranging actions and situations in which we are involved. We are never satisfied with the answer "It's just a random series of unconnected events, so leave it at that."

Dialectic has a variety of sophisticated and established methods, which are all in use today. Yet dialectic emerged from a seemingly haphazard dialogical exchange. In the movement of a dialectical argument, each step in reasoning may be framed as a question that requires an answer, which allows one to proceed to the next step—and, eventually, to the conclusion. This process can easily be dramatized, which Plato did in his dialogues: questions and answers were assigned to various interlocutors. Such dialectic was originally oral and was practiced in debates.[20] The purpose of oral dialectical debate, which was then put into a sequence of steps that could be transcribed and codified as an abstract logical proposition, was to establish what a particular thing or notion (X) was. To that end, one interlocutor advanced a thesis (X is Y), and the other, without committing to any particular position, asked simple questions that allowed for a straightforward yes or no answer.

The questioner was the dialectician (paradigmatically represented by Socrates), and the questioned was the one who initially came up with the debated thesis. Then, by asking appropriate questions, either the dialectician required that the questioned establish the truth of the thesis X is Y (a positive dialectic) or, otherwise, the dialectician made the other recognize that the original statement yielded a contradiction and was therefore wrong (X is not Y), which began the whole procedure anew (a negative dialectic). In either case, the dialectician was not committed to any claim whatsoever. Rather, his task was to test critically the initial thesis of the opponent in order to find out if it could stand. In positive dialectic, the dialectician skillfully wove an argument that would allow the interlocutors to move from a mutually shared and agreed starting point to the sought-after and accepted conclusion.

Whether positive or negative, dialectical reasoning represents a *movement of thought*.[21] It presupposes a rational procedure whose success—establishing a point through a number of steps of reasoning—is possible but not guaranteed. We find exactly the same features in the structure and construction of comic plot, which supports the claim that comedy is a rational, and philosophy a comic, enterprise. In drama, only comedy, similarly to positive dialectic, achieves a "good" end in reasoning and action. And similarly to negative dialectic, comedy prohibits, destroys (or at least suspends), questions, and ridicules wrong and oppressive social practices.

Two major versions of dialectic came from Plato and Aristotle, in antiquity, for both of whom dialectic provided an indispensable instrument for right reasoning. For Plato, dialectical argument, if successful, allowed us to know and recognize what a particular thing or notion was and how it was related to other things; and, as negative, dialectical argument destroyed a wrong thesis. Dialectic thus enabled us to gain proper knowledge and even achieve the good. Dialectic was closely associated with mathematics, which for Plato established the pattern for training in gaining knowledge by an orderly dialectical reasoning.[22] Aristotle, developing his theory of syllogism—a speech or argument (*logos*) from which, if something is presupposed, something different follows with necessity—dedicated the whole of his *Topics* to the study of the practical use of dialectic. In a sense, Aristotle attempted to appropriate a number of Platonic and Socratic insights about dialectic for his own purpose: to provide a systematic insight into the ways dialectic functioned in Plato's dialogues. Yet, for Aristotle, dialectic did not provide firm knowledge, the knowledge of being as such (*ens per se* or *ens inquantum ens*), as it did for Plato, but rather explained the functioning of dialectical syllogisms based on seemingly correct opinions and only probable premises.[23] Plato and Aristotle differed in their understanding of dialectic in that, for Plato, dialectic was the form of thinking being, whereas for Aristotle it was the form of logical argumentation.

Comedy was born out of the spirit of both dialogue and dialectic. It invites the spectators or readers to participate in the development of the plot's "argument." It draws them in by allowing them to participate in the action emotionally, through empathy with the characters, and intellectually, by anticipating the development of the action. Comedy is dialectical, for it is an artificial construction whose plot is invented and thought through by the author. Yet comedy is also dialogical, for it allows for, and even requires, a multiplicity of live independent actors—and not mere invented interlocutors—who each in their own way participate in the common action.

Being—shared dialogical cobeing with others—can be reached through comedy, as in Plato. Further, the "premises," the initial situation as the starting point for the development of the intrigue, can be only probable, that is, agreed upon by all the participants of a comedy, as in Aristotle. The action of comedy is then "dialectical" in that it requires a well-structured "argument" (*argumentum fabulae*) that allows the action to move through the complication and development of the plot to the end, where the "good" of comedy is achieved. Thus, the good of comedy is not transcendent to being (as being-human), as in Plato, but is reachable through the common efforts of the participants. Comedy allows the spectators to recognize both the humanity of the characters and the ultimate rationality of the seemingly irrational and haphazard action. Finally, the intellectual recognition (Plato's *anamnēsis*), which takes place when one manages to reconstruct, understand, and anticipate the course of action, comes as a joy for being included in the dialogical action and realization of the shared good (ending), together with other people.

Opposites

Dialectical reasoning always moves through and in reference to opposites. The opposites that were present in the questioning of oral dialectic were embodied in comedy in the double characters and paired scenes, of which I will say more below. Opposites tend to exclude each other, to get into a struggle, and yet to come to a reconciliation in the end. Achieving a dialectical conclusion or comic ending by maneuvering through opposites is never easy. It is a difficult and often painful process characterized by fighting, inevitable complications, deceit, suffering, and betrayal. There is always another position present, represented by a real other with different, conflicting, and often opposite interests. There is an opposite intention, a contrary move, which needs to be taken into account. This is why one needs to *listen to the other side*, even if one disagrees and intends to overcome the other's opinion.[24] In other words, the movement of opposites always implies negativity. Negativity is instrumental in the motion—though never the purpose—of thought or action. Yet, in the end, negativity is—or at least it can be—overcome in the proven conclusion or in a resolution of the conflict.[25]

In dialectical reasoning, seemingly incompatible opposites can be brought together in a *discordia concors*: they cease to be contradictory through the mediation of a third, or through a reconciliatory ending. This can be done without "sublating" the opposites, neither in a pure consensus nor mere dissensus but in an "allosensus," where opposites are recognized without a conflict yet without being destroyed.

Agon and Battle: The Parody of Dialectic in Comedy

Dialectic resembles a struggle, battle, strife, or competition—*agōn*—led for the sake of victory and establishing the winner. As dialectic moves through opposites, it presupposes a difficult way to either the proof or the refutation of a thesis. Thus Plato compared the philosopher and the dialectician to a warrior. Dialectical dispute is often a battle between two opposing positions—of the original thesis as established against its antithesis. In comedy, this battle was often parodied as a domestic argument—as between husband and wife[26]—or as a real battle. Thus we saw the courtesan Thais captured by a comic "army"—consisting of household servants, including a cook—led by the inept officer, Thraso (ironically compared to Pyrrhus).[27]

Dialectical debate is always carried out by at least two people: the questioner and the questioned. It can become a competition between them. Whoever wins the oral battle and refutes the position of the other is the winner. In dialectic, the intellectual war is waged, in the end, in order to win the truth of a claim. In sophistry, by contrast, persuading by any, often dialectically illicit, means available, the battle is led for the sake of personal victory, of establishing oneself in a position of authority over the other. Consequently, the feud—or battle—between philosophical dialectic (or dialectical philosophy) and sophistry began with their respective inceptions,[28] which makes them coeval and each other's necessary other.

Comedy too uses *agōn*: it competes and imitates a battle between opposite views and desires or opposing characters.[29] The comic occurs on comedy's way to completing itself as a whole, that is, in reaching its end by overcoming seemingly insuperable obstacles in a rationally judged and justified action.

However, there lies an important distinction between war and sophistry, on the one hand, and philosophical dialectic and comedy, on the other. War and sophistic battle are exclusive of others, because where there are winners, there inevitably will be losers—and the winner takes all (such as power, honor, and money). The other is then subdued or simply destroyed. Dialectic and comedy, conversely, are inclusive of everyone. Exclusion is impossible in comedy because comic plot requires the interaction of all characters. It is based on dialogue, in which everybody can participate, contribute to the commonly participated thought and action, and be recognized as such. In other words, everyone joins the fight. Here, everybody is, can, or even should be a winner: knowledge of the good and well-being is universal, communicable, and shareable with others. Such comic knowledge (*cognitio*) is achieved through a common effort. It is the knowledge of oneself and one's situation as recognized by others, which makes people better off and happy.[30] Hence, "winning" in dialectical *agōn* means establishing a point theoretically, through reasoning, or achieving a good end comically, through practical action.

Comedy is thus a dialectical enterprise, as dialectic is comic. Both are born out of the same agonistic and reasoning spirit. Therefore, from its inception, comedy—in an intentional *parody* of dialectical *agōn*—uses dialectic consciously and intentionally, as a reflection on its own constitution, ways of acting, and means of "proving" its end point through action. In comedy, therefore, we find not only a structural analogy between plot and argument but also an ironic imitation of dialectical argument and ways of argumentation. Yet the parody of dialectic is also a ridicule of sophistry, a "ridiculous" dialectic, misled (and often arrogant) thinking gone astray.

Examples of comedy's parody of dialectic are numerous. Thus, Epicharmus suggested the following "argument": A man who borrowed money refused to return it, because he claimed then to be a different person (since everything changes). Yet the creditor beat him up for refusing to pay off the debt and then himself refused to bear any responsibility for his action, as the creditor too then claimed to be a different person.[31] In Euripides, who prefigured New Comedy in important ways, such were the scenes imitative of dialectical dispute, as, for example, in the opposed speeches of Medea and Jason, in the opposed speeches of Medea and Jason, in which Jason used sophistic tricks.[32] Such were also the speeches of Helen and Hecuba in the *Trojan Women*, which were the imitations of Gorgias's fictional speeches written as rhetorical exercises.[33]

In Old Comedy, *agōn* was often represented through the song of the chorus, which, divided in two parts, supported the struggle of one of the characters against the other, as in Aristophanes's *Acharnenses* and *Equites*. Aristophanes also famously mocked his fellow contemporary Sophists in the *Clouds*, where he parodied a dialectical dispute between the personifications of Truth and Falsity.[34] In the *Frogs*, Aristophanes ridiculed the use of flawed and faulty tricks in dialectical reasoning, as in an *agōn* between Aeschylus and Euripides, or a dispute between Euripides and Dionysus about how best to govern the city.[35]

New Comedy, which grew out of the fertile soil of the previous generations' dialectical and sophistic disputes and was clearly conscious—and critical—of them and their colorful leaders, constantly ridiculed dialectical devices. Thus, in Menander we find a debate between Daos and Syros portrayed as a dialectical legal argument, in which each speaker presents arguments in support of his position.[36]

Terence's comedies were full of comic disputes, such as the one between a husband and wife, Chremes and Sostrata, a parody of a dialectical engagement that nevertheless followed dialectical rules.[37] In the *Dyskolos*, Knemon spoke in rather simplified sweeping statements that made much use—or rather, abuse—of quantifiers, such as "all," "nobody," and "nothing."[38] In the *Eunuch*, the courtesan Thais reproached her smart maid Pythias for speaking in riddles,[39] which implied dialectically opposed answers: "I know—I don't know."[40] A remarkable parody of the Sophistic abuse of dialectic was presented by Terence in the *Eunuch*, where Gnatho, a hanger-on, used a purely opportunistic tactic of referring to opposites in order to pursue his own interests: "Whatever they say, I praise it; if they say the opposite, I praise that too. They deny, I deny; they affirm, I affirm."[41]

In Terence, there was also the intended parody of the Sophistic abuse of dialectic, even though the latter claimed to be capable of proving any point—and its opposite—if only it would please the speaker. Such an exchange was utterly unprincipled, for each speaker helped the other only insofar as both were interested in winning a case, no matter what the truth of the matter might be. Such Sophistic "mutual aid society" was mocked in Plato's *Euthydemus*, as well as in Terence's *Phormio*, where two young men assisted each other in Sophistic trickery: "One's on a charge, the other's there to defend the case. The second's accused, up pops the first. It's a mutual aid society."[42] Yet such a questioning only entangled the already complicated matters. The father Demipho requested legal counsel from three advisors, one of whom replied, "It is allowed," the other, "It is not allowed," and the third, "I do not know."[43] Such a "conclusive" inconclusiveness was thoroughly relativistic, insofar as one had to conclude that "there are as many opinions as there are people."[44] As a result, Demipho was totally perplexed and could only complain, "I'm even more uncertain than before." In other words, such "dialectically" obtained advice in fact *paralyzed* any action. Later in the play, Phormio ridiculed the inconsistency of the two fathers' attitudes and decisions, of which, however, he himself was the main cause, so that his ridicule was double-edged and thus profoundly ironic: "I will, I won't; I won't, I will again; take it, give it back; what was said is unsaid; what was agreed before is cancelled."[45]

Modern comedy, up to Woody Allen, also deliberately uses and parodistically abuses dialectic. Thus, Shakespeare made the clown Feste imitate a dialectical dispute by paradoxically "proving" that enemies are better than friends: "Marry, sir, they [friends] praise me and make an ass of me. Now my foes tell me plainly I am an ass; so that by my foes, sir, I profit in the knowledge of myself, and by my friends I am abused; so that, conclusions to be as kisses, if your four negatives make your two affirmatives, why then, the worse for my friends and the better for my foes."[46]

Thus, comedy ridicules dialectic that has been misused in Sophistry for the improper purposes of establishing not a right understanding of a thing but one's alleged superiority over the other person by any available means of persuasion. And yet comedy itself uses dialectic for achieving its end in a way very similar to philosophy's use of dialectic for establishing a justified argument. Both comedy and philosophy ironically imitate, and thereby criticize, sophistic reasoning, which appears to reproduce the formal steps of an argument yet mostly recurs to fallacies (e.g., of ambiguity, *ad hominem*, etc.) and has as its main purpose the persuasion of the listeners. Thus, not only did Plato's Socrates constantly ridicule the Sophists themselves, but he also criticized Agathon for writing tragedies in the genre of "sophistic tragedy," imitative of sophistic reasoning.[47]

Comedy and Rhetoric

In its composition and organization, comedy also bears close similarity to rhetorical speech. Curiously enough, the beginning of rhetoric was ascribed in Terence's time to the fifth-century BCE Sicilians Corax and Tisias.[48] Like comedy, rhetoric originated in Sicily yet developed and flourished later in Athens. Rhetoric—with dialectic—was the very foundation of education in ancient schools. The two disciplines were closely related. As Aristotle famously said in the opening sentence of his *Rhetoric*, rhetoric is the "counterpart" (*antistrophos*) of dialectic, insofar as each one is within the knowledge of all people.[49] Like rhetoric, dialectic is capable of speaking "about everything," not only about a particular science. Thus, dialectic can use the conclusions and general principles of *all* the sciences without itself being a science of general principles, as it does not consider self-evident and general statements of the kind: "about every thing either an affirmation or a negation is true."[50] Both dialectic and rhetoric refer to and make use of *logos*, which everyone already has and thus can master in reasoning and speaking. Similarly, comedy speaks about and to everyone, insofar as everyone participates in public life and follows its implicit and explicit *logos*, translated into social rules and structures.

Moreover, both rhetoric and dialectic are capable of refuting false arguments by means of speech and reasoning in reference to *opposites*, assuming that "the true and the just are by nature stronger than their opposites."[51] It was not by chance, then, that the very first of Aristotle's *topoi*, or general schemata of rhetorical argument, was from opposites, in which "one should look to see if the opposite [predicate] is true of the opposite [subject], [thus] refuting the argument if it is not, confirming it if it is," to which he later added arguments from contradictions and from comparison of contraries, which are also based on reference to opposites.[52]

Comedy too is concerned with opposites and embodies them onstage through opposite characters, double identity, and paired scenes and moves within a plot. Both dialectic and rhetoric are thus *logical* disciplines, insofar as both refer to *logos* and produce logically justified conclusions. Each one is an art (*tekhnē*) of reasoning and persuasion that seeks the best available means for achieving its goals. They differ in the kind of their conclusions and the type of logical reasoning they use. Thus, for Plato, rhetoric established a persuasive conclusion, whereas dialectic established a true one.[53] For Aristotle, however, the difference between rhetoric and dialectic consisted in the structure of their respective syllogisms: unlike a dialectical syllogism, a rhetorical syllogism is an *enthymeme*, a "shortened" syllogism that omits certain premises and steps in reasoning as either evident, easy to surmise, or already known for the sake of shortening the argument, of making it less tiresome and easier to follow for the listeners. An enthymeme, then, can be either demonstrative or refutative and seeks appropriate means of proof in each particular case.[54] Conversely, a dialectical syllogism meticulously lays out all its premises and does not skip a single step in reasoning, as it seeks to establish a correct opinion that would be universally acceptable to each interlocutor.[55]

Important differences exist, of course, between rhetoric and dialectic: rhetoric is concerned with the means of persuasion in particular cases, whereas dialectic is concerned with the means of achieving a justified conclusion in a syllogism acceptable in all cases. Moreover, unlike dialectic, rhetoric not only persuades by arguments but also by taking into account the "moral" character (*ēthos*) of the speaker and listeners, their passions and emotions, as well as the style (*lexis*) of delivering the speech.[56] As Cicero famously said, an orator must be able to win over the audience's sympathy, to prove what is true, and to stir their emotions in the desired action.[57] In this respect, comedy remains true to dialectic, though by making use of rhetorical devices in showing human silliness and bringing out human goodness by speeches. These qualities appear through diction and style and are embodied in different characters.

Rhetorical speech is a particular rendering of *logos*, which is already inherently structured. Therefore, it too should have a *taxis*, that is, subdivisions, measures, proportions, and clearly identifiable and ordered components. At the very least, a speech should have two parts: a statement of the subject (*prothesis*) and a proof or argumentation (*pistis*). In other words, beyond saying *what* is the case, one must demonstrate *why* it is the case: a thing should be explained by its cause(s).[58]

Comedy and Mathematics

Comedy resembles mathematics, which carefully constructs its proofs and uses the rules of deduction to move from premises to a conclusion. The plot of comic drama, too, is carefully constructed and verified at each step before it is embodied in the publicly staged *logos*.

Comic plot is a problem.[59] First, it must be solved by rational and imaginary construction by the author, and then it must be brought into action on the stage. Similarly to a problem, a comedy must be constructed and "solved" step-by-step before it is recognized as "valid," when it achieves its required and desired end and is then released and shared with others. In each case, the construction of a problem or of a plot is only *a* solution and does not exclude other possible ways of achieving the required end.

However, once a problem is solved by construction, an analysis is needed to demonstrate its validity. According to Proclus, such an analysis includes six clearly distinguishable subdivisions or parts: enunciation, exposition, specification, construction, proof, and conclusion.[60] In its makeup, a mathematical proposition, if not altogether isomorphic, is similar to dialectical argument and rhetorical speech, because, as said, all three arise as a structured step-by-step development and explication of a *logos*, whose implicit structure they reflect in their respective layouts and various subdivisions. Thus, the number of components in an argument, speech, or proof can vary according to a particular discipline, task, or principle chosen for a *taxis*. Too many subdivisions might become "empty and ridiculous," as Aristotle puts it.[61] And yet there should be clearly identifiable distinctions, which are both *descriptive*, as the guideposts of the motion of thought and action, and *prescriptive*, as the suggestions for its proper course.

As I have argued, comedy is a rational and well-calculated enterprise that is similar to philosophy in its very work, which produces subtly developed arguments that move from premises through a number of deductive steps to establishing an argument as demonstrated.[62] The *logos* of both comedy and mathematics is spun out of itself as it is present in the beginning, in the premises, down to the end (by "synthesis"), so that the beginning implicitly contains the end. But then, such *logos* should also be verified as reachable "backward," from the end to the beginning (by "analysis"), in which case the end justifies the beginning. Both moves are meant to develop and preserve a unified whole of the argument from the beginning through a climax toward its end.

The Structure of Comedy

Comedy thus has a clearly established structure, obtained already in Menander and different from the structure of Old Comedy, which used the spectator-addressed parabasis and sometimes rather loosely related episodes. Yet there is no recipe for writing a good comedy. It is rather brought about by the playwright's art of writing and the actors' skill of performing. Comic narrative follows Aristotle's prescription that a whole can exist only where there is a beginning (*arkhē*), middle, and end.[63] But this is the structure of *logos* itself, which, as Aristotle explained, is either a definition or a demonstration. Demonstration starts from a beginning, goes through middle and extreme terms, and has an end, which is the syllogism (inference) or conclusion.[64] Logical demonstration is thus isomorphic with comic plot.

The *arkhē* is the beginning of an action: it captivates us, and we are unable to avoid it. The middle presupposes a necessary complication and the use of appropriate means toward reaching the end. The end itself—which occurs *through* action—is the purpose and resolution of action. In other words, the beginning is already in the end, and the end is achievable through the middle only because of the beginning. Therefore, the "whole" of action must be structured in such a way as to be rationally constructible and reconstructible and (reflectively) recognized as such.

Evanthius, of whose *De comoedia* only excerpts have been preserved, followed Aristotle in distinguishing the constituents of comedy, with the addition of the prologue. Thus, for Evanthius, comedy has four parts: *prologue, protasis, epitasis*, and *catastrophe*.[65] The prologue is an introduction to the plot addressed to the audience; the *protasis* is the first act of the play that partly explains the story and partly leaves it to the spectators to anticipate; the *epitasis* is a complication in the development, the "rolling" of the story; and the catastrophe is the resolution and explanation of the story.[66]

Similarly, Gustav Freytag's pyramid presented the structure of dramatic action as comprising five moments. The five steps are: introduction, rising up, climax, going down, and denouement. The division of the comic play into five acts, commonplace in Renaissance scholars,[67] might correspond to the rise and fall of action as described by Freytag's pyramid, when the dramatic action undergoes a clear development from its exposition through complication to resolution. Comedy thus follows Aristotle's schema of beginning-middle-end, and Freytag's pyramid seems to be a particular version of Aristotle's "whole" structure, where the "middle" is taken as climactic.[68]

Comic Plot

As I have argued, the rationality of comedy can be seen in the resemblance of the structure of its complex and intense plot to a long and sophisticated logically structured argument. To achieve its end, comedy uses (literary) plot, while philosophy uses (rational) argument. In its complexity, comic plot is like a game of chess: a winning chess combination is similar to a rational argument that proves its point. Of course, both can fail, yet both carefully try to avoid such an outcome.

A comic plot is more a product of a carefully calculating and demonstrative reason than of productive imagination, because at the end the action should arrive at a mutually acceptable state of affairs.[69] Comic plot and philosophical argument are both well and carefully structured with clearly distinguishable components.[70] Both begin with accepted premises: comedy has an exposition or prologue, while argument presents its terms, which are either postulates or are deduced from other arguments. Both go through development: comedy's has an unwrapping of its plot, while argument develops through deduction. And both end in a solution: comedy has a resolution of the conflict and a rectification of errors, while argument ends in a conclusion. Both comic plot and philosophical argument are "complete": they must "logically" move through each stage of their unwrapping toward a resolution, being careful to avoid missing or confounding any step in their deduction. Both are free inventions of the mind and yet have to be well conceived and thought through, to follow (often implicit) rules of logical or dramatic inference, by which they justify every act, so that nothing remains redundant or obsolete in their composition. And yet both are relatively independent of their author, thinker, or narrator, for they follow and show immanent rules. The conclusions of both comic plot and philosophical argument have to stand and be independent of any particular interests, purposes, and strivings. The ways of bringing about a conclusion may differ widely for both: one can arrive at the same end in many different ways, through various methods or plots. Thus, there can be *many* different (good) comedies and (right) arguments, even if both are relatively rare. But both must have a "happy ending": in comedy by obtaining the desired that exhausts the desire;[71] in argument by reaching the desired logical conclusion.

Yet, despite its well-calculated plot, comedy also allows for spontaneity and thus for freedom. Comedy always has a place for suddenness, which comes as novelty, surprise, and rupture of a seemingly steady flow of action. Suddenness is often present in a pun, which comes in an unexpected ending of an enthymeme in a joke. Yet even more often comic suddenness comes out of the expected resolution of an entanglement of the plot, which, unlike in Kant, does not end in nothing but rather in a good ending. Despite its established and anticipated course of action, which tends to suppress the surprise ("surprise" the new), comedy is capable of improvisation (already in the mime), of real novelty in the twists and turns of a complex argument, in the details that lead to the ending. While comic action tends to break and be left undecided at every particular moment (the sign of which is fate), actors are capable of stitching it together. In the elaboration of characters, suddenness testifies to the spontaneity of life, which constantly shimmers through every action and becomes apparent and triumphant in the end.

Plot and Fabula

Plot (*mythos*) and character (*ēthos*) are two central constituents of drama among the six Aristotle gives in the *Poetics*. Plot-*mythos* (*fabula* in Roman comedy) is the story shown by action and narrated in the dialogue. As mentioned, this is given not directly by the author but through the characters' rejoinders. Both tragedy and comedy have entanglement and solution, and both use the *protasis-epitasis-catastrophe* structure; yet, in comedy, the action must be such that it brings the event to a satisfactory resolution and a mutually acceptable state of affairs. As such, comic plot should be highly inventive in its construction: it must follow the established structure while being different each time. For every human life resembles any other and yet is different and unique.

A comic poet creates a narrative (*logos*) and a plot (*mythos*). Moreover, he produces a properly reasoned (dialectical) relation between the two. In jail awaiting his execution, Socrates wrote poetry—for the first time in his life.[72] Facing death, he wrote a hymn to Apollo, meant as an expiatory sacrifice, and *versified fables*, because—as he explained—the poet produces myths, not reasonings or arguments.[73] According to Socrates's own (as always, ironic) testimony, lacking in imagination, he was obliged to borrow fables, or myths, from Aesop, which he knew by heart. Thus, *the* poet for Socrates (ironically) was Aesop, who (seriously) was the creator of fables or myths. Yet the plot of comedy *is* "myth" or fable.

In the prologue to Terence's *Brothers*, the *argumentum fabulae* stood for the "outline of the plot."[74] Yet the dramatic "argument" does not give the plot of a comedy in advance, as does the later added synopsis. The "argument" exposes its "fable"; that is, it renders the myth gradually more explicit as the comedy progresses. This occurs partly through the speech of the characters (in their explanations and dialogues) and partly through action and plot. The "argument" thus "shows" or "demonstrates" comedy in two mutually complementary ways: by the dialogical *word*, which makes the plot evident and opens it up, and by the interactive *action*, which both moves and follows the plot.[75] Comedy thus employs what Cicero called the "narrative argument," which allows for an account of a story that is invented and yet probable and as such establishes a blueprint that may be imitated, followed, and reproduced in real life.[76]

As an "argument," comic plot is thus a careful construction of thought. Menander's *Dyskolos* and Ben Jonson's *Epicoene, or The Silent Woman* are exemplary in the perfection of their construction, complexity, and subtlety of plot: nothing is redundant, and all the parts contribute to a whole action that moves from a beginning, through an entanglement, to an end. Comic plot is crafted according to a pattern and the rules of its production: it is the same in form though it differs each time in concrete elaboration. Plot is thus fictitious (fully invented) but normative at the same time, which is why it should be devoid of historical or mythological events, as both Diderot and Heller have argued.[77]

Thus, plot is both simple in its general structure yet complex in its concrete realization. The general structure of comedy is already known, yet the whole plot is known only at the very end. The point of view, the "summit" from which we can nondiscursively see the whole of action, should be achieved by following and "gathering" the action carefully and discursively. Consequently, while the fabula is present in its entirety at any moment, it is known only partially and must constantly be rethought and reevaluated. If we follow the Formalists, fabula is the order of events as they are restored and reconstructed by the spectators, whereas *syuzhet* (choet) is the way these events have been narrated and represented in a drama.[78]

Yet our capacity to hold the whole of the plot and reconstruct it from details when reading or watching a comedy is limited. We get tired when the plot becomes unnecessarily complex, obviously incoherent, or superfluously episodic, which—when we do not already know the outcome—is boring. As Plautus remarks, "The loins grieve from sitting, and the eyes from watching."[79] Here, again, the distinction between the written and the oral is apparent: the written can be indefinitely long-winded, whereas the oral should be of fitting magnitude. We should be able to understand it comfortably without confusing the steps in the plot's development. Comedy, like philosophical reasoning, must be written down in order not to be lost or forgotten, for the use of actors and readers. Both a dramatic (comic) plot and a philosophical argument can be simple and clear in their formulation yet quite convoluted,

long-winded, and sometimes painfully complex as they develop from premises to conclusion and from the beginning to the end.[80] Hence, a good plot
is not too long, it is graspable in its entirety, it is understandable in each of
its steps, and it can be narrated to, or reproduced by, the other. This implies
the classical principle of the unity of time, place, and action: the action of
comedy should be brief and, as such, should fit within one day.[81] Comedy
must be prudent in its economy and structure, in which nothing should be
in excess.

Simplicity and Complexity of Plot

New Comedy, whose form is preserved in modern comedy, was therefore
rather simple in its main outline yet extremely complex and infinitely different in its details. Later critics thus unduly and disparagingly called it a
"comedy of manners," presenting but a mere a variation on the same theme.
Yet comedy resembles life, both descriptively and prescriptively. This already
made the ancients wonder who imitated whom—Menander or life? In a
sense, life is always the one and same life we all live—but it is also always different. This is the comedy of life: it has a prologue, that is, a prehistory into
which we are born, a concrete social and linguistic environment loaded with
institutional practices and family habits; it has a *protasis*, that is, birth and
edification; an *epitasis*, that is, the different concrete lives we live; and a catastrophe, that is, the end of life. The end is an event that is "catastrophic" yet,
nonetheless, can and should be comic: life ends well as fulfilled. This signifies
a life well lived, recognized as such, and preserved and appreciated by others.

Similarly, there is the one and same comedy, which is always different, the
one and same story in manifest versions, which is lived through onstage.[82]
Young people fall in love, which inflicts pain and anguish (*acerba ex amore*),
for they are prevented from being together by irritated and grumpy old
men.[83] Yet everyone becomes involved in the actions and is helped by the
comic character (who is oppressed and as yet unfree). And thus, at the end,
the conflict comes to a happy resolution, and everyone gets what he or she
wants: young people receive love; old people receive appeasement for their
anger, as well as safety, power, and recognition, symbolically represented as
money; and the oppressed receive freedom.

Viktor Shklovsky, a founder of Formalism, noted that "plots are
homeless."[84] Not only are literary plots "homeless," but so are thoughts.
The "homelessness of plots and thoughts" might mean that they belong to
everyone, that they migrate and are variously appropriated in various circumstances. Everyone who tells the same story, who thinks the same thought,
coincides, then, with the other, thereby suspending but not cancelling

space, time, and language. The other often remains anonymous yet is still the real other who has acted through the same thought, even if in an entirely alien context. Yet the "homelessness of plots and thoughts" might also mean that plots as particular thoughts and acts are universal, that all (comic) plots are in a sense variations of one and the same. Thus, even if spectators already know the plot, they are still interested in the details of its development. All lives are different, and as such meaningful and interesting, because they vary in their details, which can be indefinitely (re)interpreted. Similarly, all comic plots vary, and so all comedies are different. Accordingly, we always want to engage again with a new, but same, comedy.

Contamination

Modern subjectivity constructed itself as unique and original, as the center of all produced meanings, and hence as the most important thing worthy of attention. Such subjectivity wanted novelty always to prevail, because uniqueness is new, and the new is unique for a time being. Hence, modern subjectivity perceived repetition of the same as boring, as mechanical, and (in Henri Bergson) as an infringement on its spontaneity and freedom. Yet the new is either a discovery or a construction of a new *form*, genre, or species, present through a multiplicity of prescriptions or a system of rules. *Qua* form, it is identical with itself and always the same, and yet it is infinitely variable in its concrete presentations and, thus, other and always different. This phenomenon is seen in Monet's series of pictures of the same Rouen cathedral, which is portrayed in a different light each time.

Greek New Comedy discovered a new dramatic form, anticipated in the previous drama but distilled and properly formulated only in Menander. Once the genre of comedy was established, one could reproduce it in new versions with new details. This led Roman comic playwrights to borrow plots freely from already existing, mostly Greek comedies, sometimes merging them. This was the practice of "contamination." For the modern subject, it was a humiliating practice, for it failed to recognize the subject's autonomy and originality, making it heteronomously dependent on what others had already thought and said. Any borrowing should have been put into either exalted or condescending quotation marks: this was a way to recognize the *old*, with a touch of admiration or disdain, and to indicate that one was going to make a better, *new* move. Failing to recognize the old—somebody else's—thought or saying was an infringement on the other's (intellectual) property as the extension of the self and was thus deemed plagiarism and theft.

However, there is really only a single form of comedy and a few already known good plots, which fulfill the purpose of comedy. And a single, isolated, autonomous subject is not really the center of comedy, which is rather played out in a dialogical interaction within a community of actors. Therefore, the free borrowing of plots is fully justified and does not need an excuse. Plots freely migrate within the space of comedy. Being "homeless," they are recycled and thus purify and distill comedy by "contamination." Philosophy, to a great extent, is also contaminated, since it mostly borrows, reinvents, or resuscitates old thoughts to address new problems.

Roman comediographers freely borrowed from the Greek originals and even from each other. *Contaminatio* was widely used by Plautus and Terence. If the watershed between the "ancients" and "moderns" could indeed be drawn as one between Old and New Comedy, then the proud and autonomous modern subjectivity was already present as a critic, reader, and spectator of the New Roman Comedy, which historically came after the Greek Nea. It is well-known that Apollodorus of Carystus was the source for Terence's *The Mother-in-Law* and *Phormio*; Diphilus's dramas were adopted by both Plautus and Terence; and Menander was the most frequent source of plots for Plautus, Terence,[85] and other Roman comic playwrights.[86]

Terence readily confessed to borrowing and combining from ancient plays, admitting not only that he did not regret it but would do so again as a remedy against dreary pedantry (*obscura diligentia*).[87] The goal of comic drama for Terence was not a good translation of the originals (*bene vertere*) but good writing (*bene scribere*). In the prologue to the *Brothers* he also recognized having borrowed from two skillful constructors of plots, Diphilus and Menander; however, he argued that this should not be considered a theft (*furtum*) but rather a borrowing,[88] which did not exclude some rearrangement of the plot(s) and the introduction of new characters. Terence had to defend himself against critics who reproached him for using Menander's *Eunuch* and *Flatterer* as well as the plays of Naevius and Plautus: one did not have to strive for originality, since it was hard to say what had not already been said.[89] Rather, one had to write a good play. Conversely, Terence's purist critic, who translated well but wrote poorly, made bad Latin plays from good Greek ones.[90]

Terence himself preferred a liberal attitude toward Greek originals, having no attachment to a literalism that would require undistorted translation. Thus, he defended the carelessness of Naevius, Plautus, and Ennius in their dealings with the originals, preferring a "negligent" freedom to a pedantic stringency. Only in this way can the spirit of the "immortal comedy" be saved without deadening it by meticulously sticking to the letter. Only a free attitude toward the original can renew a comic glance at contemporary things and events. A good comediographer thus places himself or herself within an already developed and sophisticated tradition without restraining his or her own spontaneous creativity. In doing so, a good dramatist follows a "golden mean," a "middle way" between meticulous copying of the original and arbitrariness of the imaginary. In other words, a good (comic) writer is neither a philologist nor a mathematician but still a bit of both.

Roman comedy was thus not a mere redressing of Greek comedy, as the *comoedia palliata*, just as later Roman (Neoplatonic) philosophy was not a mere rehash of classical Greek philosophy. Roman comedy was already a modern literary genre and remained such in modernity. New Comedy was a *new* form of comedy, which borrowed freely from an original in an *original* way. This form of New Comedy realized itself as standing in a particular relation to tradition, which it always supplemented with an original commentary and invention. This originality was unmistaken yet unstressed and inevitable, which distinguished it from eclecticism. Both components are important here: not only the break of the originality (which Terence humbly tried to hide) but also the continuity of the tradition.

The parallel with philosophy is rather evident: a philosophical work freely borrows, combines, and contaminates arguments, notions, and ideas from the extant tradition, which it does not even always acknowledge, for, apparently, the readers already know the source and are capable of recognizing it. Thus, Plato's argument against writing, at the end of the *Phaedrus*, to a great extent coincided with that of Alcidamas, in his essay against the Sophists, so that each might have "borrowed" from the other.[91] And yet philosophical work does not plagiarize the original, for it does not simply repeat a thought without reference but always tries to bring into discussion a *new* way of seeing an old problem. In this sense, in a genuine philosophical discussion, plagiarism is impossible, but contamination is necessary.

Comedy and Detective Story

In its outline and structure, comedy very much resembles the detective story.[92] If (New) comedy is one of the oldest surviving literary genres, the detective novel is very recent and modern: the first detective story written was Edgar Allan Poe's *The Murders in the Rue Morgue* (1841), followed by many masterpieces, which include Dostoevsky's *Crime and Punishment*, G. K. Chesterton's novels, and others. Yet the similarities between the two genres are also striking.

There are not too many good plots in comedy. Comedy may even recur to one and the same self-reproducing plot: it is defined by its beginning, involves a conflict, reaches a climax, and moves toward a resolution at the end. The attraction of a good comedy lies in the innovative use of its devices, the detailed rearrangement of the plot, and the subtle nuances in the portrayal of characters. Likewise with the detective story, which also employs variations of the same repeated plot: a murder in the beginning, a complex (rational) search for the truth of the case, and a good ending—the discovery and apprehension of the criminal and thus the restoration of justice. Both comedy and the detective story *end well* (a comedy in a desired ending and a detective story in establishing justice). In John Ford's *Young Mr. Lincoln* (1939), the young lawyer solves a complex case and, by asking appropriate ("dialectical") questions, contributes to the acquittal of two innocent young men accused of murder. Therefore, he plays the role of the "dialectician," the mastermind behind getting things right.

Yet despite a seeming repetitiveness of the story—which the readers know in advance, as they know the story in comedy—the detective novel invariably enjoys popularity. For while, in the elaboration of the story, each novel differs in its concrete constellation of details, a detective story allows the reader to participate emotionally and intellectually in tracing the development of the plot by following its minute hints and details and anticipating the wrongdoer. Finally, guessing the course of action in comedy implies a joy or satisfaction of understanding and recognition of the way things are, which is also invariably the case in the detective novel.

Both comedy and the detective story are deeply engaging and, consequently, never boring: they captivate the attention of the reader or listener. Further, both are rational and highly reflective: they involve deliberation and rational calculation (which, however, is oftentimes defied by the calculation of the author).[93] Again, both use a plot that is unified, subtly constructed, and defined by the *protasis-epitasis-catastrophe* structure. Both comedy and the detective story are conceptually written but medially can be written and oral (a detective story is easily turned into a dramatic theatrical piece). Both are based on the dialogical interaction of people. Finally, in both there is a mastermind who allows the action to move forward. Thus, the detective story is a specifically modern version of New Comedy, meant for the reader who is made to believe that tragedy (murder and crime) is the human condition. Comedy reappears, even if under a different guise.

CHAPTER 4

Whatever Works: Structure and Topics of Comedy

Constituents of the Comic Plot

In the discussion of the structure of comedy, I mostly follow Evanthius's distinctions.[1] I have already mentioned all four of them: *prologue, protasis, epitasis,* and *catastrophe.* In the present chapter I reveal how the first three function (catastrophe is addressed in the following chapter) with reference to several known comedies. This also includes a discussion of several comic *topoi,* or "topics"—the strategies of "argument" central to any comedy that lead to hilarity, confusion, and much laughter but also ensure resolution in a good ending. These strategies reveal that, often, in comedy "whatever works," and yet—not just anything goes.

Prologue

The introductory part of a comedy, the prologue, which existed already in ancient drama, remains somewhat aloof from the *protasis-epitasis-catastrophe* structure. According to Evanthius, the prologue is "the first speech" that opens a play and precedes the real development of the plot.[2] In ancient drama, there was quite a bit of experimentation with the prologue. Aeschylus had no prologue, and Sophocles's prologue introduced spectators into the play rather than telling the story. However, Euripides began his plays with a prologue that explained the plot and thus told the whole story in advance.[3] In this respect, a prologue is similar to a philosophical argument: it announces from the very beginning what it intends to achieve in the end. Aristophanes used a prologue, though not in Euripides's sense.[4] In Old Comedy, as in Sophocles, the prologue announced the action and introduced the spectators into the play. In New Comedy, as in both Plautus and Terence, the prologue presented a *sui generis* "literary criticism," an extraplot reflection on literary work as such as well as on this particular one.

Terence's prologue displayed features of reflectivity. Thus, the second part of the prologue to *The Mother-in-Law* was presented as an advocate (*orator*) in the guise of a prologue.[5] It was a prologue embodied as a speech, implying itself as it addressed the audience. The role of Euripides's explanatory and expository prologue was taken over by the Hypothesis to Menander's *Dyskolos*, written perhaps by Aristophanes of Byzantium, and by the Synopsis to Terence's plays.[6] In modern comedy, a prologue was sometimes used as an extradramatic address of the author to the readers as a justification for the play.

A modern reader or spectator is astonished that the whole intrigue is explained already at the very beginning of a play or novel. If one already knows the end, what is the point in suffering through the whole of a novel, in exercising one's wit in guessing the outcome? The difference lies in our perception of the role that plot does or should play in a written or staged piece. As Gregory Sifakis suggested, in contradistinction to ancient drama, modern drama functions within "the theatre of illusion," where the plot, similar to a real story, is always new and defies any established pattern. As he writes,

> When the play begins we know nothing about these individuals, and their actions are entirely unpredictable; but when the play ends each person should have emerged as a fully drawn personality through what he did and said on the stage. The essential elements, therefore, of realistic drama could be defined as follows: (a) the story is original and its outcome unpredictable; (b) the dramatic situations truthfully imitate situations of everyday life; (c) the characters are individuals psychologically portrayed by the way they act and react on the stage . . . None of the characteristics of modern realistic drama can be found in Greek (or Roman) drama. The stories were old—in tragedy even believed to be true—or conformed to a traditional pattern; so their end was known (tragedy), or predictable (Old Comedy), or actually predicted in the prologue (Euripides, New Comedy).[7]

The method of revealing the plot in advance runs contrary to the intentions of modern drama. Modern drama is expected to tell a story that defies our expectations and captivates our attention by moving through unknown territory. The "old" is a boring déjà vu; the "new" should be original and engaging, maintaining our interest as the action develops toward an end. Conversely, in ancient drama, the end was already known: it was death and suffering in tragedy and well-being in comedy. Hence, the audience's interest lay in the subtle variations on an already well-known theme.[8]

Yet Terence's New Comedy was modern in a further sense. For him, the prologue served not as a way for the author to explain the whole plot in advance but rather to address the audience directly, to lay out his own position and answer the critics, and also to recognize the (Greek) sources of the play.[9] As spectators or readers, we ourselves will—perhaps, *must*—learn something from the play. There is, therefore, always something unexpected in any play, which we need to guess at and anticipate—even if the general structure and outline of a comic play is constantly reproduced. And yet there is also some latitude for us to understand and interpret the play for ourselves.

Protasis. The *protasis–epitasis–catastrophe* structure organizes the action and exposes the comic plot. In the beginning of comedy, there is a *wrongdoing*. A transgressive act—usually, an illicit love—upsets the order of human relations, which then needs to be restored, not legally but by a concerted effort of the participants. Similarly to folktale in Vladimir Propp, where action was initiated in the violation of an interdiction or in villainy, comedy's plot is propelled by *harm* or *lack*.[10] As Chaerea in Terence's *Eunuch* said, "Often a great friendship has been forged from an incident of this sort [illicit love] and a bad beginning."[11] Without an initial man-made harm to an innocent (beloved) person or a lack of moral justification to an act (of love), there is no comedy. For, then, there is no problem to be "solved" by comic action. Similarly, in the media today, only news that reports a harm to others or a chronic lack of some basic life supplies makes "breaking news."

The story of a comedy, which was often already told in the prologue, began to unwrap in the *protasis*, the exposition that introduced the intrigue by partly explaining it and partly leaving it to the spectators to anticipate. However, in Terence the prologue tended to be a "literary critical" self-defense, an explanation of the author's motives as a writer. Thus, a further exposition—"foreplay," so to speak—became a necessary constituent of any play. In Terence, and often in later comedy, an exposition was always a separate opening scene, which was usually a dialogue between two interlocutors. These speakers introduced the problem and outlined the "premises" for the action, often voicing the opposing views or theses that would struggle throughout the comedy in order to be reconciled at the end. A remarkable example of such introductory (here, ironic) dialogue is found in the opening scene of Molière's *Les femmes savantes*: two sisters, Armande and Henriette, present opposite views on marriage as an oppressive social institution with the possibility of rejecting it in favor of philosophy as the life of the mind.

The exposition could also be a long monologue. However, this was always in fact a dialogue in which one introduced the action while talking to oneself, thus somewhat schizophrenically impersonating the other (in a dialogue "to oneself"), as Argan did in Molière's *Le malade imaginaire*. Yet, as always, monologue did not hold in either comedy or life and ceded to dialogue. Thus, *Brothers* was Terence's only play that opened with a lengthy monologue.[12]

In Menander's *Dyskolos*, the expository scene was a monologue by Pan, who explained the whereabouts of the characters and outlined the intrigue but who then played no further role in the development of events. Sometimes, the exposition was a combination of a monologue, which addressed a silent or absent character, followed by a lengthy dialogue, as in the two opening scenes of Terence's *Brothers*, which constituted the entire first act.[13] There, Micio, and then two brothers, Micio and Demea, laid out the beginning of the plot and introduced two competing approaches to education and life, one liberal and the other conservative, which too would be reconciled in the end, when the liberal one prevailed.

Sometimes, in the opening dialogue, one of the interlocutors did not become involved in the subsequent unfolding of the plot's argument, being only an addressee for the other speaker who explained the action.[14] The only role of this so-called *prosōpon protatikon* was to listen and understand the exposition and thus collectively represent the spectators or listeners onstage.[15] The term *protatikon* literally means "capable of advancing a proposition" and refers to *protasis*, Aristotle's general logical term for *proposition*: a speech or argument (*logos*) that either asserts or denies something about something.[16] It could also designate a premise in a syllogism or simply refer to a proposed problem. All these meanings were present in the comic *protasis*. In mathematical use, comic *protasis* corresponded rather to three parts in Proclus's division of proof—enunciation, exposition, and specification, insofar as a *protasis* identified the "given" starting points for the development of the plot and specified what the comedy sought to achieve.

A *protasis* was thus the "logical" beginning and comic "origin" of action through which the comic story developed toward a resolution, implicit in the exposition yet only fully explicit at the end. Therefore, a *protasis* was justified only through the full and complete action that moved—by the joint and consorted action of its actors and spectators—to the end, which, in turn, justified the beginning.

Epitasis Topics

The exposition, or *protasis*, was followed by the *epitasis*, that is, by the complication, development, and climax of the plot. Literally, *epitasis* means "intensity" or "increase in intensity." Aristotle used this technical term in his physics to describe the intensification of motion.[17] *Epitasis* was thus the central, longest, and most complex part of a comic play. Put again in logical terms, it corresponds to the motion of a syllogism from the premises through the middle term. In dialectic, it stands for the ordered step-by-step motion of reasoning in an argument. And in mathematics, *epitasis* corresponds to construction and proof, insofar as it produces the desired result, explaining that the sought-after is achieved and how it is achieved.

In Aristotle's *Rhetoric*, the discussion of the rhetorical syllogism, or enthymeme, was immediately followed by a description of 28 different *topoi*, or "places." These were "strategies of argument," as Kennedy calls them, or the most general forms of reasoning, persuasion, deliberative action, and conclusion.[18] These "common topics" were applicable not only to rhetorical reasoning but to any valid form of reasoning, including logical, dialectical, mathematical, and dramatic. For example, one could reason from contrasting opposites (this was topic 14) when faced with a dilemma where one had to make a judgment and act (or not act)—in a situation where opposite positions both entailed a certain disadvantage.[19]

The comic *epitasis* was complex: it had various methods, devices, and ways of proceeding. Thus, here, I mention only three common *topoi* of comedy, followed by a discussion of three "fallacious" common places.[20]

(i) Gnome or Sententia

The *gnome*, sententia, or maxim is a first *topos* or "common place" of comedy. A *gnome* is a short, condensed formulation of a thought that can be easily memorized and uttered on the right occasion. The *gnōmē*—literally, *thought* or *judgment*, and translated into Latin as *sententia*—was an old Greek literary device, already found in Homer's poems, at least by his later readers who never tired of extracting quotations from him.[21] In the sixth through fifth centuries BCE, the genre became not only well established in elegy but also in philosophy.[22] Epicharmus, the probable originator of comedy, left a substantial number of gnomes.[23] Moreover, he explicitly said that "all living beings have reason [*gnōmē*]."[24] This is an interesting case of a self-reflective and self-referential gnome about gnome, which shows that the gnomic tradition was not only used at the time but was also used consciously and deliberately. Drama, and comedy in particular, already abounded in sententiae or maxims, which were often quoted within other dramas and literary texts and have come down to us as "fragments" of ancient writers, carefully selected, arranged, and edited by conscientious philologists. Euripides, Menander, and Terence all used maxims, skillfully weaving them into the fabric of the plot. In this way, a maxim within a drama was not an isolated saying but communicated and presented an important thought, often central to a play.

Terence was particularly abounding in the sententiae department, for which he was already known in antiquity. Some were old proverbs, like the famous Pythagorean proverb "Friends share everything in common."[25] Many others were invented by Terence and became proverbial and commonly cited, such as "Their silence is praise enough"[26] and "You'll hear all the quicker if you keep quiet."[27] In his *Aesthetics*, Alexander Baumgarten referred to Terence when speaking about his "laudable absolute brevity."[28]

In fact, many maxims became such once they were quoted out of context by other authors. Thus, the famous "homo sum; humani nil a me alienum puto" was usually meant to say that, being a human, I share in all human weaknesses, and hence a particular weakness is excusable, since nobody's free of it.[29] In Terence's play, however, the character (Chremes) meant to say that he took on other people's work and business (by laboring on his own farm), because he acted out of a sense of humanism and solidarity, and thus could help his son by providing him additional income.

The very brevity and thus indeterminacy of the maxim made it an attractive item for reinterpretation and quotation in a new context. Even Saint Paul quoted Menander's *Thaïs*—"Evil communications corrupt evil manners"—without much caring for the source or the original context.[30] Some maxims became so popular that they turned into proverbs (many coming from the Bible), some of which we use to this very day without an understanding of their pedigree. A gnome could take the form of aphorism or apophthegm, a "terse pointed saying," often produced on purpose in order to enhance the rhetorical effect of what was said, as in the famous Laconic sayings.[31]

A gnome was thus a concentrated and condensed thought. It was a thought distilled and fragmented on purpose, in order to reflect the whole of an argument in a brief maxim. For this reason, as said, a gnome bore similarity to a joke and often replaced a joke in later comedy, since a joke too was a coagulated narrative. A gnome, then, could be used for both narration and proof.[32] The gnome was a "zipped" argument, intended to be unfolded by the spectators, readers, or listeners. They thus exercised their autonomous hermeneutic and detective abilities. As they became involved in the action, the comedy thereby became interactive. Some famous maxims (such as "know thyself") were not at all evident and were contrary to popular wisdom. Being paradoxical, they invited people to think for themselves, often together with others. There was thus much affinity between gnome and logical or rhetorical syllogism. Aristotle dedicated a whole chapter to maxims in his *Rhetoric*,[33] which comes right before the discussion of enthymeme or rhetorical syllogism.[34]

A gnome was a particularly appropriate comic device, as it could speak in universal terms about what was not universal. By using incongruence (e.g., when "all living beings are endowed with reason" referred to a stupid man), a maxim could produce a comic effect. Yet the maxim's thought could also arouse passions, which was especially suitable for drama, including comedy.

Because a maxim expressed a thought, speaking in maxims fit those who were more experienced in making judgments.[35] Perhaps the maxim was an archaic "pre-Enlightenment" tool that expressed wisdom by stating *what* was the case without discussing *why* it was the case, that is, without an explicit argument or explanation. However, as Aristotle argued, a maxim was in fact similar to a syllogism, since a maxim was an assertion of a generality and hence a sort of minimal enthymeme. In other words, a maxim was more condensed than an enthymeme, which at least stated some of the premises explicitly, whereas a maxim gave only the conclusion, supposing that the presupposition, premises, and argument itself were evident or could be easily restored. A gnome or maxim was thus an important comic *topos*, insofar as it condensed a particular argument and presented it through a character's thought and thereby also reflected the whole argumentative, rational, and "logical" structure of the plot.

Aphorism and Fragment

A gnome thus "rounded up" a thought, made it into an aphorism, which literally was a delimitation, or assignment of boundaries. An aphorism thus shaped thinking into a compact and beautiful form: it could be remembered and withstand time. Once a thought had been thought through, it could become an aphorism. A thought was put into this form in order to prevent forgetting, if not the long and complex process of reasoning, then at least the conclusion.

Modern authors—as different as the marquis de Vauvenargues, Ludwig Wittgenstein, and Nicolás Gómez Dávila—often used the genre of aphorism. In ancient philosophy and comedy, a gnome was a result of the work of reason, which was meant to be appropriated by everyone, universalizable in (philosophical) thinking and (comic) action. Modern subjectivity, however, favored aphorism as a written and published "*pensée*" for a different reason. An aphorism testifies to one's uniqueness: it is *mine*; I produced it. And even if modern solitary and monological thinking still aspired to wisdom, it marked this turn by authorship: wisdom was not an anonymous saying of a Delphic pythia but testified to the wit of—and thus glorified—*this* individual. As Pascal noted aphoristically, "the delight of glory is so great that one loves any object that one attaches to it, even death."[36]

Moreover, aphorism in modernity was transformed into a fragment— literally, a "splinter"—which was a way to break away from a monoconscious thinking that distilled itself into a verified logical system. A fragment, then, was a shatter of a broken systematic whole that was not preserved, because the whole was considered impossible to achieve. In particular, fragmentation became the way of thinking about past art and thought. Many texts of pre-Socratic philosophers that survived in the quotations of other authors, and thus became fragments, are now *only* fragments. The "broken" and fragmented whole of a thought, a philosophical system, or a literary work is only implied but remains inaccessible.

A fragment, which can be an extended form of aphorism or even an enthymeme, can become its own subject matter. However, Epicharmus spoke about the gnome in a gnome: thus, a reflection on the role of fragment might be appropriate in fragments, precisely as a reflection of an unobtainable whole. And if a fragment happens to contain a thought and say something that can be shared with others, it is therefore comic, because it then achieves its purpose and comes to a "good ending."

- Can one write philosophy in fragments? A fragment is isolated, and yet it is a whole, even if incomplete.
- Fragmentation in writing corresponds to fragmentation in thought: if discursive thinking means constantly going from one thought to another, then each thought, even if a step in reasoning, is discrete. If nondiscursive thinking is an understanding, an insight that we sometimes get, then the thought or "idea" obtained in such understanding is also discrete. Perhaps, then, a fragment stands for and reflects an independent, though not isolated, thought, either in discursive or in nondiscursive thinking.
- Because each thought is not isolated, it therefore possesses an inherent relation to other thoughts (maybe even to all thoughts?) that one moves through. In this sense, thinking and writing in fragments is justifiable. However, this "inherent" connection between fragments may come from a certain systematicity within thinking itself—or from a coherence of the character of a thinker, which is determined not only culturally but also individually, as one's "personal other." It seems, then, that an intrinsic connection between fragments is differently established in these two cases.
- A fragment differs from an aphorism, for an aphorism is a sharp and pointed *bon mot* meant to be said on occasion, whereas a fragment may (and perhaps should) be left as it is, stylistically imperfect and rough-edged, a trace of a thought that happened once and will never be repeated again in exactly the same way in the same circumstance.
- A fragment is a minimal compromise between a continuing thinking and its written molding into an acceptable form. Thoughts are many, and hence they can be forgotten; fragments save them from oblivion.
- A fragment is also a minimal act of politeness to the reader: there are many lengthy books with valuable insights, yet to extract their thoughts is not easy, for one is often intimidated by the sheer amount of work.

Through its conciseness, a fragment is capable of explaining itself in "two or three words." Of course, its insight might be nil, but at least we are not vexed by spending a life on it.

- But a fragment can equally catch one's attention. As such, it may be either an incentive for thinking, when one suddenly realizes that there is something in there (*il y a quelque chose là dedans*), even if one cannot quite grasp what it is. Or a fragment can suddenly clarify what one has been thinking yet was unable to bring together: a fragment can thus be a "coping stone," the last piece in a puzzle without which one cannot get the whole picture.

- A thought represented in a fragment may appear different at another time, or at least it can be seen as differently connected to other thoughts. What one said at one time might be opposite to what one says now: one can be mistaken either then or now. In that case, one of the thoughts behind a fragment should be rejected as wrong, since two mutually contradictory statements can be said but not thought at the same time. And yet the very act of thinking—of having had a thought—is indubitably present in each of the thoughts. *Si fallor, sum.*

(ii) Monologue

The monologue is another *topos* of comedy. Comedy is monological in its plot, which is an artificial construction or "argument" of the author. Yet comedy also needs a plurality of independent voices and characters to take part in the commonly shared action through their dialogues. Monologues are abundant in comedy, but in fact they are not monological. A pure monologue, a distilled soliloquy, a speech that does not seem to have an addressee, was the invention of a modern subjectivity that was satisfied with itself and was therefore solipsistic and did not need the other. But in comedy's action, as in life, everyone is engaged in common action and hence always in need of an other. Thus, pure monologue is a *contradictio in adiecto* and is impossible.

Monologue is therefore already implicitly dialogical. A comic monologue is meaningful only once an implicit inner dialogue is presupposed—a dialogue between a character and herself, between different characters, or between characters and spectators. A comedy, as said, often began with a monologue in the prologue, which, however, was dialogical because it addressed not only a *prosōpon protatikon* but also the listeners. Besides, a monologue could amount to the retelling of a previous dialogue within a dialogue with another person.[37] This was a common device in many of Plato's dialogues, such as the *Parmenides*, where a character retold a dialogue that had taken place between other people, which he had presumably heard or overheard. Comedy also favored monologues of eavesdropping as a means of plotting. However, it was only meaningful when the eavesdropping character responded with a mono-logue in the presence of the implicit response of the listeners.

A monologue is lengthy and slow, whereas a dialogue consists of short rejoinders and is therefore quick. Monologue represents what Socrates called "long speech" (*makrologia*), which either ignores others or condescendingly allows them to listen but not to join in.[38] A lengthy monologue is self-defying, not only because it is boring but also because it prevents itself from expressing a meaning it intends to convey—for nobody's listening. Thus, Chrysale's long monological speech in Molière's *Les femmes savantes* was meant as a rejoinder in a dialogue with his sister, and it was performatively self-contradictory from the very beginning, because the very length of such a "rejoinder" would not allow the other to respond and properly join in the dialogue. The speech, which was a philippic against women's education as allegedly causing harm to a household, exposed its own untenability by the very act of its uttering in the presence of educated women.[39] The self-defeat of the speech became ever more apparent as it continued unwinding. Paradoxically, within the plot of the comedy Molière himself wanted the speech to mean what it claimed, yet, ironically, the speech eventually defied not only itself but also the intention of the author. Such *double irony* can be considered another comic device—a speech ironically defying and cancelling the originally intended irony put into it by its author.

Dialogue, in contrast, is energetic, brief, and fast-moving.[40] Quick dia-logue consisting of short rejoinders was a favorite tool of comedy. Shakespeare and Molière used it often. Because dialogue is swift and attends to others, it always consists of a series of mutually interrupting rejoinders. Thus, Terence's *Phormio* presented a dialogue between three people consisting practically of one single word ("sold," *vendidit*) repeated four times;[41] and, in *Andria*, seven rejoinders of a dialogue fit within one single line![42]

(iii) Recognition

Recognition is an important comic *topos*. The motif of recognition is com-mon in all cultures and myths.[43] Recognition is a cognition, a cognitive act confirming another person's true identity, showing who she or he is. The other person becomes fully "real" and human only as a result of being recog-nized as such by others.

Recognition is both possible and necessary because of an initial misrecog-nition. Thus, recognition is based in negativity, in a mistaken acceptance of "what" or "who" the other is. Thus, in Terence's *The Mother-in-Law*, the young man Pamphilus married a woman whom he first did not recognize as the woman he loved.[44] Besides, recognition is a reflective act, because in order to recognize the other properly one must, first, recognize one's own initial misrecognition or mistake; second, recognize the necessity of correcting it; and third, come to understand who the other is. Recognition therefore begins with the recognition of misrecognition; it continues with the recognition of the importance and necessity of recognition; and ends (or should end) with the recognition of the other's identity, which the other now recognizes too as a result of the reflective act of recognition.

Recognition thus implies a kind of "repentance" as the recognition of misrecognition. In the Greek tradition, this was the repentance of the author, the poet who had wrongly transmitted the foundational myth of the whole culture—of the rape of Helen and her abduction to Troy. As the tradition goes, Helen was not really brought to Troy—only her image or "apparition" was—but spent the whole time in Egypt waiting for the end of the war. The punishment for telling the untruth of Helen's abduction to Troy for the poets was blindness. However, Stesichorus was able to recognize his mistake by writing a so-called song of repentance (*palinōidia*) and, as a result, was able to see light again, whereas Homer stubbornly persisted in his misrecognition and, as a result, remained blind.[45] "Repentance" leads to a sudden and unexpected, yet necessary and thus predictable, change in one's understanding of other people.[46]

The final moment of the recognition of the other's "who" requires certain devices and, in modern society, certain institutions and democratic practices and procedures.[47] Most importantly, it requires that one recognize one's own recognition of another person and, thereby, her recognition of such recognition—at which point the act of recognition becomes complete and fully reflective. In this way, recognition is capable not only of grasping a unique other's "who" but also the other's humanity, which one now shares with her as an equal in a mutual dialogically established recognition of each other.

Comedy thus establishes a mutually recognized comic identity that is not a given but a task to be *achieved*. It is comic because the attempt of recognition succeeds, or "ends well," which is by no means guaranteed in advance, particularly because recognition is a complex act.

In New Comedy, recognition was usually triggered by a "sign," or the testimony of a witness, which revealed a character's identity.[48] In modern comedy, this procedure was common too, as in Shakespeare's *Twelfth Night*, where "maiden weeds" assured Sebastian that he had indeed found his sister Viola whom he considered to have perished.[49] Comedy shares this feature with its modern sibling, the detective story, where a piece of evidence makes it possible to find the criminal.

Recognition by a token or by testimony was commonplace in late tragedy, particularly in Euripides, in whom, however, it worked toward a different end: characters would suffer or face death as a result of their actions. Thus, in Euripides's *Iphigenia in Tauris*, Iphigenia recognized her brother by calling his name; and in the *Electra*, Orestes was recognized by an old man at Electra's country estate. A foundling whose identity was revealed later in the course of action was also often present in Euripides. In the *Ion*, Ion was recognized as the son of Creusa with the help of the things he was found with (a basket and baby linen).[50]

A token was a "symbol" (Greek *symbolon*) or "sign" (Latin *signum*) that made recognition possible. "Symbolon" originally meant the half of an object that two parties kept and presented to each other on occasion as proof of identity, which they thus mutually recognized.[51] A "symbol" is therefore a *sui generis* "password" that allows for a recognition of who one is by others and also by oneself: I do not know who I am until my "symbol" fits the other half and until I am recognized by others. The object of recognition is therefore also a "signum," a sign or mark, which is also a *proof*—again, of who one is in a mutual recognition. In Menander's *Epitrepontes*, a child was recognized through the tokens he was found with;[52] in Terence, a box with tokens was presented as proof of a girl's identity.[53] The token here is a "monumentum," a memory or recollection, a memorable sign or "monument"—a testimony to what happened in the past, which makes it possible to understand oneself in the present and thus come to a future resolution of a current conflict.

The act of recognition is thus necessary for comedy. However, finding the "symbol" in a thing or a testimony, as evidence that establishes one's identity, is itself accidental and contingent. Yet this contingency *should* happen, so that its appearance in the plot is itself not contingent. The apparent contradiction between the necessity and contingency of recognition in drama is solved by an appeal to fate, which I discuss in what follows. Fate is responsible for contingent events that are at the same time necessary and are thus guided by both chance and necessity.

"Fallacious" Topics

After having discussed various rhetorical *topoi* in the *Rhetoric*, Aristotle moved on to exposing "fallacious" topics (e.g., from an accidental result), which render an argument or enthymeme logically invalid.[54] In comedy, however, the situation is different. Although, as I have argued, comedy uses sophisticated dialectical ways of structuring its plot or overall "argument," as well as particular scenes and rejoinders, it does not care much for the logical validity or truthfulness of its premises as the starting points for action. Comedy is pragmatic: it is interested in making sure its action works and that it comes to a good ending. Certainly, this does not mean that total licentiousness is permitted or that anything goes. New Comedy unambiguously distanced itself from the abusive recklessness of Old Comedy, assuming that to take an immoral course of action to straighten an initial moral and physical harm made a good ending self-contradictory.

Yet comedy accepted certain strategies of action that looked highly suspicious and "fallacious" to modern monological moralistic consciousness. Their "fallaciousness" appeared in comedy's use of illusion—as well as in the breaking of scenic illusion—and of that which could not be controlled by the rational will of the actor, that is, fate. Comedy even used a seeming deception, which employed doubles and ruses, and which sometimes turned into the double deception, deceiving the deceiver. Thus, Pythias took revenge of Parmeno, who had deceived her, by deceiving him herself, which she did by telling an invented story.[55] In this way, she reentangled the action that Parmeno had tried to disentangle; yet in the end she disclosed the truth to Parmeno: "I've worn myself out laughing at you."[56] The truth was thus restored through double deception. However, that moral action might employ deception was utterly unacceptable to a modern deontological Kantian subject: such an action was morally suspect, as it ran contrary to this subject's autonomous rational activity. And yet this subject was itself comically suspicious and compromised in its self-satisfaction, with its righteousness directed primarily toward itself and not toward the other person.

When comic characters and the author used "trickery," they did so because they always acted in a situation of uncertainty. They were only certain of the certainty of the outcome, namely that current difficulties could and *should* be resolved. An apparent "fallaciousness" of comic *topoi* thus consisted not in a logical falseness of the premises that might yield a true conclusion but in a comic response to the contingency that necessarily converges on a mutually acceptable conclusion or good ending.

(i) Doubles Truth-Telling and Deceit

Comedy was the dramatic forum for dialectical reasoning: thus, comedy was carried through by dialogue and propelled by opposites, which were embodied in coupled rejoinders, paired characters, and double scenes. In such pairs, one rejoinder, character, or scene opposed yet answered, complemented, and presupposed the other. In Aristophanes, there were few paired scenes and characters (e.g., Aeschylus and Euripides); by contrast, in New Comedy they were rather typical, necessary to the "dialectical" development of the action throughout the "argument" of the plot.

Two was the minimal number of characters for a dialogue and interaction: to show a development of thought or to stage a dispute, the playwright needed the one who asked and the one who replied. In Old Comedy, the minimal dialogical duality was presented by the collective body and personality of the chorus, usually divided into two parts. Thus double characters are rare and are mostly secondary in Aristophanes.[57]

New Comedy was abundant with duos—paired characters who embodied dialectical opposites and supplied them with a soundtrack.[58] Double characters were common in Plautus: two old men, Nicobulus and Philoxenus; two young men, Mnesilochus and Pistoclerus; and two courtesans bearing the same name of Bacchis in the *Bacchides*. And double characters were pervasive in all of Terence's plays: two old men, two matrons, two young men, two (silent) young girls, two slaves, two brothers, two courtesans, and, of course, two lovers.[59] Two independent yet mutually responsive characters and voices were also a mark of modern comedy, abundant in Shakespeare and Molière, in Beckett (*Waiting for Godot*) and Ionesco (*The Chairs*). Several months before his death in Stockholm, René Descartes was writing a comedy (left unfinished) in French, which, judging by Leibniz's brief note, was a new comedy that celebrated the life and love of the two main characters, Alixan and Parthenie, disguised under a double identity.[60] Importantly, the comic double was a *real* person, not a mirrored image of the self, as was Fyodor Dostoevsky's Double in the *Notes from Underground*, who was the double of the same, of a modern subject that looked in vain for the other within itself as its own mirror.

Comedy constantly referred to, implied, and provoked opposite *feelings*, passions, and emotions. For example, first there was mistrust, and then there was trust: "You want me to believe that, when it's unbelievable? I believe you."[61] Comic catharsis followed, as the "purification" of the passions by opposite passions. As Pamphilus in Terence's *Andria* exults at receiving unexpected news that in part resolves the complex intrigue said, "I am in a jumble of emotions, fear, hope, joy."[62] Or, as Parmeno lamented, "To love someone who's taken a dislike to you is stupid twice over."[63] Yet this was the way of comedy. Comedy always allowed for the resolution of a seemingly irresolvable conflict: through the exposure to two equal possibilities (in emotions and in action) that made them seemingly impossible—as when Pamphilus ordered Parmeno to stay and run at the same time.[64] The comic resolution, however, differed from the tragic or elegiac one in which one had to accept the unacceptable in a sublime heroic or desperate defying gesture, as in Catullus's "I love and I hate."[65] The comic solution of a dramatic human problem involving opposites did not "sublate" the opposites in a supposed reconciliation. Rather, it provided a sophisticated rational and dramatic construction resembling a dialectical argument. Therein one moved through the interaction of opposites, allowing for a well-conceived resolution of the conflict and a dramatic—though not speculative—reconciliation of opposites.

Comedy, as mentioned, was agonistic: it always presupposed a fight. Opposing, double characters disagreed and struggled in verbal duels and battles, which were often framed as double scenes or even double intrigues. As comic plot goes through intense action, complication, and struggle, double scenes were an effective device for presenting a comic conflict.

Double scenes and double intrigues that paralleled and responded to each other were also abundant in comedy. For example, Menander's *Dyskolos* and Shakespeare's *The Taming of the Shrew* end in two marriages.[66] Plautus's *Miles gloriosus* uses a twin-sister intrigue and a pseudowife intrigue, and Terence masterfully uses a double scene in *The Woman from Andros*, where two characters are talking to each other and two are eavesdropping,[67] which creates a complex dynamic interaction between the two duos and a whirlwind action in which spectators also become inescapably involved as listeners and involuntary eavesdroppers.

A double scene signified an important moment in the development of the plot: it would lead to a resolution of the complication by an even further complication. Double scenes often implied a seeming *deception*, which, however, was a way of telling the truth and steering the action in the desired direction.

Thus, the very name of Plautus's Pseudolus suggested a double deception: *pseudos*—falsehood, deception, fallacy, or false conclusion—and *dolos*—bait for fish—hence, a cunning contrivance for deceiving or catching. Pseudolus came to truth by provoking the untruth to expose and to ridicule itself, thus unmasking the untruth through untruth. A typical comic ploy was to read a fabricated letter about the supposed financial collapse of the family, in order to try two grooms: one groom sought to marry the daughter in hopes of a rich dowry but, having heard the news, quickly withdrew; the other offered all the help he could possibly give and, as a result, after the ruse was exposed, happily married the daughter.

In a double scene in Terence's *The Woman from Andros*, Davus talked to the maid Mysis in such a manner as to let the old man Chremes overhear the dialogue, without making Chremes know that he overheard it.[68] In this way, imitating dialectical reasoning,[69] Davus revealed the true identity of a woman and a child, which he could not reveal straightforwardly, for Chremes would not have believed him: "It was the only way we could make him believe what we wanted."[70] For one believes the conclusion if one arrives at it oneself. In order to accept a solution of a problem, one needs to be able to reproduce every step along the way of its construction in reasoning or (in the case of comedy) acting. Therefore, in order to tell a truth—which is a difficult under-taking that requires courage—one sometimes should not speak sincerely and naturally but rather with a premeditated intention or by acting a part.[71]

Thus, Davus did not lie, though he intentionally spoke ambiguously: "If you discover I've told a lie, put me to death."[72] And yet this ambiguity was interpreted unambiguously by the listener (or eavesdropper). That the ironic, dialectically framed, ambiguous dialogue nevertheless yielded a unique answer is the art of comic reasoning.

The truth in comedy can sometimes be gained by seemingly avoiding it, by putting on a mask and playing a new role.[73] Thus, in *The Self-Tormentor*, Chremes said to his slave Syrus that another slave was supposed to "invent something, devise a trick to get money for the young man to give to his mistress, and to save the bad-tempered old man in spite of himself."[74] Per-plexed by the suggestion of such a "strategy," Syrus asks, "Hey, tell me, do you approve of slaves who deceive their masters? – In the right circumstances, I do. – And rightly so. – Because this is often the remedy for serious prob-lems."[75] Then Syrus recognizes, "I am pretty experienced and I know how these things are done," but adds, "I'm not used to telling lies."[76] Syrus seems to mean this both ironically and seriously, for although he was capable of using the "fallacious" *topos* of double-acting, he did *not* lie in doing so, since his action, being apparently deceptive, cancelled another deceptive action and so helped others—not himself—out of a complicated situation and a seeming impasse.[77] However, in the end he helped himself, too: he received his freedom by helping others, although he did not intend to do so when act-ing. When Syrus suggested to a young man, "I do not want you to tell a lie,"[78] this not telling a lie was itself a cunning plan of the plot. The truth-telling thus implied a seeming pretense that annulled itself: in this case, a withdrawal of truth that revealed the truth. Syrus concludes, then, "I congratulate myself with great pride on possessing so much power and being capable of so much cunning that I can deceive both of them by telling the truth."[79] Syrus's crafti-ness, however, caused only laughter,[80] as did Panurge's slyness in François Rabelais, which, in this case, was a sign of relief and appreciation of the ambiguity that worked toward a resolution of the conflict.

Double Identity, Misrecognition, and Misunderstanding

The art of getting the truth by seemingly avoiding it was practiced by comedy to the point of refinement. Arriving at a truth from an untruth was pos-sible and, in a sense, necessary in comedy, for comedy began with a harm that was first disguised by a lie. Moreover, the understanding of a truth at which comedy eventually arrived always began with a misunderstanding.

However, unlike understanding, which closed a discussion and signified an end to action, misunderstanding was fruitful and *productive* and thus enabled the interlocutors to think further and move on in their search for a good ending. Since understanding is a personal and even intimate act—nobody can understand for me; I have to do it myself—comic action is engaging and never boring. Yet it is also a constant attempt at solving problems and bringing together the pieces of a puzzle.

Understanding in a comedy was not arbitrary, because, as a free act, it was implied in the motion of the whole of a plot and also in a particular question or a given dialogical situation, which, even apparently ambiguous and not understandable,[81] suggested an unambiguous answer. The ambiguous identity could also be ascribed by different characters, in a double entendre, to an act or a thing (such as a vase or a chamber pot). This could always provoke laughter and complicate a situation. Comic understanding thus began with a necessary ambiguity and *misunderstanding*, which was *carefully calculated* by the author and entrusted to one of the characters, who then became the mastermind behind the action.

This comic hermeneutic structure parallels the structure of recognition, which, as I have argued, always begins with misrecognition. For this reason comedy needed trickery and a double—mistaken—identity, as a way to grapple with the constant uncertainty of the situation. Yet this uncertainty was certain to be resolved: the comedy eventually revealed the mistake, and—often with the additional help of a token as a "symbol" of recognition of who one is—the misrecognition ceded to proper recognition.

The doubling of a character, carefully calculated and often set in a double scene, was a favorite "fallacious" *topos* of comedy. Pretending to be the other is philosophically ironic, because irony is a way of falsely enacting a false pretense, thereby showing what is by what is not, or by what appears to be other than what it is. Doubling is necessarily reflective, because it allows for *distancing* and thus mirroring oneself in a real other and discovering "the other within" as well as "the same without" in the other person.

Employing doubles in comedy thus allowed the author to question the idea of a stable and monolithic identity of both dramatic characters and real persons. By becoming—or pretending—to be one's own physical other, one allowed for a nonidentical identity, which was thus shaken and fluid, misrecognized, misunderstood, and misinterpreted. The confused—personal, sexual, or social—identity became the source of error and incongruity, which allowed for a development of the intrigue.

The comic doubling of oneself faced with the other puts one's firm identity into question. As Terence put it, "How each one resembles himself!"[82] That is to say, each disputer *resembled himself* and reproduced himself as a character and yet *did not fully coincide* with himself. For he was forced to recognize this noncoincidence as the comic action developed. In comedy, everyone always attempted to remain identical with her or his self, with an image that everyone has of such a self. And yet, ironically, everyone became nonidentical with his or her self, so that every comic character was a "twoself."

The initial recognition of oneself thus turned out to be misrecognition, a "carnivalesque" exchange of roles.[83] And yet this allowed in the end for a proper recognition of who one was—universally, as human, and individually, in a particular respect: socially, sexually, or temperamentally. The possibility of such recognition eventually realized in common action and effort testifies, once again, to the justice and goodness of comedy.

Doubling a character is also a source of *intrigue*, especially when one appears as her or his physical other—as a (false or imaginary) twin. In Plautus's *Miles gloriosus*, one of the characters, the girl Philocomasium, presented herself as her own twin sister and thus became a double lover in order deliberately to create confusion that would resolve the dramatic conflict. The intrigue with pseudoadultery and the resulting birth of twins was propelled in Plautus's *Amphitryon* by Jupiter, who assumed the appearance of Amphitryon, in which form he appeared before Amphitryon's wife, Alcmene, accompanied by Mercury, who was disguised as Amphitryon's slave Sosia.

The change of dress was a usual actor's device that allowed one to assume any temporary identity.[84] Double identity was often presented as a travesty—literally, a "disguise by dress"—which, through an intentional initial misrecognition, brought one back to oneself. Thus, for instance, in Terence, a young boy, Chaerea, dressed as a eunuch and then dressed back or "mutated."[85] In Bernardo Dovizi's *La Calandria*, Lidio and Santilla, twin brother and sister, learned each other's identity only eventually, though they looked very much alike—since Santilla dressed as Lidio.[86] In Shakespeare's *Twelfth Night*, Olivia dressed as a man in order to be able to talk to Viola about the love of Orsino. As a result, Viola fell in love with Olivia, Olivia loved Orsino, and Orsino loved Viola. The whole play was a comedy of doubles and misrecognized identity, a "comedy of errors": a trick[87] was played on Malvolio, and he was declared mad; the clown Feste dressed up as a priest; and Viola's brother Sebastian was taken to be Viola, who presented herself as a man. When finally, in the last act, Sebastian entered and Orsino saw him and his sister Olivia, dressed as a young man (Cesario), Orsino could only exclaim in astonishment, "One face, one voice, one habit, and two persons! / A natural perspective, that is and is not!"[88]

Comic identity was therefore always a double identity. Even the comic playwright himself, as said, often belonged to two different cultures, which allowed him to distance himself from each and fruitfully work between them.

This allowed the author to bring out the commonly human in all of us, which, however, was shown differently each time within a particular cultural setting. The comic actor, in a sense, had a double double identity, because, being human, she impersonated a fictional character—and because this comic character herself was often doubled on stage. Finally, the spectator, listener, or reader also had a double identity, for although she understood the ambiguity of a situation that was not understandable to the characters on stage, she was also pulled into the action whose outcome she anticipated but did not yet know precisely. In this sense, the spectator is the double of the character. But most importantly, unlike comic characters, the spectator understood that the comic action was fictitious and yet accepted it as meaningful and revealing a truth about everyone's, and thus her own, life.

A Case Study

Molière's Sganarelle. Molière's early comedy *Sganarelle, or the Imaginary Cuckold* is a fine example of the functioning of double scenes and double characters, as well as of mistaken and misrecognized identity.[89] The intrigue was based on an imputed infidelity, which was resolved at the end, when it was shown to be a sheer misunderstanding and a deceit displaying the true love. The plot of the comedy, which took precedence over the characters (who were paired as Célie and Lélie), was well conceived, calculated, and constructed: it revealed a tightly structured argument, which developed in a number of steps presented through dialogue: (1) Gorgibus, a grumpy father, wants his daughter Célie to marry Valère, a rich man who never appears on stage; yet Célie loves Lélie. (2) Célie laments her fate, drops a portrait of Lélie (the token that leads to the misunderstanding and then to the recognition of the proper identity), and faints. (3) Sganarelle sees Célie and holds her, intending to help. (4) Sganarelle's wife sees him with Célie, without being seen by him. (5) As a result, the wife becomes suspicious of Sganarelle, thinking that he is having an affair with Célie. (6) The wife finds the portrait of Lélie and praises the beauty of the man portrayed; Sganarelle sees his wife with a portrait of another man without being seen. Sganarelle makes himself known and declares his suspicion to his wife, who, however, does not understand him. Both are jealous of each other for false reasons, which neither understands. (7) Lélie returns to the scene, because he hears of Célie's betrothal to another man. (8) As a result, Lélie is jealous. (9) Sganarelle, who takes away the portrait of Lélie from his wife, looks at the portrait and offends the person portrayed. Lélie, not seen by Sganarelle, takes Sganarelle to be Célie's new fiancé, who apparently must have given the portrait to Sganarelle as a token of love. Sganarelle tells Lélie that the woman who gave him this portrait (Sganarelle's wife) is his wife, whom Lélie took to be Célie.

(10) As a result, Lélie suffers. (11) Sganarelle's wife sees Lélie, who almost faints, and is determined to help him. (12) Sganarelle complains to a relative that he saw his wife with a portrait of another man, which Sganarelle took as a sign of infidelity. (13) As a result, Sganarelle suffers. (14) Sganarelle, his wife, and Lélie each thinks they had been cheated by the other. (15) Lélie is jealous and envious of Sganarelle as the imaginary new husband of Célie. (16) Sganarelle tells Célie that Lélie was involved with his wife. As a result, Célie suffers. (17) Sganarelle suffers, too, complaining about his wife's alleged infidelity, which makes him an imaginary cuckold. (18) Célie, desolate, agrees to marry Valère, the man her father wants her to marry. (19) Célie tells her maiden about Lélie's supposed infidelity. (20) Célie and Lélie reproach each other for infidelity, yet neither understands the other's reproach. (21) Sganarelle wants revenge and intends to kill Lélie but (comically and ambiguously) is afraid of Lélie. Célie reproaches Lélie again, which Sganarelle takes as a sign of support of his intention to punish Lélie, whereas Lélie takes it as a sign of Célie's benevolence toward Sganarelle. The apex of the complication of the plot. Total confusion: everyone assumes the false identity of a cheater in the eyes of someone else. (22) Four paired characters, Célie, Lélie, Sganarelle, and his wife, are then all convinced that they are being cheated by their wife, husband, fiancée, or fiancé. The resolution of the conflict is not an accident but is brought about by the maiden, who is the master dialectician discovering the truth and setting things straight by asking appropriate questions. As a result, Célie, Lélie, Sganarelle, and his wife all understand that they had been mistaken. (23) Célie repents her decision to marry another man. Gorgibus, Célie's father, is indignant when he learns that Célie and Lélie rejected the arranged marriage of Célie to Valère. (24) Valère's father appears and informs everyone that Valère had married in secret, which raises the obstacle to Célie's and Lélie's marriage. Everyone was then happy and well-off. A good ending, q.e.d.

(ii) Breaking the Fourth Wall

Comic action thus presupposes an initial misrecognition, a mistaken identity, and hence an illusion and a fiction that needs to be overcome equally by the illusion and the fiction of dramatic action. Comedy tells a truth by withdrawing or suspending it in an act of a deliberate misunderstanding and misrecognition, in order to reveal the truth of being human and a person's true identity at a later point, as a result of a joint comic effort at establishing it. As Agnes Heller argued, comedy always implies an element of a comedy of errors. Error causes an illusion, and illusion needs to be exposed and rectified. Therefore, error is necessary for a comic plot.[90]

When Menedemus in Terence's *The Self-Tormentor* decided to be resolute in helping his prodigal son—by giving him money—and asked, "What shall I do?" Chremes responded, "Anything rather than what you are proposing. Contrive to give it through somebody else; let yourself be deceived by your slave's wiles."[91] And Menedemus agreed: "You observed that they were planning to deceive me: see that they hurry up and do it."[92] But his son and his accomplices wanted to deceive him in a way that was *different* from what he thought. Menedemus knew he would be deceived, yet he was deceived about how he would be deceived. Correspondingly, he planned a countermeasure that missed the planned deception but could indeed work exactly for the reason of having missed the ruse. Thus, comic double action is reflective yet misses itself in its reflection, precisely because it is double and thus always inevitably a "misreflection." A double action thus implies a counteraction planned as a nonaction, as the "other" action, conceived in such a way as to take into account the action plotted against it. Thereby, it recognizes this action by seemingly not recognizing it.

However, not just anything goes in comedy. It uses a wide variety of means and devices to promote human well-being. Yet comedy avoids outright falsity. Nonetheless, it often tells and shows the truth by withdrawing or suspending it, in order to make good life available to everyone, even those who apparently do not deserve it. Thus, at the end of Terence's *Eunuch*, everybody was well-off, even the stupid soldier and his hanger-on, who apparently betrayed his client yet made him happy.[93] The truth in comedy is not told plainly but demonstrated through the entire comic action by truth-telling and truth-enacting, by a seeming avoidance of telling the truth, which thereby tells it. Both the truth-teller and the spectators, although not necessarily other actors, are aware of such withholding of the truth for the sake of truth being told. Yet the truth, which was inextricable in the beginning, becomes apparent to everyone in the end.

As an author's invention, comic action is fictitious. And yet it helps us get rid of life-impeding illusions and oppressive practices and promotes human well-being. An illusory oppression is still oppression.[94] And the struggle against oppression, even an illusory one, takes courage, which is always real in its resoluteness. Free speech is dangerous, because the act of truth-telling irritates others, as it goes against the accepted conventions, which themselves are often illusions. Moreover, truth-telling that uses a seeming withdrawal, suspension, or delay of a truth irritates the modern moralistic subject, who does not tolerate untruth as a way to universal moral maxims. Consequently, nineteenth-century readers considered comedy as promoting "shrewdness rather than morality, expediency rather than right, means rather than ends."[95] It is usually the comic character of a slave or maiden who, seemingly timid, takes on the risk of violating the illusion by *enacting* the truth—again, by first suspending it—often going to the extreme of violating the very illusion of the stage.

Violating the scenic illusion, then, is another "fallacious" comic *topos* that shows truth by seemingly withdrawing it. One might say that there is an implicit and yet understood agreement or "pact" between comic characters and spectators to accept the voluntary suspension of a seemingly rigid separation between the "what" and the "is" (the "that") of characters and action. As fiction, representing something that did not happen but might have happened, comedy brackets the reality of characters and stresses *how* they act, showing the characters not by description but by action.[96] The characters themselves are not aware of their fictitiousness, but we spectators understand that the comic characters onstage do not exist. Yet this is of no importance, because it is not their "is" but their "what" that matters.[97]

Thus, comedy is always an "as-if" action, which, as illusory, is nevertheless more significant for us as spectators than most of the real-life events that remain unfinished and do not come to any ending or resolution. In its "as-ifness" comedy is still meaningful for us who cannot avoid participating in it, finding in it normative acts and patterns of behavior, recognition, and treatment of others and ourselves.

In order to stress the illusory yet meaningful character of the passions and actions onstage, comedy often breaks the fourth wall. Examples of violating the scenic illusion are numerous in both Old and New Comedy.[98] Woody Allen has often used this comic "fallacious" topic—for instance, in *Annie Hall*, where a sudden appearance of Marshal McLuhan resolved a dispute about his philosophy, which was then commented on by Woody Allen, who addressed the audience directly, saying he wished all the pseudointellectual disputes could be resolved in this way. And in *Whatever Works*, the main character addressed the spectators, thereby violating the scenic illusion, although of all the characters he was the only one who understood that it was an illusion; still he dared to reveal it, even if this disclosure went unnoticed by his fellow fictional characters.

(iii) Comic Fate

Fate, too, is a "fallacious" comic *topos*, which appears beyond human power and is thus an improbable constituent of a dramatic argument that remains within our control. The most distinctive feature of fate is that it combines opposite properties and seemingly incompatible characteristics: it is necessary and inevitable but also contingent and elusive; it is good and auspicious but also deceptive and unreliable. Yet fate is pervasive and omnipresent in comedy—and perhaps in life, too.

The Greek *Tykhē* was considered divine (in Pindar, Herodotus, and Plato) and did not obey laws—for example, even gods obey fate.[99] In classical tragedy, characters followed and surrendered to fate, which governed the events in the unfolding plot. The Latin *Fortuna*, originally the goddess of fertility[100] and patroness of women, was later identified with *Tykhē*. Fortuna too was unpredictable and could providentially bear happiness (*Felicitas*) and good luck (*Bonus Eventus*)—but also appeared as blind retribution and bad fortune.

As chance, fate appeared in later drama, especially in comedy. In Menander's *Aspis*, we find a monologue of *Tykhē* personified as a goddess, who was already personified in Euripides.[101] At the end of her speech, she named and disclosed herself as "the steward and judge controlling all things."[102] But steering them, she withheld the reasons for her actions, which were thus "not trustworthy."[103] Being blind, she nevertheless could see, which, however, is not immediately known by us but becomes apparent only as a result of fate's actions. Fate can enslave but also liberate people, which is why life is like a game of dice. She can be cruel but also benevolent, which might seem random, yet, unlike in tragedy, fate's mercy does justice to those who deserve it. As Terence put it in a gnome that has since become proverbial, "Fortune favors [helps] the brave."[104] This predictable unpredictability of fate, including her goodness, must be and actually is recognized in comedy.[105]

Some critics have found it an unnerving sign of feebleness in New Comedy that its plot is often guided by contingent events—such as the recognition of a person's identity based on the sudden appearance of a token as evidence that leads to a "catastrophic" resolution of the conflict. And yet it is contingency that testifies to comedy's universality, insofar as comedy reveals the universal in and through the particular, including the contingency of characters, events, and fate. In comedy, as in life, every action and character is directed both by chance and necessity. The very contingency is necessary in the makeup of comedy.

Comedy as a whole is determined by the plot, which, as I mentioned, is a monological construction of the author. For instance, in *Whatever Works* (2009), Woody Allen seems to have come to the conclusion that any intentionally structured comic narrative is doomed to fail and that fate, under the guise of chance and luck, is the only viable driving force in the comedy of life. For chance—under the guise of love—is the sole randomly selective, yet teleological, force that appears to work toward human good. In the epilogue, Boris, a misanthropic protagonist who is the author's alter ego, addresses the audience: "Whatever works. And don't kid yourself: It's by no means all up to your human ingenuity. A bigger part of your existence is luck than you like to admit." Yet not all of our existence is luck. In its very contingency, fate appears as an author's construction, indispensable for the plot. What Woody Allen does not notice is that he himself as the author takes over the role of fate and chance by producing the plot as a work of fate, which is therefore not accidental.

Comic human fate thus displays itself as both chance and necessity, for fate helps to establish that which is already anticipated in the plot. As Chremes said, "How often things come to pass purely by chance which you wouldn't dare to hope for!"[106] Chance therefore expresses the undecidedness and necessary concreteness of the situations in which comic characters have to act and make decisions toward a resolution of a conflict. Such indeterminacy causes fear that can, however, be overcome through resolution and courage and reliance on others in a shared action.[107]

Besides, while comedy allows for a proper recognition of distinctions such as birth, gender, social standing, and language, it also allows for their suspension in favor of human well-being, which is already not contingent but rather necessary. The necessity of comic fate is that of a good ending: that is, well-being in the form of being together with others. Comedy then comes to an equally manmade resolution as equals—a recognition that comes about through comic dialogical and "dialectical" action. Thus, fate is present in comedy as both contingent *and* necessary.

Common action under the "spell" of fate is always possible. For it is supported by other people who also must act in the situation of contingency and necessity. But comedy needs at least one savvy and skilled comic character, who accepts the universal responsibility for the contingency of this common action and tries to change it. As Terence said, "Life is like a game of dice. If you don't get the exact throw you want you have to use your skill and make the best of the one you do get."[108]

The end of comedy is to overcome sheer contingency and blind necessity. Every person, despite a lack of predetermination, should be free. Everyone in comedy should become a Stoic: capable of recognizing what one can and cannot change and thus accepting and bearing one's fate, yet also trying to improve one's situation to the extent that one can understand and change it. And thus, comedy always allows for freedom, as it provides a place for improvisation and participation, understanding and interpretation, and, hence, for life in an open (onstage) dialogue with others.

CHAPTER 5

The Catastrophe of the Good Ending

The epilogue is the "catastrophe" of comedy. A seemingly oxymoronic catastrophic good ending is a most important defining characteristic of comedy, resting on the principle "all's well that ends well," which was formulated by New Comedy long before Shakespeare. We need to clarify, therefore, the meaning of *good* and *ending*.

All's Well That Ends Well

The bitterest conflicts can be resolved in comedy, which, through its very structure and devices, offers ways of finding effective solutions to human disputes and misunderstandings. In comedy, as Aristotle said, enemies leave the stage as friends, and, unlike in tragedy, nobody dies as a result of other people's actions.[1] Euripides already prefigured comedy's good ending in some of his tragedies. And yet, on its way to emancipation from tragic death as the end point of action, comedy preserved some traces of tragedy's "bad ending." Thus, when the priest in Shakespeare's *Twelfth Night* wanted to indicate that two hours had passed, he said, "Since when, my watch hath told me, toward my grave / I have traveled but two hours."[2] Yet the whole comedy cannot but end well, in proper recognitions and marriages and the celebration of love.

Comedy has a bad beginning but a good ending. Despite human beings' poor treatment of each other—which is the beginning of human drama— people can come to a peaceful coexistence. This requires a common effort and the use of comic devices. Comedy always begins (in the *protasis*) with a man-made complication: a clash of interests, an illicit act, a violation of norms, or a crime.[3] Comedy then comes to an equally manmade resolution, which, how-ever, does not appear out of the blue as an act of a *deus ex machina*: although it is supported by chance, it is a carefully calculated solution to a problem set within a complex comic "argument." As Corrigan put it, "Opposition, frustration, malice, lust, prejudice, and greed can and do inhabit the world of comedy, but these divisive powers are always overcome."[4]

The comic epilogue is a "catastrophic" act: it literally "overturns" the comedy by "returning" to the beginning at the end with a resolution of the conflict. Thus, comedy solves an apparent paradox within the incessant and desperate human striving for happiness: it seems that if one is *desperate* to be happy, one cannot be happy.[5] And yet comedy allows one to be happy *in the end*, precisely as a result of one's desperate striving. The comic ending is already implicitly present in the beginning, in the "premises" of the *protasis*. In this respect, again, a comic ending resembles a logical or mathematical conclusion, which is already implicitly (analytically) contained within the premises and is reachable through the steps of the proof or construction. Moreover, one can always go back to the beginning, to the initial conflict, and reevaluate it from the perspective of the end. The beginning and the end in comedy are thus mutually reachable in the double movement in which the end explicitly suspends and changes the beginning, and the beginning implicitly bears and brings about the end.

The Possibility of Well-Being

But how and why is a good ending possible? The "how" is provided by the structure of comic argument. The claim that a (good) ending is reachable in comedy may be taken in at least two different senses: either as a statement whose validity must be demonstrated by a philosophical argument or as a situation that is concretely implemented through a series of actions and events, in which, at the end, human well-being is achieved by comic means. A good comic ending is achieved in the second sense: comedy brings about human well-being at the end,[6] to which it comes through a number of well-thought-through steps using the *topoi* I have discussed.

Even if comic devices are in place, it is not yet guaranteed that a good ending will actually be achieved. And yet, *there is* a good ending to comedy. But such a good ending seems paradoxical, for we *already* know the end of comedy and nevertheless still follow it with interest. We know that comedy should and will end well, but we do not know exactly how it will come to a good end. As with a good life, comedy is never boring—for, even if its end is always the same, its action is always different. There is thus an oxymoronic "anticipated suddenness" to a good ending—a well-known secret, a surprise that is always expected.[7]

The "how" of a good ending lies in the characters' ability to work together, not only for one's own good but also for the good of others and thus for the common good. Unlike their tragic counterparts, comic characters were not sublime heroes who acted at the limit of human capabilities but ordinary people from all walks of life. Along with common human limitations—such as stupidity and the inability to rise above immediate self-interests, as well as shortcomings such as greed, envy, and vanity—comic characters always showed, especially in the end, human goodness, kindness, and empathy.[8] Enduring humanism was thus a distinctive mark of New Comedy and modern comedy. Consequently, the good ending of comedy, which overcame, or at least suspended, human suffering, was possible because of the mutual benevolence of other people. Characters in comedy worked toward a good ending, even if they often lacked an understanding of their actions. By acting with others toward a good ending, comedy allowed for the individual's realization of human being as comic cobeing, that is, as being in dialogue with others.

Still, human goodness is not a given (*Gegeben*, to use Kant's term). In fact, in the beginning of comedy, human goodness seems quite improbable: it is thus a task to be achieved (*Aufgegeben*). Human goodness is not a perennial "human nature" but must be realized and worked out with other people, enhanced by a common effort, and directed by a comic character. A good ending thus comes about because of human goodness, which is neither guaranteed nor taken for granted but is *possible* in comedy.

The goodness of comedy consists, then, in its capacity to overcome suffering and to suggest ways of doing so. Minimally, the end of comic action should be such that nobody gets hurt or hurts others. However, comedy actually achieves much more than that. The ultimate goodness of comedy consists in its capacity for a complete *apokatastasis*: reconstitution, restoration, and recovery—which allows even the grouchy and ignorant to be well—from an original wrongdoing; thus it comes, often without ever having known it, to the seemingly undeserved good ending, which is a grace from others. At this point—in the end—one achieves and celebrates the "absolute present" (to use Heller's term)[9] of the other person, just as epic celebrates and forever retells the "absolute past." This "absolute present," however, is not realized once and for all but only for a time being and thus needs to be constantly maintained and renewed, as a task to be accomplished. The moments of well-being (love fulfilled, freedom achieved, aspiration realized) do not last long and need to be regained and renewed again and again, as does human life itself. For the good always appears as *a* good, both in comedy and life, achievable not by luck but through a shared and reasoned common effort. The very transiency of the "absolute present," an apparent sign of our limitations, is a fortunate feature of comedy. For it allows us to live on without getting bored by the repetition of the same as the good ending.

The Normativity of Comedy

Comedy ends and must end well, for a good ending is implied in the very notion of comedy. But comedy is not a hedonistic desire-fulfilling mechanism preprogrammed to end in a fulfillment of dreams and wishes. Comedy represents, reproduces, and describes ("imitates") human affairs. Yet comedy also "distills" life by representing it onstage. Comedy is thus also *normative*: it *prescribes* the end to be achieved and suggests a course of actions toward human well-being. Yet, again, although a comic ending gives meaning to the whole of comedy's action, the end is not inevitable but a normative task to be achieved. Nothing guarantees that the end will actually be reached, although the "justice" of comedy, the equality of people and their well-being with others, is always possible as a result of fair-minded[10] dialogical interaction and common (political) action.

In comedy, we are moved by a sense of justice, namely that we and other people *should* be well-off.[11] Not even the author can violate the requirement of a good ending. For example, in Ben Jonson's *Volpone* the main character tried to trick others out of their money by pretending to be gravely ill and promising to leave his fortune to each of them after his death. In the end, the hoax was exposed and the author punished Volpone by putting him in prison and making him suffer from all the diseases he had invented. However, to his surprise, Jonson discovered that the spectators found such a punishment much too cruel and revolting—it was incompatible with the very idea of comedy.[12]

Reflection: The Good Ending and Knowledge

Comedy not only provides appropriate means for achieving a comic ending; it also comes with the awareness of the possibility of doing so. Thus, in Terence's *The Mother-in-Law*, a young man, Pamphilus, was hesitant to reveal to his father the whole story of his love for Philumena, who by then had happily become his wife. Pamphilus says, "There's no need to [tell him], not even a whisper. I don't want what happens in comedies to happen here, where everybody finds out everything. In this case those who need to know know already; those who don't must not find out or ever know."[13]

Apart from its face value, this rejoinder is a double comic self-reference to comedy, which understands itself as resolving the initial (love) conflict through its entire plot, in which an original error and offense is disclosed, exposed, and rectified at the end. At this particular place, at the *very end* of comedy, one of its main heroes claimed that comedy is a device that allows people—both characters and spectators or readers—to *know*. This is knowledge of the way others act throughout comedy, yet it is also knowledge of oneself. Hence, it is reflective knowledge or self-knowledge obtained through knowledge of others and in communication with others. Put otherwise, those who need to know are those who *want* to know—to find out or get to know how things will turn out through acts of human goodness, even if such acts are initially muddled by a mistake or wrongdoing. From the very beginning, people *already* know *what* and *how* things human are. They just need to get to know *that* they know, which they find out in a (comic) interaction with other people that moves to a resolution or good ending. In this sense, the development of a comic plot in its entirety provides an almost Platonic or Socratic *anamnēsis*, or "recollection," of how things are, can, and should be: in the comedy of life, everyone should be well-off, and things should be understandable and simple *in the end*. In its justice and goodness, comedy unknots apparently irrevocably entangled human affairs.

But what does "good" mean in comedy's good ending? As Aristotle argued, different kinds of rhetorical speeches are defined by specific ends.[14] Similarly, each dramatic form and each form of action is defined by its proper end. Any action may have an end, but only comedy has human well-being and the celebration of goodness as its end. Similar to life, the resolution of a conflict at the end of comedy appears different and provisional each time, yet it always prevails for the time being, when people come to their comic being as cobeing with others.

Love and Life: Being toward Life

Autonomous, monological, and single, the modern subject is lonely, facing an inevitably tragic end. Its mode of being is being-toward-death.[15] In contrast, comic being is shared by all participants of comedy; although it is not easy to realize, comic being is being-well that is achievable through a joint effort. If tragedy celebrates death and human finitude under the guise of mortality, comedy celebrates life in its various forms and promotes the life of well-being with others under the guise of life-renewal.[16] The seemingly irreversible can be reversed in comedy. By showing human goodness, comedy teaches us how to live. When the young Clitipho in Terence's *The Self-Tormentor* suffered—or thought he suffered—the "slings and arrows of outrageous fortune," that is, seemingly unrequited love and a loss of means, his father, Chremes, told him, "First learn how to live, for heaven's sake. When you know that, if you don't like life, you can try the other way [i.e., death]."[17] Yet, when one learns to live through comedy, one realizes that life is worth living. For it makes death redundant and, in fact, impossible. Death appears to be irrevocable, until it is overturned by life's renewal, which makes death only a comic "as-if" event. Thus, comedy often uses fake dying and coming alive, as well as fake illness and quick recovery (as in Molière's *Le malade imaginaire*), which are versions of the "fallacious" *topos* of double action.[18] The comic mode of being is thus alive as being-toward-life. In order to continue, life should be comic.

Laughter, Joke, Wit, and Humor

Many scholars stress the centrality of laughter for comedy.[19] Laughter is engaging and obvious, though difficult to grasp. Further, it is a clear indication of being well and alive. Thus, laughter shares and connects the features commonly distinguished in comedy, namely its propensity toward absurdity and transgression, as well as toward vitality and life-renewal.

As with comedy, many attempts at the understanding and definition of laughter have been tried. Thus, the *Tractatus Coislinianus* took laughter (*gelōs*) as the "mother" of comedy.[20] John Tzetzes, a Byzantine commentator of the twelfth century, also emphasized that comedy was "moulded by laughter and pleasure."[21] Giraldi took laughter to be comedy's purgative and instructional means for improving people's lives. Among modern writers, it has often been taken for granted that laughter is essential for the understanding of comedy.[22]

D. H. Monro provided an apt classification of various types of theories of laughter: superiority, relief, and incongruity, or a combination of them.[23] Thomas Hobbes famously argued that laughter comes with a pleasurable sense of alleged superiority.[24] And yet both the superiority and its pleasure must be recognized as such, and they can be recognized very differently by the one who feels superior, the one being derogated, and the spectators (if there are any). For the superiority is an alleged one, which can be perceived in mutually incompatible ways by various parties. If it is, laughter becomes ambiguous and may not have any object at all. As an expression of (alleged) superiority, laughter is derogative and veils an implicit aggression. Thus, Gotthold Lessing distinguished between sympathetic laughter and ridicule, *Lachen* and *Verlachen*.[25] Laughter based on superiority, then, can either express the joy of accomplishment (the "divine" laughter of "I did it!"; e.g., when climbing a mountain) or the sneer (the "diabolic" laughter of *schadenfreude*; e.g., when seeing the opponent fail in an argument or slip on a banana peel). Ridicule can target the other, as in the political caricature in Aristophanes, or be directed against oneself, in which case it has a liberating, therapeutic effect. But such laughter should never target the other person, for in this case it becomes offensive. Cyrano can laugh at the length of his nose, but woe to him who dares to do the same.

Laughter expressing superiority is communal, as it must be directed at, and recognized by, others. Such laughter is both *with* others and *against* others.

Laughter might appear solitary, at the moment of thinking or reading, but community is still implied here, even when purely imaginary. Thus, laughter transgresses the distinction between individual and community, because it is *personal*: everyone laughs, but we can recognize someone by the way she laughs, for everyone laughs differently.

Laughter as subversive is common to both the superiority and relief theory, because it signifies an (anarchic) fight against authority and thus both liberates from oppression and establishes the superiority of the right against the wrong. In his book on Rabelais, Bakhtin stresses the antiauthoritarian character of laughter. He concludes that every act of world history is accompanied by a chorus of laughter, for laughter is capable of breaking repressive rules and underlies common political action against oppression.[26] And so, the righteous are suspicious of laughter. Unsurprisingly, the Puritans, who found laughter sinful, forbade comedy: "Woe unto you that laugh now! for ye shall mourn and weep."[27] And yet such an understanding of laughter is beside the point, for laughter precisely liberates against unreasonable prohibitions, including the prohibition of laughter itself. Besides, one might take Luke's claim as emphasizing not the "laugh" but the "now," that is, those who *now* laugh *later* will inevitably cry, because the present joy will be balanced by a later pain, and if one wants to avoid it altogether, one should strive to achieve *ataraxia*, a peace of mind.

Bergson's famous account in *Le rire* depicts laughter as a "correction," "a slight revolt," against the improper infringements on social life, as a ridicule of rigid mechanic encrustation and its incongruity with vitality.[28] Laughter as incongruity can assume different avatars. Laughter, as Agnes Heller argued, can be understood, then, as a rational reaction to the impossibility of bridging the gap between the social and the natural in us. This is liberating, for it is a celebration of life overcoming death, or at least the fear of death.[29] As rational, comic laughter is also reflective and judgmental, for, even if one cannot speak when one laughs, one can always explain afterward why one laughed. (Conversely, elementary crying is not reflective.)[30]

As incongruous, laughter can appear absurd, which, according to Elder Olson, produces "a relaxation of concern" and thus is equally liberating.[31] Incongruity signifies the distance between who a character is and what is intended by her appearance and acts. Thus, it may refer to an ambiguity of situation, action, or mistaken identity—both of things and of people (in doubles and travesties). Incongruity is also perceived in the ambiguity of reference to two things as one (to cow and bride in *Fiddler on the Roof*) or in the ambiguity of meaning—for example, in a pun. Thus, in Molière's *Les femmes savantes*, the exchange between Bélise and Martine—"Veux-tu toute la vie offenser la grammaire? / Qui parle d'offenser grand'mère ni grand père?"—plays with the phonetic similarity between *grammaire* and *grand'mère*, grammar and grandmother, which is further strengthened by the "offense" to the grammar of the sentence by its wrong use.[32]

Laughter as incongruity can signify a sheer contradiction in our being, as for Charles Baudelaire, for whom laughter was "a token of an infinite grandeur and an infinite misery—the latter in relation to the absolute Being of whom man has an inkling, the former in relation to the beasts."[33] Put more strongly, laughter is an expression of utter absurdity, a loss or absence of any meaning in our words and actions. For Georges Bataille, the laughable might be in principle unknowable, so that it is the unknown, the *non-savoir*, that makes us laugh, precisely because it is unknown.[34] Laughter, then, is provoked by the absurd inaccessibility of its object. Following this logic of "un-logic," Simon Critchley takes laughter as an acknowledgement of human finitude, which inevitably comes with a performative contradiction, insofar as finitude cannot be affirmed, because it cannot be grasped.[35] However, unlike for Bataille, here, we should apparently know *what* we laugh at, although we do not know *why* we laugh.

Laughter caused by something shameful or ugly is also incongruous.[36] Riccoboni claims that we laugh at "a certain fault and ugliness without pain, lacking a destructive force."[37] Laughter, then, is a recognition of the right and proper, evident in a perceivable representation of the wrong ridiculed in the "painless" ugly. On this account, comedy might be taken as an incongruous exaggeration of a well-constituted propriety, in which *decorum* is offended intentionally but not repulsively. This type of comedy often gives rise to farce and slapstick.[38] Deformity distorts either a person's moral character or physical appearance, which is why it is often perceived as shameful, though pardonable.[39] A laughing face is always disfigured, sometimes to the point of becoming unseemly. As such, laughter is an expression of passions (gut laughter—the opposition between "nature" and "convention"[40]), but it is not joyous. The deformed face of Marsyas appears as an insult to the serene beauty of Apollo's, which is why, despite being close to laughter, smiling is also quite different from it. For, as Plessner argued, more subtly nuanced and much less distortive, a smile lightens and brightens the face, expressing friendship and serenity of mind.[41] The contorting incongruity of laughter is further seen in the fact that, when laughing, one loses the most human of all the capacities, the "*logos*" or the ability to speak, whereas one can smile and speak at the same time.[42]

Laughter is often a response to a joke—and to joke means to provoke laughter. For this reason, jokes have been considered the defining feature of comedy.[43] Like laughter, a joke can express superiority, release from restraint, or incongruity and ambivalence—or all of them together. A joke can be a "very short narrative," told in a few words or even shown in a gesture. The attraction of a joke consists in its ability to get the listeners, readers, or spectators actively involved in filling in the details of its story. Thus, listeners become participants, actors, and cocreators of the comic action. To be fun and subtle, a joke has to be witty: a witty joker has the capacity to quickly conceive and spontaneously crack a tasteful and sophisticated joke as a condensed play or convoluted enthymeme. An epitome of this wit is Jerome K. Jerome's *Three Men in a Boat* (to say nothing of the dog, of course).

Jokes are often made by a buffoon or fool, which means that he is not really a fool after all, for one must be smart in order to utter a joke and even pretend to be a fool. Viola understands this well when she describes the clown in the *Twelfth Night*:

> This fellow is wise enough to play the fool, / And to do that well craves a kind of wit. / He must observe their mood on whom he jests, / The quality of persons, and the time; / Not, like the haggard, check at every feather / That comes before his eye. This is a practice / As full of labor as a wise man's art; / For folly that he wisely shows, is fit; / But wise men, folly-fall'n, quite taint their wit.[44]

Serious wisdom may be deceptive, as it fails to assume an ironic reflective distance to itself, whereas a seeming foolishness can be truly wise, insofar as it knows that it pretends to be foolish.

Hence, joke is a sign of wit, of an enlightened and civilized intellect, which became an indispensable social norm starting with the Renaissance.[45] Thus, Ben Jonson considered not laughter but wit as providing comedy's purpose,[46] and in Restoration and eighteenth-century comedy, wit was commonly valued over decorum. Wit is thus an expression of intellectual excellence,[47] even if it is often a way of showing off.

The expression of wit is humor, which is frequently taken as the defining moment of comedy, together with laughter and joke. Meredith clearly expressed this attitude when he claimed that comedy "laughs through the mind, for the mind directs it; and it might be called the humour of the mind."[48] The modern notion of humor was introduced into comedy by Ben Jonson as a "generall disposition," which originated in ancient natural philosophy and medicine.[49] Humor can be vulgar, bawdy, and brusque, as in George Colman's "Broad Grins." It can also be carnivalesque, turning everything upside down, as in Bakhtin's story. In both cases, humor is an expression of the life of the comic mind or wit. Critchley, following Antony Earl of Shaftesbury, considers humor a form of common sense.[50] Yet common sense is a rational faculty that implies a (proper) judgment; as the application of reason in solving a particular problem, it might not be funny or laughable or imply a joke, in which case it has nothing to do with comedy as a witty enterprise.[51]

In fact, comedy might not be about laughter at all but rather, as I have argued, about the structure of common action. Laughter is not central to Terence, who follows the ancient tradition of *spoydogelaion*, the serio-comical; thus, Donatus does not provide a theory of the ridiculous in his account of comedy. Surely, comedy is neither agelastic nor misogelastic, that is, it does not have to be nonlaughing or serious or abstain from jokes. Comedy can be funny and can even laugh at itself; laughter abounds in comedy. Laughter can be liberating (as a release from restraint and tension, an imitation of orgasm), yet comedy can be liberating without laughter. As L. J. Potts famously argued, later joined by David Farley-Hills, many comedies contain little to no laughter or humor; thus, comedy must be defined in other terms.[52]

Love and Erõs

If comedy renews life and overcomes death, it cannot do without love, for only love produces and reproduces life in its constant self-renewal. As imitative, comedy *reproduces* life. Yet, as normative, comedy *produces* life in its various appearances—as birth, love, and the life of the mind. It artfully creates artificial situations, which do not occur in life yet which show life as distilled and separated from the boredom of repetition and the inconclusiveness of everyday action.

However, life-asserting love is present differently throughout the whole action of comedy. In the *protasis*, love appears as desire and the seeming impossibility of love; in the *epitasis*, as striving toward the loved that complicates the action; and in the catastrophe, as the fulfillment and completion of love at the end.

Love has a double function in comedy: On the one hand, it is the driving force that provides an impulse for comic action, complicates the situation in the beginning, creates havoc along the way, makes lovers strive toward their beloved, and then helps characters move to a resolution, release, and fulfillment of their aspirations in the end. On the other hand, love is also the consummation and completion of comedy as its end. Being both the moving force and the end of comedy, love is therefore *ambiguous*. Philosophy is well aware of this ambiguity, which it tries to explore and explain already in Plato. Philosophy is itself an erotic enterprise (a love for an elusive wisdom that appears desperately unthematizable), and so its self-reflection is also erotic—and often comic—when it comes to a resolution of the discussed problem in a philosophical dialogue with others.

Erōs is an insuperable and unpredictable—divine—power, which played a central role in the Nea. Thus, in Menander's *Dyskolos* a young farmer, Gorgias, said that he had never been in love, as he was prevented from it by thinking about hardships. His interlocutor, who was in love, replied that it was not up to him but to a god (in this case, Pan) to make us fall in love.[53] Ambiguous and double-edged, *erōs* can enslave us by making us unable to make a judgment about right and wrong, but it can also liberate us by assisting us in moving toward a good life in its constant self-renewal. Yet the very "project" of comedy and philosophy presupposes not the elimination of *erōs* but the search for ways to keep it in check by comic and philosophical means, making *erōs* work for our good, as it can otherwise become utterly destructive.

Philosophy and comedy share the same driving force, which strives toward an end and is extinguished when it comes to a resolution (a good ending or the conclusion of an argument)—but never to a last stop. For life must move on, continually starting from scratch, facing another complication and trying to solve another problem, in order to come to another new, yet provisional, ending. Love's end can be achieved but never once and for all, for, just as life renews itself, it should be constantly renewed. Thus, life always has an end in its self-renewal and reproduction, in others (in new life) and in each individual (insofar as one keeps living). As an attempt at grasping both love and life, philosophy is comic, and comedy is philosophical. Both are performed as constantly renewed and repeated symposia, which are the same in the structure of their action and moving forces yet are always different in the concrete problems they address and try to solve.

In comedy, love comes to an end in people's (well-)being-together, shared and recognized as such, which is usually realized as a marriage or a union of people.[54] In comparison with the sublime suffering of tragic heroes at the end of tragedy, an association of people living together appears banal and vulgar; and yet it is a fulfillment of the possibility of being-together with other(s), a realization of well-being in its plain commonality and everydayness, available for, and accessible to, all people.

Passions

Love's capacity to arouse different, often conflicting passions makes it ambiguous. Sometimes people act like rational beings, but they are always passionate beings. And although they cannot get rid of their passions, they can guide, rule, and "purify" them. Comedy is precisely a mechanism that allows people to restrain and balance their passions, both with the help of, and resistance from, others.

Love, which begins as unfulfilled, should bring the most contentment in life. At the moment when love comes to its completion and consummation, it begins its striving afresh. In this sense, love works exactly as life and comedy do: it can achieve its end but always only provisionally, and thus its end should be renewed. The comic *"conditio humana"* is being alive and always in love, that is, capable of being well-off and yet also dissatisfied with one's situation: "In general, this is what we human beings are like: we're dissatisfied with our own lot."[55]

As I have argued, personal comic identity is always double, implies misrecognition, and presupposes nonidentity: One is "beside oneself"[56] and must be reconciled with oneself at the end, but never in a finalized way, through the recognition—by others and by oneself—of what one is. Hence, in comedy love is accompanied, opposed, and temporarily suspended by hate, anger, and irritation.[57] As Terence said in the prologue to the *Eunuch*, the passions or emotions of comedy are "love, hate, suspicion."[58] Although the list could be extended (e.g., to include Darwin's emotions), each of Terence's passions is present at each stage in comedy; yet the *protasis* is dominated by hate, the *epitasis* by suspicion, and the catastrophe—by love.

Comic Sex

A most fertile and productive incarnation of love in comedy is sex.[59] The model for a seemingly muddled action that comes to a good ending is the sexual act, which is a resolution of love and the origin of life. In Aristophanes, there was plenty of sex but no love;[60] in Menander, Terence, and later comedy, in contrast, there was plenty of love but mostly only hints at sex.

Sex is always a *provocation*, as it arouses, awakens, appeals to, and invites (as meanings of *"provocare"*) the participants, both actors and spectators, to share the action by getting involved in it in one way or another. Besides, sex is vulgar in its appearance. This, however, it has in common with comedy, which always bears a flair of vulgarity as an expression of comedy's "popularity," "ordinariness," or "everyoneness," of its being there for each and all. The *vulgarity* of sex is further associated with its *ambiguity*, which is appealing to the participants, since ambiguity can be a source of both laughter and new and engaging hermeneutic interpretations of the current situation.

The ambiguity or ambivalence of sex in comedy betokens an inevitable *negativity* implied in the sexual act. In its negativity at the beginning of comedy, sex is not just vulgar but also illicit, a force that brings havoc and creates the ensuing chaos in human relations, which seems impossible to dissolve. Hence, sex originates an action that in the beginning is forbidden, shameful, dangerous, hurtful, and violent, often fuelled by hate, anger, and irritation. Without rational plotting, winning the other over, and the justification of one's actions, sex is not much different from rape (e.g., in Terence's *The Mother-in-Law*). The uniqueness of comedy consists in its unsurpassed ability to address, incorporate, and resolve the initial negativity of the act of domination and aggression that upsets the course of events. Only comedy can make a difficult and, in the beginning, quite improbable transformation of violence into mutual care. Yet comedy does so not by legal or moralistic means but by communicative and dialogical ones, by plotting and acting in a reasoned way. Thus, people can be in love in the end, attending to each other, being together, and finally realizing—and recognizing—sexual acts as desire-fulfilling and mutually enjoyable.

In comedy, sex is thus a celebration of life and freedom. Comedy not only liberates the soul by helping it overcome, release, and balance the negative affects of passions; comedy also liberates the body in the end by fulfilling, and recognizing as legitimate, bodily desires. However, there are limitations to such recognition, for sex is inclusive of an other or others yet *not* of everyone, which is the meaning of marriage and the free union of people. In this sense, unlike dialogical communication and interaction, sex cannot but exclude the majority of other people. For this reason, it is *erōs* and not sex that is the universal driving force of comedy, because *erōs* can appear under very different, often quite unexpected, and not obviously sexual guises and can serve as an inclusive, rather than exclusive, principle of human interaction.

Nonetheless, the overall structure of comedy coincides, in a sense, with that of the sexual act: beginning with the aim it wants to achieve and moving through negativity, complications, and persuasion, comedy achieves its goal with a sense of relief and satisfaction that is appreciated individually but shared in its various expressions with others. Similarly, the sexual act is a relief from tension, is liberating, and should have a good ending, after a long unwinding story of initial (sometimes subtle) aggression, followed by courtship. Yet, as I have argued, the makeup of comic plot coincides with that of logical or philosophical argument, which means that (dialectical) argument and the sexual act, as particular incarnations of *erōs*, are isomorphic and have the same structure. Or, once again, philosophy and thinking are profoundly erotic, and *erōs* is philosophical. *Erōs* and (demonstrative) thought always follow one another. I leave the question of which one is primary open; at least, both *erōs* and thought are unmistakably comic.

Comic Money

Money played an important role in New Comedy and modern comedy. Comic money is to be had not by everyone but only a few. Those who spend money borrow it from others, and those who have it keep it to themselves. The comic archetypes of money-spenders and money-keepers are the prodigal son and the greedy father: "A miserly father makes a prodigal son."[61] However, a prodigal son also contributes to a father's being miserly, which suggests that comic money is double and ambivalent in its function. On the one hand, money provides security and safety against misery, but as such, money generates greed, suspicion, and deception (which, in a sense, parallel the "negative" passions associated with sex—hate, anger, jealousy, and irritation). Thus, money compensates for pleasure that one wants but does not— or cannot—have. On the other hand, comic money is used for merrymaking, amusement, and pleasure and, as such, is associated with lust. Hence, father and son represent opposites within the duality of money's functioning in comic life. This changes as the comedy progresses and the plot develops: at the beginning of comedy, money, in its negative aspect, is kept to oneself and spent on oneself; later, money is given to others and spent on others—a sign of attaining the comic good ending and thus taking proper care not only of others but also of oneself.[62]

In both these aspects, money is an embodiment of the possibility and capacity of acting as one pleases and having what one wishes—though not, of course, everything. Spending, keeping, and gaining money signify the moment of happiness as wish-fulfillment—though not of every wish and desire. One can have sex for money but not love; one can gain servility but not freedom; one can acquire property but not the recognition of others. Money's capacity to obtain what is desired is limited, for it cannot buy life, love, and freedom, which should be accessible to everyone. Therefore, comic money was the equivalent of possession or property[63] but *not* the universal equivalent of well-being, as it is in modernity, where money became a general possibility and capacity for acquiring anything, a sign of the autonomy of the subject, signifying his freedom to spend and to increase (invest) money any way he wants.

Comic money was not the result of hard work but was rather a gift. Its accumulation was not an end in itself: money was meant to be (re)*distributed* and *spent* to give pleasure and a happy life. As desire-fulfilling, comic money was similar to food, which could be bought, consumed, and given out to others. In this respect, comedy's money was premodern: it was not meant to be increased, invested, or grown for growth's sake. Comic money was not capitalist, Calvinist, or Weberian. Indeed, the figures of the miserly father and the prodigal son were parodies of the capitalist. While modern money came to require rationalization, thriftiness, and the ability to calculate, comic money was associated with exuberance, extravagance, and a lack of thought in those who spent it (often a young man or a boastful reveller).

As David Konstan noted, in Molière erotic passion and fixation on wealth were paralleled; yet, if in the *Miser* Harpagon's attraction to a particular woman is similar to interest in a buried treasure, in *Dom Juan* the hero's passion for women corresponded to his evasion of debt. Thus, Dom Juan reduced "all women to the single currency of sex, that renders his passion a figure for the nascent capitalist's indiscriminate interest in commodities and in their common denominator, money."[64] If comic money was concrete and often vulgar, modern money became abstract and anonymous. As a general aim in itself, modern money disregards other fellow human beings; it is a universal measure for *having* anything, rather than *being* happy with an actual possession.

Freedom

The Humble Freedom of Comedy

Human freedom is realized in comedy—and, thus, human freedom is comic. Comic freedom permeates comedy from the very beginning—even while limited by the author's freedom to construct a plot—as the freedom to act and think. Freedom, as the goal of comedy, then, should be gained in the end.

In his "On the Aesthetic Value of Greek Comedy," Friedrich Schlegel claimed that the ideal of Greek comedy was "sublime freedom."[65] Yet this sublime freedom is the appropriation of tragic freedom by the modern subject, whereas the freedom of comedy is humble and immanent to comic action—to thinking about action and in action—in a situation shared by all its participants. As freedom-with others, comic freedom is often ridiculous and awkward, sometimes indecent—but it is always humane. Such freedom is not sublime and divine but mundane and human, inscribed into everydayness.

Yet, according to Jünger, comedy displays a struggle between two unequal parties. This is paradoxical exactly because they are unequal: there is no point in struggling, since one party is already recognized as stronger and superior to the other.[66] Comedy, therefore, seems to entail a pragmatic contradiction. Jünger recognized such a conflict as comic but left it open, without resolution. And yet comedy has powerful means to resolve such conflict by structuring its plot as an "argument": either the discordant parties are eventually reconciled, or the character originally in an inferior position is recognized as equal with others. Thus, comedy is capable of providing freedom and justice to its actors—by rational and argumentative comic means.

Moreover, freedom borders on love, for it is motivated by the desire for liberation, which is a form of erotic striving. And yet love is itself paradoxical in its relation to freedom: it is a sort of oxymoronic "unfree freedom," for one does not choose whom to love and what to desire. Still, love connects a person with an other or others and hence liberates one from oneself, from solitude. It allows, in a shared action, for one to suspend and check unmotivated decisions and actions, driven by the utterly negative capacity to reject any good reason.[67] To be free, a comic character should act *for others* and thus (and only thus) achieve *her own*—now deserved—freedom. Comic freedom is thus *for all* (in which respect it differs from sex and money). The universality of comic freedom rectifies the possible injustice of the initial distribution of life roles with their social, gender, family, economic, political, and other inequalities. Unlike Christina of Sweden, who, dying in her room in the Palazzo Corsini in Rome, reportedly said, "I was born free, lived free, and will die free,"[68] in comedy, not everyone is lucky to be born free, but—since comedy is a normative enterprise—one can and should *become* free as the end of the shared human action, *freed* and helped by others to obtain and realize one's freedom.

Freedom-From and Freedom-For as Freedom-With

The duality of freedom is present in comedy, for everyone is subject to fate but also free to act and make decisions. However, this is not the modern freedom of the isolated autonomous subject, who makes decisions independently of others. Rather, while comic freedom is achieved—despite the contingency of one's situation—by one's own effort, it is always done together with others, in interaction and dialogue with them.

Comic freedom is first and foremost a *freedom-from*: the freedom from oppression, coercion, and compulsion. In this sense, comedy is subversive: it destroys stereotypes of a whole society and thus liberates politically and socially, by ridiculing and questioning oppressive practices and patriarchal prejudices and thereby establishing a person's right to dignity, a good name, and a good reputation as well as the right to have (nonexcessive) property.[69] Such freedom is never simply posited in the beginning as a given but is a task to be achieved. The struggle for liberation is dangerous: it takes much thinking and plotting—the work of comedy. In order to gain freedom, the comic truth-teller often jeopardizes his own freedom and acts at his own expense, seemingly against his immediate interest: he reveals the truth about oppression and injustice (frequently done by truth-withdrawing), and he risks ridicule or even repression and punishment. The comic revolutionary not only dares to speak up but also clears space for the speech of others who were silenced, mute, and tacit,[70] helping them regain their voices. The truth-teller is thus both unpardonably ironic and sincere, going against the taste of society and thereby making a fool of himself.[71] Comic freedom-from, therefore, is *dangerous*.[72]

And yet comedy also heals the individual psyche in a "vomedic" catharsis. It liberates and recognizes desire—by balancing, and not abolishing, passions—as legitimate. Personal psychological liberation is thus an important therapeutic constituent of comedy: it even helps to overcome death, although not *as such*—for death is not a part of one's personal experience and thus cannot be shared with others. Accordingly, the portrayal of death is rare in comedy; at least, main characters do not die. Comedy helps to overcome the *fear* of death, and the bitter taste of lonesome finitude, through the celebration of love and life with others. In comedy, one does not have to die in order to understand that in the comedy of life—while one is alive—death does not exist. Comedy, then, enacts love and life but *not* the beautiful. The beautiful appearances of characters are deceptive, and their mischievous actions are often ugly.

The social aspect of comic freedom appears in the spectators' and readers' capacity to identify themselves with the characters' affects and circumstances and with the normative demand of comedy. This identification is what makes possible our ability to say "we," insofar as *we* all participate in the same liberating comic motion. Personal, social, and political liberation was always present in comic plot as a prized goal in the good endings of New Comedy. All who were oppressed in the beginning—a slave, a mistreated and silenced woman, a person in a position of dependence—dreamt of liberation as the highest goal in life.[73]

Yet comic freedom is also a *freedom-for* well-being, achieved through spontaneous and live being-(in-dialogue)-with others. This is a different sense of freedom from the one Schiller associated with comedy: he saw comedy as liberating us from passions, once we have accepted the absurdity and utter contingency of life, shrugging it off with a smile.[74] Rather, comic freedom is freedom-with others as mutually recognized in the always renewable and renewed end of the comedy of life.

The freedom to act in comedy presupposes the freedom to think and judge. Comic action, therefore, is always mediated by reflection and understanding, which, once again, supports the claim that comedy is a collective, rational, and reflective enterprise. The reflective understanding *that* one is unfree allows one to understand *why* one is unfree, what to do in order to be rid of an oppressive practice, and how to move toward freedom for well-being. Reflection makes it possible to obtain a proper *distance* from oneself in order to recognize oneself in one's situation. But the same is true of the spectators who exert hermeneutic effort toward understanding comedy and identifying with it, which also requires a reflective distance between the interpretandum and interpreter. This may coincide in an act of comic self-cognition, while still maintaining the difference between comic characters and comic spectators, listeners, or readers. In other words, without distance, in comedy, freedom can neither be gained nor preserved.

Through reflective, interpretative action, one can achieve freedom as being with others: then, one knows not only *that* one is free but also *why*. The liberating effect of comedy is not immediate but a result of a joint action performed with, and in the presence of, others. The full realization of freedom as freedom-for and freedom-with comes only at the very end. Freedom, then, is never a given but should be achieved anew within a reflective *process*: one moves from an initial misrecognition, through the "argument" of the plot, to the understanding of who one is as mutually recognized by others. Liberating its characters and spectators, who also reproduce freedom in their lives, by participating in the onstage comedy, comedy makes life meaningful and brings well-being into life. Comedy is thus *the* place for the realization of human freedom.

PART III

Ethics of Comedy

CHAPTER 6

Foolish Wisdom: The Philosopher as a Comic Figure

Plot and Character

What is the role of character in the comic universe? Are comic characters just functions of the plot, or are they independent of it? Or, perhaps, is the plot defined either by the individual "logic" of each character or by the "logic" of the whole of the interaction of characters?

For Aristotle, plot (*mythos*) takes precedence over characters (*ēthē*), for drama presents an action (*praxis*) that alone can lead to well-being, not a quality (*poiotēs*) that determines a character in a particular way of acting.[1] Perhaps, then, comic plot uses its various contrivances to organize and direct human action toward the goal of a good ending. But this would mean that comic characters are just rivets in the grand mechanism of comic plot that hold it together and allow it to function toward the preconceived end. In this case, comic characters are sketchy, being perfunctory and stereotypical representations of certain psychological types ("qualities"), fully predictable in their reactions in preset situations.[2]

For others, comic characters are fully independent of each other, unique individuals, just as humans are. Consequently, all the action of the plot follows straightforwardly and univocally from the characters' interaction with each other. Thus, Otto Ludwig, Leonid Grossman, and Bakhtin proposed the idea of "polyphony" as a way to understand the ensuing interaction of fully independent characters.[3] According to this reading, the plot develops and comes to its end solely from within the inner consistency of characters.[4] Thus, the plot is fully inscribed into, and determined by, individual characters.

Against the extremes of these two interpretations, I argue that plot and character, while they have different functions, bear equal importance and weight in comedy. Plot is monological and fictitious; it is an author's invention and construction. But even if some characters appear sketchy and sometimes dependent on the development of the plot, the major comic characters are true to life: they both imitate life *and* offer us normative models of behavior (in this respect, characters are sometimes even "truer" than life). Such characters each have their own voices and are capable of real dialogical interaction with other characters and spectators. Interestingly, spectators have the advantage of knowing the progression of the plot, which each character knows only in part. Nonetheless, comic characters are active in comic interaction, whereas spectators do not participate in the action directly but rather follow the characters and exercise their activity in the understanding and interpretation of the action. Hence, the spectators live a "theoretical" life in comedy, that of observation and possibly learning from earning from what they see, whereas the actors live a "practical" life, that of action.

A relative autonomy of the plot is therefore always balanced in comedy by the characters' being true to life, even if they often carry and reproduce a mistaken or misinterpreted identity.[5] The being of comic characters appears as "as-if" being, because they have only a realistic "what" (or "essence") but not a real "is" (or "existence"). Yet the characters' "what" is fully human in that it is—or at least it can be, in a good comedy—meaningful to us, spectators or listeners, whose "is" is real.[6] We can communicate, imitate, and disagree with comic characters as with fellow human beings.

As interaction between characters, the action of the comic plot testifies to their dialogical being—that is, as being together with others—in which other characters and spectators can participate. Thus, dialogical being is always present at any moment in comedy: implicit in the beginning, it unfolds through the development of the plot and becomes fully realized as well-being with others in the end. Comic characters are revealed through comic action as dialogical interaction and not by an objective description of their appearance or of features of their "character" as a psychological type, which would pinpoint and objectify them. Comedy is therefore not solely plot-driven, and its characters are often finely portrayed with much psychological nuance and subtlety as fully human beings.

Comic Character: Individual or Universal?

But does the comic character *represent* a universal type or an individual? This question, as Silk noted, "is eminently discussible in respect of Menander,"[7] as it is in respect of all later comedy. The very development of comic character seems to suggest the movement from the representation (and mocking) of a concrete individual in Old Comedy toward a rather schematic yet universal,

Aristotelian character and then to the finely tuned portrayal of a real individual who bears universal features in New Comedy.[8]

The comic character's distinctive features are suggested by his or her name, which is often indicative of the character's social position or behavior. Unlike in tragedy, where many characters are either known mythological personages or invented individuals, in comedy we often encounter either typical names (such as *Davus* for a slave) or "speaking names" (such as *Onesimos*, the name of the "useful" slave in Menander's *Epitrepontes*).[9] Sometimes, what is typical is presented in a character as a function of a family relation (son or daughter), social characteristic (page), or psychological trait (miser). Nonetheless, a straightforwardly simplistic pure type is rare among main characters, who are usually psychologically nuanced. As in a many-figured painting, some figures are portrayed in more detail, and some remain sketchy.

An important source of our knowledge of the types of characters from the beginning of New Comedy is Theophrastus's brief treatise *Characters*,[10] which presented thirty different types of characters, though in a much less sophisticated way than Aristotle did in his three treatises on ethics. Theophrastus did not provide any clue as to the sequence of and principle(s) for the classification of characters; in each case, he gave a brief definition of a type and then listed several examples of it. Thus, *irony*, with which the treatise opens, is defined as *pretense* or *affectation*, implying self-derogation in speech and deeds. Irony, of course, is the most conspicuous feature of Socrates, and the example Theophrastus used was typical of Socrates as someone who kept saying "I cannot believe this" or "I cannot grasp this."[11] Among other characteristic types we find flattery, garrulity, rusticity, obsequiousness, incredulity, petty ambition, stinginess, ostentation, and faintheartedness. The treatise was composed after 319 BCE, and, since Menander studied with Theophrastus, it is quite possible that Menander knew this work on characters. Each of Theophrastus's types can be found in Menander and later comic characters (for instance, in Gogol's *Dead Souls*), although rarely in a "pure" and isolated form: usually, they appeared as a feature characteristic of a comic personage in his or her interaction with others. Thus, the common translation of Theophrasus's work as *Moral Characters*[12] is somewhat misleading, for in Theophrastus and Menander a "moral" character presents a psychological type or propensity, which depicts particular kinds of actions of both humans and dramatic characters. In fact, each of Theophrastus's character examples can be easily embodied and presented onstage either in a mime or in a comedy. And, unlike Hegel's comic self, Menander's characters did not take off their masks.[13]

Nevertheless, comic characters are universal *and* unique but not abstract, for, on the one hand, they display typical or universal features and, on the other, they are all uniquely recognizable through their acts and voices. This is especially true in Terence, whose characters were far removed from the grotesque vulgarity of Old Comedy and always tried carefully to preserve decorum, that is, proper and decent ways of speaking and behaving. They were thus not mere masks in their appearance but appearances and voices subtly modeled in a true-to-life way. Universal features do not yet make comic characters into abstract types, since each figure (at least, among the main personages) is also a unique individuality, which is not entirely covered or exhausted by any one psychological type or a combination of them. For one cannot say that a dramatic character or a real person is fully characterized by the features 2, 3, 17, and 21 out of Theophrastus's list of characters or any other classification. Everyone, every character and every human being, embodies *many* different characters, which transpire in the dialogical (inter)action. Yet no one can be fully thematized, objectified, or reduced to a particular character or even several types. For every human being always faces an other that is never entirely thematizable, even if fully meaningful at each particular moment. This is the other of another person and also the personal other of oneself, who cannot be rendered objective, defined, or described through a finite number of features but is rather revealed only in a dramatic or live dialogue.[14] Therefore, comic characters are "concrete universals," which nonetheless do not represent an imaginary situation of sublime suffering but are capable of interaction and well-being with other characters and people.

The Smart Slave

The clever slave or maid was a central figure in comedy: it appeared already in Old Comedy, increased in important and omnipresence in New Comedy,[15] and survived into modern comedy as the maid[16] or servant, epitomized by Sancho Panza in Miguel de Cervantes—all the way down to Lurcio in the *Up Pompeii!*

The slave stands out by being "the other" of everyone else. The comic slave was conspicuously different from other characters even in appearance: he was redheaded;[17] he had a big belly;[18] and he was an almost epic, colorful, "heavy," and bizarre figure. The slave bore a typical name that immediately pointed to his otherness: often, it was simply the indication of the slave's place of origin,[19] which effectively obliterated all traces of personal identity. In any event, the slave's look always bore pejorative connotations, therefore excluding him from being accepted as an equal and relegating him to the margins of society. Thus, a slave's testimony in court did not have legal power;[20] and a clown in Shakespeare spoke *in prose*, which was typical of characters of lower social standing.

As Plato argued in the *Laws*, comedy depicts base and ridiculous things and therefore should be left to slaves and foreigners.[21] A slave was a foreigner and a stranger. He was *strange*: outlandish and marginal, he was a comic figure, for he spoke, acted, and looked different, in stark contrast to the homogeneous morals of a community of the like-minded and like-looking. However, a foreigner or slave is never a bore, exactly because he can see—and tell—things differently. In this sense, a philosopher is a comic figure and a foreigner to his own country, as both Hans Blumenberg and Agnes Heller have noted,[22] because he despises the common sense that he lacks and is (or should be) ready and capable of thinking beyond the accepted social and political divides and cultural prejudices. In fact, the classless intelligentsia always consists of such comic dissident characters.

The slave's irritating and defiant otherness provokes others who, looking at him, realize their own difference, with which they are neither able nor ready to cope. Traditional society requires loyalty and discretion[23] from a slave, and when others find a much more complicated personality behind the slave they tend to reduce him to a being over which one exerts power. The uniform self-repeating and self-reproducing idle class, which undeservingly enjoys the benefits of life, gets frustrated by those who are meant to be dependent on their masters yet prove to be independent by being other and thinking differently. This dissatisfaction—which in fact is frustration toward oneself and one's unfulfilled life—leads us to establish negative clichés about slaves as supposedly lazy, garrulous, deceitful, and outright stupid. Such was the idle, acid-tongued, and deceitful Xanthias in Aristophanes's *Frogs*[24] and Terence's loquacious Parmeno, who ironically "recognized" chattiness as his greatest failing.[25] All these biased descriptions show a profound frustration with the slave's otherness. This would seem to evade the immediacy of his appropriation as a useful tool rather than a dignified person. Yet the masters cannot live without a slave, not only because they rely on him in everyday subsistence but even more so because they cannot survive without his otherness, which they incessantly reject. Without the other, no communication, no conversation, is possible, and no action can take place: life stops, and love is impossible within an ever-boring and suffocating repetition of the same.

Split Identity, Ambiguity, and Ambivalence: The Fool

The marginalization of a slave is inevitably unsuccessful. Seemingly other to "normal" characters, a slave is a most human and humane character, ready for compassion and forgiveness[26] and even self-sacrifice. Unsurprisingly, then, the audience, while heartily laughing at the slaves and maids, always sides with them and not with their masters. For, even if with a touch of

Schadenfreude ("not me"), spectators, who turn coactors, are always on the side of the oppressed.

Yet the slave was not only an important figure in comedy: he was the *central* figure, who rescued everyone from an apparently inextricable situation, leading them through the twists and turns of the plot and out of the impasse. The slave was the "conductor" of an undisciplined orchestra of comic characters; he was the "director" of the intrigue who staged the whole of the drama within the current drama, steering the action toward a resolution and the right end. He conducted the action and directed the unruly comic orchestra sometimes by tricking the players and sometimes by postponing the planned action by keeping silent, which became the precondition for gaining the knowledge that could propel the action forward: "You will know if you can keep quiet."[27]

The slave, then, was the mastermind, the "head" of the intrigue,[28] the one who suggested the plan of action,[29] as were Syrus in the *Brothers* and Parmeno in the *Eunuch*. He was the unrecognized *one* who allowed a whole dialogical community of *many* actors to become well-off. But, as I mentioned, unlike the tragic autonomy of the single modern subject, comic autonomy is collective, that of one *and* many, which appears oxymoronic to the modern subject, who is the one exclusive of many. Comic autonomy is realized in a communal comic action, guided by one particular comic character—the "comediagogue"—toward a good ending.

Consequently, the slave was not only recognized as equal to others but became the embodiment of practical reason: through the organization of action, he was capable of solving apparently irresolvable problems. As Agnes Heller puts it, "the social roles are frequently reversed in comedies. The maid tells the mistress that she is acting like a fool. Servants, slaves have no social prejudices. The fools are often the clever ones since they can see through the socially created 'fog' of the learned." The slave, then, was someone who could find a *remedium*, a solution to a problem.[30] This readily brings to mind the Greek *pharmakon*, famous (or notorious, according to some) for its ambiguity, meaning both *cure* and *remedy*, as well as *poison*, *spell*, and *enchanted potion*.[31] In comedy, the slave was no longer discrete and silent but had a right—and even an obligation—to speak. The slave thereby became the inspiration behind the development of the comic plot.

The slave was a carnivalesque character: he was both foolish (as commonly perceived), for he needed to carry out his intended plan without raising suspicion, *and* also very clever (as he truly was), for he needed to pretend to be foolish while carrying out his plan (which tended to go awry). Moreover, he had to be patient in order to carry out the plot and hopeful that everything would come together in the end. He had to be smart enough to crack a joke or improvise an aphorism, which was the slave's prerogative in comedy. Consequently, the slave was a profoundly *ambiguous* and *ambivalent* figure. Not only did a slave intentionally speak ambiguously, but his identity was always a *split* identity, which could be reconciled only at the end of comic action. Smart and foolish at the same time, he bore both Apollonian and Dionysian features, neither of which he could disavow. He was not recognized by others (as equal), yet he was still recognized as the person needed most (for the action): without him the plot stood still, and the complication could never be resolved in the denouement. The slave was thus both almost indiscernible and the most important figure in comedy.[32]

The slave was a profoundly *ironic* figure. While most comic characters were satisfied with a finalizing identity, rooted in their social or family roles, the slave was truly complex but appeared—and *pretended*—to be a simpleton. For he could never entirely "gather" himself; he was not fully thematizable by a stable and definable "what"; in fact, he existed only in the moment of interaction and dialogue with others.[33] Furthermore, he both had to hide and reveal himself through what he was not, in his actions and intentionally ambiguous rejoinders.[34] The slave appeared both as intentionally humble, underappreciating himself (*eiron*), and as intentionally boastful, overappreciating himself (*alazon*). Inevitably ironic, this mastermind of comedy wanted to hide his cleverness and to show it: he wanted at once to help others achieve their goals and fulfill (erotic) desires and to help himself achieve personal liberation and recognition as an equal. The irony of being foolish, then, consisted in the fool's *pretending* to be a fool, while in fact he was the smartest character in comedy, of which not only others but even the slave himself might not have been aware.

The slave's situation thus entailed a paradox. He appeared to embody the logically impossible conjunction of opposites: he was a smart fool and thus embodied both wisdom as knowledge in its entirety and its utter lack. However, unlike Freud's unconscious, which is "the realm of the illogical," the slave's ambiguity did not violate the laws of logic, including the law of noncontradiction—for the implied contradiction was only an apparent one, since the slave embodied and displayed these opposite qualities *in different respects*.

The slave knew that he did not know (the course of the whole action). Wisdom in comedy consisted in the knowledge that in order to act well (to the benefit others), one should—and yet cannot—act with full knowledge of everything that should happen on the way to a good ending. Comic wisdom was thus paradoxically an abdication from knowledge that suspends itself—and thus allows for both reasoned and spontaneous action. Therefore, in order to be a fool in comedy, one had to be a clever thinker and a sophisticated actor.[35] Only the fool was a wise person, whereas (seemingly) the wise person was foolish.[36] One should *know* how to be a fool. For the fool was the one who outsmarted everyone else, without their even noticing it, not for his or her own sake but for the sake of others.

Even at the level of prejudiced public perception, the slave was considered both stupid and crafty and shrewd.[37] However, shrewdness was not insolence but often a disguise for a timid and shy person who nevertheless took the risk of telling and enacting the truth. And stupidity stood for knowing that one does not know, which is already a sort of knowledge. Therefore, when Menedemus said he was not very smart and could be considered stupid,[38] he showed that he was not at all foolish; thus, he acted as a slave. For the very capacity to think reflectively and critically about oneself is already a sign of intelligence. The conceited and self-righteous is in fact foolish, because, unable to have a proper dialogue with the other, he is unable to have a reflective distance from himself and thereby know his not knowing of himself. As the clown in Shakespeare rightly observed, "Wit, an't be thy will, put me into good fooling! Those wits that think they have thee do very oft prove fools; and I that am sure I lack thee may pass for a wise man. For what says Quinapalus? 'Better a witty fool than a foolish wit.'"[39]

A delicate balance between opposite poles is difficult to maintain. Thus, the fool sometimes slipped into roguishness and trickery; yet as a trickster, plotter, and schemer, he lacked guile. Since the fool primarily helped others—and only in this way helped himself—he was selfless and belittled himself. Rejecting and (often unwillingly) sacrificing his own self for others, he embodied what others did not have—a foolish wisdom—and regained himself in the end, along with others. Since at any particular moment the fool did not coincide with himself, he was always more and always less than he was. This split (but not "illogical") identity—being both a sublime hero and a cunning "antihero"—is seen even in the figure of Odysseus. Hence, the fool combined in himself something divine (the "holy fool" in the Byzantine tradition) and something animal. As such, he was often represented by a cunning and witty animal.[40] The fool was essentially good, although his human goodness, situated between divine and animal, was not well understood by the modern solitary and moralistic subject.[41] But only a clever fool could guide the plot, playing in and with it—through thoughts, actions, gestures, and words. The clever fool is thus an indispensable and fitting figure in a comic play.

Freedom for One, Freedom for All: The Paradox of Freedom

The whole point of comedy is to assert and establish—in the end—the humanity and equality of all the people involved in its action, especially of the oppressed. Comedy is a dramatic procedure that allows for the recognition and acceptance of the other and of oneself. It allows for liberation from oppression in its various kinds: personal, psychological, family, social, and political. Thus, the end of comedy is the abolition of slavery in all its forms. Yet freedom never simply happens or comes about by itself, as a stroke of luck or gift of fate: one has to strive, plot, act, work, and fight for liberation together with others.

The slave's ambiguity was also notable in this struggle: he was both the mastermind of action toward freedom and the most oppressed figure. Fighting for the liberation of others, he also fought for his own freedom. As the acting director of comedy, the slave is also lazy: as Socrates reportedly said, idleness is the sister of freedom.[42] Yet the slave almost never explicitly set personal freedom as the end of his actions, although he always hoped for freedom as the most prized and dearest goal, especially for one who does not have it. One cannot be well-off unless one is free. This is, however, the minimal accomplishment. The slave helped others to resolve a seemingly irresolvable situation, and only then could he receive recognition and liberation. But the maximal accomplishment is to realize that one cannot be free unless *everyone* is free. Thus the cranky and stingy father, who found himself happy and liberated (perhaps only for a moment) when he saw others free and happy: the son with the woman he loves and the slave liberated.

Comedy implied the universality of human equality, as it depicted the contingency of social and class distinctions. For the liberation of the most oppressed in comedy implied a paradox. As a "practical" philosopher, a thinker-in-action, the comic slave was capable of transgressing social differences, showing that they are only a matter of convention that have nothing to do with the human condition. This was to achieve a good ending through comic action and deliberation. As Euripides said, the slave's infamy existed only in name, that is, it was just a convention, but if he was well-doing and right-minded, he was no different from a free man.[43] The contingency of social and class distinctions was apparent already in Aristophanes: in his utopian polity, birds carried no purses[44] and thus had no corruption or distinctions based on money; only those birds who were formerly humans employed servants[45] and thus were already corrupt; and slaves, foreigners, and the disenfranchised were all welcomed into their commonwealth.[46] In Greek New Comedy and especially in the later Roman comedy, which reflected the growing cosmopolitan and multicultural world, there was a clear understanding of the utter arbitrariness of class differences.[47] In comedy, it was the slave who was wise and the master either greedy and stupid (the old man) or self-indulgent and inexperienced (the young man). It was the slave who helped his master out of a difficult situation and sometimes cheered him up by entertaining him with (often rude and obscene) jokes.[48] In the opposition of bright slave and dull master, the former "enlightened" the latter and allowed him to become more humane.

Here, then, is the paradox of liberation in comedy: the slave, who needed liberation more than anyone else, was *already* free. For, while he helped others become free before he himself was liberated, he also was a thinker—*the* thinker of comedy. As such, he was capable of free thought and free speech,[49] although often in a disguised form. And free thought and speech are risky and dangerous, for they are provocative and go against the moral, social, and political conventions of the age, especially when uttered in the face of someone in a position of power.[50]

The moment of the slave's liberation, in the conclusion of comedy, solved the paradox between being already free (as a rational and dignified human being) and not yet being free (from the lack of recognition of his freedom from others). Long before Hegel, the comic dialectic understood and embodied onstage the relationship between master and slave.[51] Steering and directing the comedy, the slave proved to be the master of comedy—the master dialectician, the mastermind and architect of its plot. And the master turned out to be the slave of comedy, insofar as he had to follow the twists and turns, the traps and solutions, along the way of the action and the "argument" of the plot, which often dragged him along.

Structures of Domination and Strategies of Liberation

While the comic character was portrayed as an individual, he also bore typical traits. Three conspicuous types of comic figures were the parents (fathers and mothers), the children (sons and daughters), and the servants (male and female). These three character types were the three foci that defined comedy and its action. The comic triad established three pairs, each of which was characterized by a particular type of interaction. The common comic representatives of these three pairs were father-son, son-slave, and slave-father. In each pair, there was a clear opposition of domination, of the oppressor to the oppressed. In contrast, the modern idea of domination was based on a rather simplistic dual opposition: Hegel described this in the famous master-slave opposition, which defined a moment within a *linear*, even if intricate, development (of the spirit), which presupposed that opposites were capable of interacting (or "struggling") without mediation.

An interaction based on three, and not two, agents presented an altogether different type of power distribution. Three points define a plane. The progression of the plot could always be reconstructed (but only retrospectively) as a linear argument moving through a number of steps, except for those cases when it was deliberately broken or interrupted. Such a progression, however, is in fact much more convoluted, implying many side moves rather than evident steps and obsolete relations: it is a meander rather than a straight line.

In a triadic structure, each element is independent and yet equally important: it is neither subsumed under nor derived from the other two. Therefore, the third character in comedy was not a mediator between the other two or a "sublation" of the uneasy relation between them and did not represent a "synthesis" of the "thesis" and "antithesis." The triadic structure of comedy *prevented* a total domination of any one of the three constituents. Each one "prevailed" over one of the three and was in turn "prevailed" upon by the remaining one.

The comic triadic power structure was similar to the structure of the rock-paper-scissors, rochambeau, or morra cinese game where, depending on a particular combination, each one could prevail (rock over scissors, scissors over paper, and paper over rock). This type of interaction, which establishes a balance of domination and being dominated, and thus the structure of oppression and a strategy of liberation, was pervasive in New Comedy. Thus, the father overpowers the son (through family and economic relations), and the son overpowers the slave (through a social hierarchy), but the slave overpowers the father (by outsmarting him). Even if this structure did not really cancel the oppression altogether, at least it spread opportunities to prevail evenly, thus giving everyone a chance. The liberation, as I have argued, came only at the end of comedy, as a result of the concerted action orchestrated by its mastermind, the slave. Thus the role of the slave, the most oppressed in a linear top-down hierarchy of domination, was extremely significant: first of all, he turned the unhealthy vertical hierarchy into a rochambeau triangle (or circle); and second, his clever but not evil trickery allowed for the liberation of everyone in the comic *apokatastasis*.

Numerically, tripartition also provides a better and richer distribution of possible relations in dramatic action: In the case of a duo, there is only one relation, which can easily become too stiff and overexploited. In the case of a quartet, there are six possible relations between the actors, which is simply too much: some of them will inevitably become perfunctory, sketchy, and hard to follow. But in the case of a triad, there are three relations, all of which can be actively explored and become equally important while providing a more balanced distribution of power. It is perhaps not by chance, then, that Montesquieu's split of the branches of government into three—legislative, executive, and judiciary—proved to be the most stable power arrangement.[52]

Woody Allen marks a remarkable case of the realization of the rochambeau triad in modern comedy. He is probably the only comedian who managed to unite all three comic hypostases in one persona. In his earlier comedies, he is the son who wants to be happy with the woman he loves, the father who originally prevents himself—through implicit self-imposed taboos and unnecessary regulations—from being happy, and also the smart trickster, the real thinker, the paraklete or "comforter," who in the end liberates himself from his own oppression. (For example, in one of the final scenes of *Manhattan*, he explains to himself why life is worth living by listing, in the mood of Coltrane, his "favorite things.") In fact, Woody Allen embodies even more than that—he is also the playwright who hovers over the comic trinity of himself.

Dianoia

The slave is thus the fool, who is cleverer than everyone else but who reasons covertly, often forced to think within the confines of the circumstances in which he finds himself. But it also appears that he *likes* to think, for thinking brings satisfaction both as an activity targeted at itself and inasmuch as it brings about a good ending for everyone. For the well-being of others is a much greater reward than the well-being of only oneself, as isolated and "autonomous" well-being is a contradiction in terms: well-being is well-being with others, for to be is to be (in dialogue) with others.

In Terence, a character was sometimes revealed through his or her *mores* (morals), sometimes through the *ingenium* (way of thought), and sometimes through a combination of both. A smart slave's thought or intelligence was the always partial thinking of a proving and calculating discursive mind (*dianoia*) in action, which needed a number of steps to eventually realize something or establish a conclusion. Such thinking was not an all-embracing intellect (*noys*) that could grasp any point without reasoning, in a simple act of thought (incomprehensible for a recursive thinking). In Plato, and especially in the later Neoplatonic tradition, *dianoia* was *the* "faculty" of philosophy and dialectic. It was therefore also the faculty of the slave as the thinker in comedy.

"Thought"-*dianoia*, one of Aristotle's six structural components of drama, was one of two constituents (together with "character"-*ēthos*) that distinguished a dramatic character. In the already mentioned *Tractatus Coislinianus*, *dianoia* represented either opinion or proof.[53] Renaissance authors, however, who mostly had difficulties with the explanation of the term, translated it as *sententia*.[54] As Arbogast Schmitt has argued, "thought" should be understood within Aristotle's distinction between moral or "ethical" virtues—habituations that allow for making the right choice and acting according to a mean—and "dianoetic" virtues based in thought.[55] Moral habituation-*ēthos* is thus always complemented by thinking-*dianoia*, not only in ethics but also in drama, insofar as such thinking is a reflection, imitation, and normative pattern of human activity.[56]

If comic plot as a whole, as I have argued, represents a "macroargument" that makes love, life, freedom, and human well-being possible, then thinking-*dianoia* allows for a "microarugment" made by a character within the development of the major argument of the plot. *Dianoia*, then, is a capacity for discursive thinking that makes it possible to move from premises to a conclusion in a number of reasoned steps. The nondiscursive intellect-*noys* supposedly makes it possible for one to intuit the right conclusion immediately, as already contained in the premises, without a necessary "discourse" or "running" of reasoning: thus, it requires no drama of thinking. But for *dianoia*, the process of thinking and reasoning is indispensable. Such thinking is itself a drama and becomes comedy if it manages to arouse and direct affects, passions, and emotions and arrive at the desired end or conclusion.[57]

Such thinking is practical and "poetic," insofar as it directs the action and guides the dramatic production by practical means: comic characters do not theorize much but *act* concretely out of a difficult situation according to a plan, steered by the smart slave who, however, often does not understand it in full himself, until it is fully disclosed in the end.[58] Comic characters thus think in action often without even knowing, until the very end, that they think through acting—through exactly what they do. Hence, comedy needs reasoned thinking expressed in saying (*legein*) that discloses an act of reasoning (*logos*) enacted together with other people. Such thinking-in-action shows what is and what is not and establishes what is universally valid and possible in a particular case—of a thought in an argument, of life and freedom for a person. Proceeding by affirmation and negation (*kataphasis kai apophasis*), discursive thinking-*dianoia* is capable of proof and refutation and of making an appropriate judgment, which is often sedimented in a maxim-*gnōmē*. Comic thinking, then, deals with what can be reached and arranged by the embodied speech and reasoning: it is therefore "logical" and dialectical.

Dialectician in the Situation of Uncertainty

As I have argued, the overall structure of comedy imitates, reproduces, and assimilates the structure of a dialectical argument, that is, a rational construction realized through a motion of discursive thought-*dianoia* from premises to conclusion. The flow of a dramatic dialectical argument is propelled by questions and answers that refer to opposites, use dialectical means, and are carried on and out by at least two interlocutors in an agonistic exchange: the one who asks and the one who replies. But the interlocutors are not symmetrical: The dialectician is a questioner who takes the risk of suggesting, through appropriate acts and questions, the direction of the development of the plot. The one who answers, on the other hand, is initially responsible for the debated thesis or claim and provides the answers to the questions.

Human thinking, and comic thinking in particular, is always partial and incomplete and therefore presupposes the *process* of searching and acting and only rarely the *act* of understanding. Such thinking, therefore, needs a supporting *skill*—art, knack, *tekhnē*, the ability to act and plot—which is dialectic, the art of reasoning in philosophy and of reasoned action in comedy. From the very inception of this technique of reasoning in the Greek Sophistic Enlightenment, the dialectician knew *which* question to ask at a particular junction of the dispute; that is, he was capable of formulating a carefully constructed question that would yield an answer that advanced the reasoning toward the desired end. However, a dialectician did not know *why* he knew which question was the right one at any juncture in reasoning and what the next correct logical move at that point would be. Consequently, dialectical questioning is not a strict discipline or science but an art, structurally similar to the art of developing comic dramatic plot through dialogue. The characters of dialectical or comic dialogues did not know why they were asking the questions that would turn out to be appropriate from the perspective of the end. Only the author of the play might have known this, but he usually did not reveal it, so that the readers or spectators themselves had to guess and restore the "logic" of a dialectical or dramatic plot. As an art, ancient dialectic differed from modern dialectic, which, although inspired by its ancient model, understood itself as a science and universal method of correct and precise reasoning. The dialectician, then, was a logical artisan and skillful mastermind behind the construction or destruction of a complex dialectical argument and (comic) dialogical plot.

Yet, if the slave was *the* thinker in comedy, his thinking, as mentioned, was still partial and his knowledge incomplete: he did not grasp the whole of the dramatic "argument" at any particular moment. Although he hoped to reach the (good) end by comic reasoning, nothing guaranteed in advance that the sought conclusion would or could be reached. His wisdom was the knowing of his Socratic not-knowing: the slave was the philosopher of comedy. The slave knew that he thought (intentionally), but he did not know whether he would succeed in thinking, which he could not gather until the very end. The slave was thus comedy's *dialectician*. Yet, as one who reasoned, he inevitably had a split identity, for reflective discursive thinking is profoundly ambivalent, often by making mistakes and digressions, not having at each particular moment what it looks for. Moreover, oftentimes none of the available strategies and devices seem to work, as Geta realized when thinking about how to appease the old man's wrath by tricking him: "Tell him? It'll inflame him. Say nothing? It'll provoke him further."[59]

When comic action is directed dialectically, each act is defined (often implicitly) by reference to opposites (contradictories), one of which is the negation of the other: do this and do not do this. In this privative opposition (A and not A), as Roman Jakobson has argued, the privative, "weaker" part (not A) has more volume ("not red" in "red and not red").[60] Therefore, in action, the "not doing," or "not happening the way it was planned and conceived," which is the privative part of the (logical) opposition, should always be further specified. For this reason, the planning of an action is always a struggle with the indefiniteness of the situation, which is expressed in the privative opposite. To carry out a determinate action, then, is to make it into a definite and defined contradictory opposite, that is, into the other, and not just another, action. Yet in life there is always indeterminacy, a "surplus" that cannot be fully dissolved and resolved by means of a rational action and decision. In most cases in comedy, the smart slave-dialectician plotted an action, though he was never quite sure whether it would work. The rest was assigned to *tykhē* (the *topos* of [good] fortune), which in fact was a *communal working* of people acting toward a shared good ending, often without noticing it. Thus, the goodness of comedy was entrusted to peoples' mutual reliance and dependence, which, in the end, overcame (or at least temporarily suspended) the initial division, exclusion, oppression, and lack of freedom.

The dialectician, therefore, knows that he does not know (how to act) but acts nevertheless, for he possesses the intelligence to plan the action, although he is not capable of seeing all of its consequences at any particular point. The dialectician does *not* know the precise course of the argument or plot that might make temporary loops and come to provisional dead ends. He can only guess, apply his skill, and try to calculate and anticipate future events, which, however, is possible only to an extent. This is exactly how a dialectician proves an argument, which is meaningful at every step yet, before and until the conclusion is reached, is not yet established. As Syrus said to Demea: "That's real wisdom (*sapere*) . . . not merely to see what lies under your feet but to foresee the future."[61] Yet Syrus said this ironically, for he could not be sure of the success of the dramatic intrigue until the very end, when everything came together and thereby justified the dialectical comic action *post factum*. As he was never sure of the outcome at the moment of reasoning and moving through the steps of questions and answers, the slave-dialectician did not make his "art" conspicuous, even for himself. He was therefore a profoundly ironic figure, who had to conceal himself and his skill in order to make his not-yet-knowing knowledge work. Thus, the smart slave proved himself to be the master dialectician of comedy.

Terence's *The Mother-in-Law* provided a fine example of such dialectical comic action. At the very end of the comedy, Pamphilus said with gratitude that Parmeno had helped him without knowing it, but Parmeno responded that he knew perfectly well what he did, although part of it was done unwittingly rather than on purpose.[62] In other words, Parmeno did what he intended to do, even if he was not altogether sure that his plan would succeed. That is, the "dialectician" Parmeno knew that he did not—and could not—know (everything in advance), whereas the master Pamphilus, who was well-off at the end due to Parmeno's actions, did not know even this not-knowing. When acting, Parmeno used his skill to the best of his ability and left the rest of the inadvertent action to the necessity of chance, in a concerted action carried out with others, which allowed the overall "argument of the plot" to succeed in the end.

The Cook

The figure of the philosopher as the smart comic slave and the ironic master dialectician bears a clear similarity to the cook. As a parody of a true dialectical argument, Plato had the Sophist Dionysodorus argue that, since it is proper for every master to do what he is supposed to do—in particular, for a cook to cook—then if someone were to cook a cook, he would do the proper thing.[63] Such an "argument" is, of course, ironic, since it is immediately understandable as fallacious, because the reader is aware of brilliant examples of proper dialectic, so often practiced by Socrates, who was also Dionysodorus's ironic interlocutor.

Famous cooks were celebrities of their time, and food was an important feature of comedy.[64] In Old Comedy, the performance was often accompanied by throwing food to the audience, and comedies often ended with a banquet, as did Aristophanes's *Ecclesiazusae*, where women presented and ate *the* food—a dish that incorporated all possible fish and meat delicacies, whose syncretic name was the longest word in Ancient Greek.[65] The colorful figure of the cook (*mageiros*) was also common in fables.[66] Middle Comedy was full of food, and the important major buffoon character was a cook.[67] The cook appeared regularly onstage in New Comedy, as also in modern comedy.[68] More recently, we had Woody Allen himself trying to cook a lobster in *Annie Hall*.

The importance of the figure of the cook lies in his mock similarity with the slave and the dialectician. Both the dialectician and the cook are (improperly) curious.[69] Besides, the cook (the master of the kitchen) and the slave (the master of comedy) are similar in that both have a lower social status yet both are absolutely indispensable for making people happy. Besides, both the cook and the dialectician make a valuable, useful, and memorable product that sustains and promotes life: one the life of the mind, and the other the life of the body.[70] A culinary recipe has the same structure as a dialectical argument and a comic plot (as well as a rhetorical and mathematical proof): it starts with the necessary components, blends and transforms them by various methods, and comes up with a tasteful ending. The comic weaving together of efficient and beautiful speeches is therefore very much like cooking: one should add an exact number of components and process them in a precise order—but also demonstrate one's skill for overcoming the uncertainty and necessary contingency of a concrete situation and producing a good food for body and soul in the end.

Socrates and the Figure of the Slave

Since the inception of philosophy as thinking that arrives at and justifies a conclusion through an argument, Socrates has been the embodiment of the figure of the dialectician. Socrates is *the* comic figure of philosophy, the cook of its arguments and the conductor of its plots. In comedy, the slave played the same role as Socrates did in dramatized dialogue: he liberated others. The former directed the plot, and the latter steered the dialectical argument. Both the slave and Socrates seemed somewhat simplistic; both deliberately wore an ironic and ever-ambiguous guise behind which we quickly discover a powerful and sophisticated mind. Hence, both were dialecticians: the slave was a practical thinker, leading us through the labyrinth of a plot; and Socrates guided us through the maze of an argument, even if often toward a negative outcome. Both selflessly promoted the freedom and well-being of others: the slave by directing them toward a resolution of the conflict and Socrates by steering others to the freedom of and in thought. Both freed themselves by helping others (or, rather, being already free, they are recognized as such by others as a result of their actions): the slave was often rewarded for his deeds with the highest gift, that of freedom;[71] and Socrates was free in the knowledge of his apparent not knowing: not limited by any fixed knowledge, he kept striving toward finding out how and what things were.

Yet Socratic dialectic was usually (but not always) theoretically negative—that is, it destroyed a wrong statement or argument—whereas comic dialectic was always practically positive, as a good comedy came to a resolution of the dramatic conflict and a good ending. However, the positive result of the negative dialectic was to learn the skill of dialectical reasoning that allowed those who practiced it to come to a desired conclusion through a dialogical interaction with others.

Socrates constantly reached across the classes of his society. As we know from Plato and Xenophon, he preferred talking to ordinary people without paying attention to their social position or age. Both fellow citizens and slaves were his cherished interlocutors, as a famous example with a slave boy demonstrates, where the dialectical discussion was comic, since Socrates guided his interlocutor from a total impasse toward a "good ending": the resolution of a geometrical problem.[72] Socrates's dialectic is realized in a comedy of errors (eventually exposed by Socrates), as, for instance, in the *Euthydemus*, where two Sophists, brothers Euthydemus and Dionysodorus, produced seemingly valid yet in fact deeply flawed and confusing arguments, all based on some error, usually that of equivocation.

During his lifetime, in his relentless critique and subtle mockery of the Sophists, Socrates continuously ridiculed "serious" (often flawed) arguments by reproducing and often reducing them to a farce. Even on his deathbed, Socrates remained a comic figure who refused to take his situation as tragic: his death was clearly a comic event for him, since, as we learn from Plato's *Phaedo*, Socrates hoped—and argued—for the best as the ultimate end of his life's comedy.[73]

Moreover, Socrates was a colorful stock figure, an indispensable character in any ancient collection of anecdotes, often compared with Silenus, a "stranger" who was not immediately understandable in the bright Apollonian world. Later, Diogenes of Sinope, a student of Antisthenes, who himself was a student of Socrates, was assimilated to the figure of comic slave and readily parodied in comedy.[74] Diogenes criticized accepted conventions by advocating the life according to nature, yet he still lived at the "margins" of the city life, of which he was a staunch political, philosophical, and cultural "comic" critic. Like Socrates, he thought critically with and in front of others, yet unlike Socrates, who was a purely "oral" philosopher, Diogenes wrote books. He not only used theoretical deliberation but also argued for a good life with others as achievable by practical and comic action.[75] Both Diogenes and the comic slave were dispossessed: reportedly, Diogenes reproached even Socrates, who was famously poor, of indulging in luxury, because Socrates had a house, a bed, and sandals.[76]

In his somewhat eccentric fame, Socrates was similar to Aesop, a flamboyant prephilosophical thinker who put his moral deliberations in the form of fable.[77] Perhaps it was no chance that shortly before his death, in order to bring his life to a meaningful conclusion, Socrates turned not only to arguments but also to poetry, which creates myths in fables.[78] Facing the end of his life, Socrates turned back to philosophy and dialectic: he cathartically purified himself through poetic creative work by, in a way, becoming Aesop.

Unsurprisingly, then, Socrates became a comic character already in Old Comedy: for Aristophanes, Socrates was the epitome of the skilled dialectical thinker. In later comedy Socrates was transformed into the figure of the smart and witty slave. Thus, in Plautus's *Pseudolus*, the master Simo explicitly compared the crafty slave Pseudolus, famous for his skills in argument, to Socrates.[79] The ensuing discussion between the master and slave parodied a dialectical dispute, at the beginning of which Pseudolus even compared himself to the Delphic oracle who only tells the truth.[80] This "self-description," however, was profoundly ironic, as the oracle neither reasoned nor speculated in order to get to truth: the oracle already knew it. Simo thought that he outsmarted Pseudolus in the debate, but in fact the slave skillfully fooled the master, without the latter even noticing. Later, in a monologue directed explicitly to himself and implicitly to the spectators, Pseudolus appeared as a nondialectical tragicomic *raisonneur*, speaking about the illusion of striving toward a desired end in life, about suffering and death. Yet, at a certain point, he abruptly interrupted himself, saying, "Enough of philosophy,"[81] for rather than engage in idle talk, one must return to action.

Philosophy thus originated in a comic dialectical action guided by a comic figure—Socrates, the master dialectician of philosophy, transforms into the slave who directs comedy as a dialectical philosophical enterprise capable of reasoned action, free speech, and a good ending for all.

Conclusion

A conclusion to a book on comedy would naturally mean a good ending. Philosophically, a "good ending" is achieved when the argument arrives at the sought-after conclusion, often in a way that is different from the manner in which it was originally intended. Everything that has been said suddenly, and often unexpectedly, receives meaning and justification; the effort is repaid, and the thought is gathered together, so that nothing is left obsolete or redundant. The same is true of comedies.

As we have seen, from its very inception, New Comedy absorbed all available philosophical thought, approaches, arguments, and techniques. It appropriated them for its own purposes and reflected on them (often through the use of parody) through its comic action. Platonism, Aristotelianism, Skepticism with elements of Cynicism, and especially Stoicism and Epicureanism were all in one way or another present onstage right through modernity. Often we do not notice them, represented and embodied in comic characters and their actions, though we nonetheless learn from them. In fact, comedy was aware of its affinity with philosophy in its various guises. Thus, in Molière's *Les femmes savantes*, the women mentioned all the existing philosophical schools: those of Aristotle, Plato, Epicurus, the atomists, the Stoics, and also—because they kept up with the modern development of philosophy—Descartes. And Descartes himself knew the ancients and tried systematically to develop his philosophy as a comic enterprise, guided by the rules of reasoning and based on the method of achieving the desired end.[1]

From what I have said about the comic character and the structure of the comic plot, it follows that comedy is Platonic in its diction and dialogue, in the use and appropriation of dialectic and methods of reasoning, and in the idea of the good as its end. But comedy is Aristotelian in the "logical" and "rhetorical" arrangement of the constituents of its plot and the use of the comic "topics." And, as we have seen, comedy also displays similarity to Stoicism and Epicureanism, which were the most important postclassical philosophical schools that attempted to appropriate and synthesize the then-existing philosophical vocabularies. Both were contemporary with New Comedy, and both flourished in later antiquity and survived into modernity, although Epicureanism in a more implicit and suppressed form.

Most importantly, the Stoics were the first philosophers to systematically stress the fundamental equality of humans as rational beings in possession of "*logos*," which made all social distinctions only accidental. In this respect, Stoic ethics was particularly modern. The modernity of comedy could also be seen in its ethical position, which could be fairly characterized as Stoic. In comedy, each character was free to do whatever he or she thought best, yet each action was always inscribed in a concrete situation that in turn developed along with the action. A Stoic accepted and bore his fate but also tried to improve his situation through interaction with others—to the extent that he could understand, change, and transform it. Geta was a Stoic when he said, "Whatever fortune brings I will bear it with equanimity."[2] Human moral "comic" knowledge consists, then, in the ability to deliberate well, in order to be able to distinguish and accept what we can and cannot change, and to work together with others on what we can. Epictetus, himself born a slave, expressed this Stoic attitude in the maxim that we should not be afraid of what is not within our control and proceed cautiously with what is.[3] On the basis of such knowledge a comic moral character can decide how to bring a situation to a resolution and a good ending—to the desirable conclusion and satisfactory closure. Comedy and philosophy are thus capable not only of understanding how things are—but they can also change them for the best.

The Cynics, who were a source of influence and inspiration for the Stoics, stressed the practical side of philosophy as a way of life. Later, the Skeptics developed systematic strategies of questioning the feasibility of purely theoretical research and argument. Comedy uses skeptical doubt but always as an instrument for easing a situation. The Academic Skeptics[4] attempted to justify their doubt of the possibility of rational access to truth, which arises once one takes the *comic* abuse of dialectic too seriously. Purely negative, skeptical dialectical reasoning assumes that, if one is simply skilled enough, one can in principle prove any thesis, as well as its opposite. By contrast, comedy persists in mocking speculative dialectic yet at the same time using it for the construction of its plot.[5]

Moreover, the Cynics stressed the universal equality of all people and hence the freedom one can gain if one lives a *simple* life ("according to nature"), which becomes available as the end of one's effort at gaining it together with, and in front of, others. Such a life, without fear and shame,[6] is displaced to the outskirts of the now corrupt existence of the polis and is thus removed from the harm that can be incurred by those who still live according to the tenets of human social, political, and economic distinctions and inequalities.[7]

One can—and should—become self-sufficient, as Diogenes kept arguing and showing throughout the comedy of his life.

Such self-sufficiency is not the autonomy of the isolated modern subject but the autonomy according to nature, accessible to everyone as a result of her actions in an (often uneasy and allosensual) dialogical interaction with others, implying dangerous yet liberating free speech. Only in this way can one gain the freedom of a simple yet rich life.

But perhaps the most congenial comic philosophic attitude is that of the "Garden." As tradition has it, Menander and Epicurus were friends and knew each other in Athens from the time of their youth.[8] Reportedly, in one of his epigrams, Menander said that if Themistocles freed his country from slavery, Epicurus freed it from irrationality.[9]

In Epicurus's preserved texts, we find a constant return to two distinct themes, both comic: *freedom* as the freedom from the fear of death and *life* as the life of pleasure according to reason. For, as Epicurus famously claimed, when we are, death is not, and when death comes, we are no longer; therefore, death is nothing for us, and we should not be afraid of it.[10] It is pleasure that is the highest end in life: the pleasant life is a beautiful and just life based on measure, which can be achieved only through a reasoned life shared with others.[11] These two Epicurean themes are, as we have seen, *the* comic themes, distinctly present and developed throughout comedy.

Perhaps, from a strictly philosophical point of view, comedy might appear a syncretic and eclectic imitation of philosophical techniques of reasoning. Yet comedy is not a theoretical appropriation but a practical reproduction of reason, which moves from the initial complication, through a number of both carefully planned and unexpected steps, toward the resolution of a conflict through dialogue with others. Comedy therefore shows itself as philosophy in action. It helps philosophy realize itself as the comedy of thinking. Comedy thus becomes the paradigm of interaction as acting together with others toward the realization of a good ending, which is never final but always comes as a liberating statement of human goodness found in a shared well-being and the renewal of life.

Notes

Preface

1. Indeed, Emmanuel Levinas will even claim that solipsism is the very structure of reason: E. Lévinas. *Le temps et l'autre*. Paris: PUF, 1983, p. 48: "le solipsisme n'est ni une aberration, ni un sophisme: c'est la structure même de la raison."

2. As Hegel approvingly says, "Don Cesar in Schiller's 'Braut von Mesina' can rightly exclaim: 'There is no higher judge over me', and when he is punished, he must pronounce judgement on himself and execute it." G. W. F. Hegel. *Aesthetics. Lectures on Fine Art*. Vol. I–II. Trans. by T. M. Knox. Oxford: Clarendon, 1975, p. 192; G. W. F. Hegel. *Vorlesungen über die Ästhetik*. In *Werke*. Bd. 13–15. Frankfurt am Main: Suhrkamp, 1986, Bd. 13, p. 252.

3. Unlike in Epictetus's admonishment: "Remember that you are an actor in a play, which is as the playwright wants it to be . . . What is yours is to play the assigned part well. But to choose it belongs to someone else." (trans. N. White). Epictetus. *Ench.* 17.

4. Some of the ideas developed in the book are presented in D. Nikulin, "The Comedy of Philosophy," in *Engaging Agnes Heller: A Critical Companion*. Ed. by K. Terezakis. Lanham et al.: Lexington, 2009, pp. 167–192.

5. As Walter Benjamin observes, philosophy appears as ethics in tragedy and as logic in comedy, in which philosophy is "absolute" and "refined": "Was nämlich für die Tragödie die Ethik, das ist für die Komödie die Logik, in beiden ist philosophische Substanz, aber in der Komödie die absolute, gereinigte." W. Benjamin. "Molière: Der eingebildete Kranke." *Gesammelte Schriften*, Bd. II.2. Ed. by Rolf Tiedemann and Hermann Schweppehäuser. Frankfurt am Main: Suhrkamp, 1972, p. 612.

6. Historically speaking, New Comedy emerges when ancient philosophy comes to its fruition after the death of Aristotle, when the Academy and the Lyceum are already well established and Stoicism is about to appear.

Chapter 1

1. Narrative distinguishes the important from the nonimportant, forgets something, and eventually finds it impossible to fit the fullness of a live event into a

linear progression. Such incongruity at times gives rise to different, often competing stories concerning the origins of the same thing. Yet we try to reach an origin
(or *the* origin) again and again, often missing it, though doing so in interesting
and philosophically fruitful ways.

2. Aristotle, *Poet.* 1448a35–36.

3. Cf. Plato, *Theaet.* 173d. Also see S .I. Radzig. *History Ancient Greek Literature*
(*Istoriya drevnegrecheskoy literatury*). Moscow: Vysshaya shkola, 1982 (5th ed.;
first publ. 1940), p. 275 sqq.

4. Dionysus was the god of wine, ritual madness, and ecstasy in Greek mythology.

5. Jesting and jeering were important parts of a popular ritual that can be understood as carnivalesque. Demosthenes 18.122; Athenaeus 14.621e–f. Cf. M.
Bakhtin. *Rabelais and His World.* Trans. by Hélène Iswolsky. Cambridge (MA):
MIT Press, 1984. However, such mockery also parodied the heroic battle. Here,
myth was mocked, killing was substituted with verbal duels, and immortal glory
in the word of the poet was replaced by a seemingly fleeting yet constantly self-
reproducing communal fame. Battle was substituted with competition (*agōn*),
where the purpose was to win a verbal struggle. Later, in Attica, this became a
literary contest on the occasion of a communal celebration; the winners' names
and works survive even today.

6. Aristotle, *Poet.* 1448a32. M. Foucault. *Fearless Speech.* Ed. by Joseph Pearson.
Los Angeles: Semiotext(e), 2001; D. Nikulin. "Richard Rorty, Cynic: Philosophy
in the Conversation of Humankind." *Graduate Faculty Philosophy Journal* 29:2
(2008), pp. 85–111.

7. Ian C. Storey. *Eupolis: Poet of Old Comedy.* Oxford: Oxford University Press,
2003, p. 41.

8. Aristotle directly associates *kōmos* with the inception of comedy (Aristotle, *Poet.*
1449a11–12; cf. Aristophanes, *Nubes* 538–39).

9. LSJ; cf. Plutarch. *Moralia* 355E, cf. 365C (*De Iside et Osiride*); Athenaeus
14.621b–622c. According to Aristotle, an important aspect of the *phallika* is that
they were based on spontaneous improvisation (*aytoskhediastikê*). Aristotle, *Poet.*
1449a10–11. Improvisation also played an important role in the mime, as later in
the *commedia dell'arte*, which influenced the German *Stegreiftheater.* Improvisation means that the action is defined, on the one hand, by the spontaneity and
appropriateness of the moment and, on the other hand, by a use of traditional
formulaic language known to the singers and the participants. Milman Parry.
"Studies in the Epic Technique of Oral Verse-Making." In M. Parry. *The Making
of the Homeric Verse: The Collected Papers of Milman Parry.* Oxford: Clarendon
Press, 1971, pp. 266–364.

10. Cf. a parody in Plato, *Symp.* 212d sqq.

11. In ancient times, until Propertius, iambus was not a mournful song but a war
hymn and, for this reason, is often identified with epic poetry. Iambus and elegy
are both famously represented in the seventh-century BCE poet Archilochus and
the sixth-century BCE poets Simonides and Hipponax.

12. Aristotle, *Poet.* 1448b27, 1448b31–1449a6, 1449b4–5. Aristotle designates
Homer as the father of both kinds of drama: as from the sublime heroic spirit

of the *Iliad* and the *Odyssey* comes tragedy, so from the down-to-earth iambic mockery of the *Margites* comes comedy. The now lost *Margites*, wrongly ascribed by Aristotle to Homer (Aristotle, *Poet.* 1448b30–1449a1), is also mentioned in the Platonic corpus. It is a mock-heroic poem, where the main character, Margites, is to have appeared as a sort of fool and jester. [Plato]. *Alc.* II, 147c–d: "He knew many things (*polla*), but he knew them badly (*kakōs*)." Much-knowing (*polymathia*)—i.e., knowing a little bit of everything without the capacity to give an account of it and bring it into some kind of unity—is much worse for Plato than straight ignorance (Plato, *Legg.* 819a). Ignorance can be recognized, but the Socratic knowledge that one does not know, which is the beginning of an earnest self-investigation, is far from *polymathia*, which does not allow one to think critically and judge for oneself.

13. Cf. Archilochus, fr. 41–44, 46 et al. West. *Iambi et elegi Graeci ante Alexandrum cantati.* Ed. by M. L. West. Vol. I. Oxford: Oxford University Press, 1989 (2nd ed.), pp. 18–20. See also M. L. West. *Studies in Greek Elegy and Iambus.* Berlin and New York: De Gruyter, 1974, pp. 22–39; *Die griechische Literatur in Text und Darstellung. Bd. 1: Archaische Periode.* Ed. by Joachim Latacz. Stuttgart: Philipp Reclam jun., 1991, pp. 240–47.

14. 2.184–205 West; approximately sixth century BCE.

15. *Homeric Hymns: Homeric Apocrypha; Lives of Homer.* Edited and translated by Martin L. West. Cambridge (MA): Harvard University Press, 2003, pp. 46–47 (2.200–5); cf. commentary on p. 8.

16. Aristotle, *Poet.* 1449a24–25.

17. Aristotle mentions both Megara and Sicily as making claims to the origins of comedy. Aristotle, *Poet.* 1448a31–3. In Megara, the sixth-century BCE poet Susarion was said to be the originator of Attic comedy. *Mar. Par.* 39. *Der Kleine Pauly. Lexikon der Antike.* München: Deutscher Taschenbuch Verlag, 1979. Bd. 5, col. 437.

18. Aristotle, *Poet.* 1449b6=fr. A2 DK. Epicharmus reconstructed comedy from its existing disjointed constituents and added much of his own. Epicharmus, fr. A5 DK=Anon. de com. 2.4 Kaibel. Aristotle also mentions the fifth-century BCE Sicilians Chionides and Magnes among the first comic writers. Aristotle. *Poet.* 1448a34.

19. Diog. Laert. 8.78; fr. A4 DK=Iamblichus. V.P. 266; fr. B23 DK.

20. Plato, *Theaet.* 152e; cf. *Gorg.* 505e. The later tradition says that Plato himself borrowed and even transcribed much from Epicharmus. Diog. Laert. 3.9.

21. Sophron's son Xenarchus also wrote mimes. Cf. Aristotle, *Poet.* 1447b10–11. They were followed by the popular mimiambs of third-century Herodas (from whom we now have a number of fully preserved short comic scenes, mostly from ordinary life, written in Hipponax's choliamb).

22. Anon Proleg. 1.3 Westerink.

23. Plato, *Theaet.* 174a.

24. Cf. Plato, *Apol.* 19c.

25. Fr. B42 DK.

26. Plato, *RP* 607c.

27. Plato, *RP* 606b sqq.; *Legg.* 934 e sqq.
28. Fragments in *Fragmenta Comicorum Graecorum* Meineke, vol. I, p. 160 sqq. and *Comicorum Atticorum Fragmenta.* Ed. by Theodorus Kock, vol. I–III. Leipzig: Teubner, 1880, 1884, 1887. Vol. I, pp. 601–67. See also Ralph M. Rosen. "Plato Comicus." In *Beyond Aristophanes: Transition and Diversity in Greek Comedy.* Ed. by Gregory W. Dobrov. Atlanta: Scholars Press, 1995, pp. 119–37.
29. Plato, *Phil.* 31c, 48a, 50a–d.
30. Plato, *RP* 607a.
31. Plato, *Legg.* 658d, 817e.
32. Drawing on the famous Aristotelian definition of tragedy (Aristotle, *Poet.* 1449b24–28), the *Tractatus Coislinianus* defines comedy as "an imitation of an action that is absurd and lacking in magnitude [of grandeur], complete, <with embellished language,> the several kinds (of embellishment being found) in the (several) parts (of the play); (*directly represented*) *by person <s> acting, and <not> by means of narration*; through pleasure [*hēdonē*] and laughter [*gelōs*] achieving the purgation [*katharsis*] of the like emotions." *Tractatus Coislinianus*, IV; emphasis added. Plato considers comedy similarly capable of purifying the passions (or emotions). Later Neoplatonists, including Iamblichus, Proclus, and Olympiodorus, will agree with Plato. *In Remp.* I, 49.13 sqq. Kroll. See R. Janko. "From Catharsis to the Aristotelian Mean." In *Essays on Aristotle's Poetics.* Ed. by Amélie Oksenberg Rorty. Princeton: Princeton University Press, 1992, pp. 341–58, esp. pp. 347–51 and R. Janko. *Aristotle on Comedy*, pp. 143–49. Unlike tragic catharsis, which is achieved as a purification of ("conservative") passions of fear and pity, comic catharsis is achieved through communal and "anarchic" passions.
33. Lucio Olimpio Giraldi. *Ragionamento in difesa di Terentio* (1566), cit ap.: Bernard Weinberg. *A History of Literary Criticism in the Italian Renaissance.* Chicago: The University of Chicago Press, 1961, p. 289.
34. N. Frye. *The Anatomy of Criticism*, p. 41.
35. Aldous Huxley. *Antic Hay* (1923). Cit. ap.: Morton Gurewitsch. "From Pyrrhonic to Vomedic Irony." In *Comedy: New Perspectives.* Ed. by Maurice Charney. New York: New York Literary Forum, 1978, pp. 45–57, p. 55: "the human 'vomedy', Huxley's felicitous typographical error."
36. As Corrigan rightly notes, "This almost animal exuberance and vitality is probably best seen in the wide-open use of sex in his [Aristophanes's] plays. We sense neither neurotic lust nor puritanical guilt in his use of it, and this probably explains . . . why his blatant sexuality is still so inoffensive when it is read or produced on our stages today." Robert Willoughby Corrigan. "Aristophanic Comedy: The Conscience of a Conservative." In *Comedy, Meaning and Form.* Edited with an introduction by R. W. Corrigan. San Francisco: Chandler Publishing Company, 1965, pp. 353–62; p. 359.
37. Aristotle, *Poet.* 1447a17.
38. Ibid., 1448a2.
39. Ibid., 1448a16–8.
40. Ibid., 1449a32–4.
41. Ibid., 1449a34–7.

42. Plato, *Legg.* 816d–e.
43. Agathon was ridiculed by Aristophanes in the *Thesmophoriazusae* and *Ranae* 83. Agathon's tragedies were probably close to New Comedy. Pierre Lévêque. *Agathon.* Paris: Les belles lettres, 1955.
44. Plato, *Symp.* 223c–d.
45. Fr. 1 Kassel=*Poet.* 1449b21. For a comprehensive reconstruction of Aristotle's theory of comedy, see Arbogast Schmitt. *Kommentar* zu: Aristoteles. *Poetik. Werke in deutscher Übersetzung*, Bd. 5. Übersetzt und erläutert von Arbogast Schmitt. Berlin: Akademie Verlag, 2008, pp. 302–21.
46. Aristotle, *Met.* 1005b19–20.
47. Aristotle, *Anal. Post.* 72a12–14; *Cat.* 13b36–14a25.
48. Cf. Plato, *Phaedo* 103c–e.
49. Aristotle, *Poet.* 1448a5–6.
50. For a very helpful discussion of Cratinus, see Emmanuela Bakola. *Cratinus and the Art of Comedy.* Oxford: Oxford University Press, 2010. Eupolis's fragments in *Fragmenta Comicorum Graecorum*, ed. Meineke, vol. I, p. 104 sqq. and *Comicorum Atticorum Fragmenta*, ed. Kock, vol. I, p. 258 sqq. For a discussion of Eupolis's comedies, see I. C. Storey. *Eupolis*, p. 67 sqq.
51. "(The kinds) of comedy (are): (the) old, which goes to excess in the absurd [laughable]; (the) new, which abandons this, and inclines toward the serious; (and the) middle, which is a mixture of both." *Tractatus Coislinianus*, XVIII. The text, translation, and discussion of the *Tractatus Coislinianus* in R. Janko. *Aristotle on Comedy. Towards a Reconstruction of* Poetics *II.* Berkley: University of California Press, 1984, pp. 22–41 (the text of the treatise) et passim and also *Scholia in Aristophanem. Prolegomena de Comoedia.* Pars I, Fasc. IA. Ed. by W. J. W. Koster. Groningen, 1975.
52. When we find a list of writers of Old Comedy, it usually begins with Chionides and Magnes. Aristotle. *Poet.* 1448a34; Magnes is also mentioned by Aristophanes, *Equites* 520–25 and indeed, among the titles of Magnes's plays is *Frogs*, later reproduced in the famous play by Aristophanes. Another famous Attic comedian is Eupolis, ridiculed by Aristophanes in the *Clouds*. *Nubes* 553.
53. For example, there is the Great Dionysia and, later on, the Lenaia. In general, Dionysiac cult appears to be at the origin of all Greek drama, including tragedy. See Aristotle, *Poet.* 1449a10–11 and Richard Seaford. "Tragedy and Dionysus." *A Companion to Tragedy.* Ed. by Rebecca Bushnell. Oxford: Blackwell, 2005, pp. 25–38.
54. The comic poet Crates was reportedly the first to abandon iambus and begin to compose general narratives and plots (*logoys kai mythoys*). Aristotle, *Poet.* 1449b7–8.
55. This human activity comprises action-*praxis* in its entirety (Aristotle, *Poet.* 1449b24–25), as well as in its concrete acts-*pragmata*.
56. Aristotle, *Poet.* 1449b31–1450b20. Of these six dramatic aspects, plot and characters are the central characteristics of any play. The brief anonymous *Tractatus Coislinianus*, written sometime in the fourth to second century BCE, explains the Aristotelian division in the following way: "Comic plot is one structured around

laughable events. The characters [*ēthē*] of comedy are the buffoonish, the ironical and the boasters. [There are] two parts of thought [*dianoia*], opinion [*gnōmē*] and proof [*pistis*] . . . Comic diction is common and popular. The comic poet must endow his characters with their native idiom, and [use] the local [idiom] himself. Song [*melos*] belongs to the province of music; hence one will need to take its principles complete in themselves from there. Spectacle supplies as a great benefit to dramas what is in accord with them. Plot, diction and song are found in all comedies, instances of thought, character and spectacle in <not> a few." *Tractatus Coislinianus*, XI–XVI, trans. Janko.

57. One may note the etymological connections between *popular, vulgus,* and "people."

58. I have in mind such innovations as the introduction of masks, the prologue, and an increased number of actors.

59. For a discussion of Aristophanes's comedy, see Lane Cooper. *An Aristotelian Theory of Comedy.* New York: Harcourt Brace, 1922; Elder Olson. *The Theory of Comedy.* Bloomington: Indiana University Press, 1968, pp. 45–47; Northrop Frye. *The Anatomy of Criticism: Four Essays. The Collected Works of Northrop Frye*, vol. 22. Ed. by Robert D. Denham. Toronto, Buffalo, and London: University of Toronto Press, 2006, p. 49.

60. M. S. Silk. *Aristophanes and the Definition of Comedy.* New York: Oxford University Press, 2000, p. 9. Cf.: "In the parabasis, when the dramatic action is suspended, the choreuts step out of the area of dramatic myth—which is symbolized by their taking a few steps toward the spectators, the *parabainein*—and addresses the latter, speaking as members of a group of performers trying to influence the audience in their favour, although they may at times pretend that they still speak from the point of view of the dramatic character which they have been impersonating so far, and which is determined by their disguise." G. M. Sifakis. *Parabasis and Animal Choruses: A Contribution to the history of Attic Comedy.* London: Athlone Press, 1971, p. 25. Along similar lines, the *Tractatus Coislinianus*, mentioned above, identifies the following four quantitative constituents of comedy: "(1) The prologue is (the) part of comedy (extending) as far as the entry of the chorus. (2) The choral element [*khorikon*] is the song sung by the chorus, when it is of sufficient length. (3) The episode is the (part) between two choral songs. (4) The *exodos* is the (part) spoken at the end by the chorus." *Tractatus Coislinianus*, XVII. Cf. Aristotle. *Poet.* 1452b15–17. Interestingly, qualitative aspects of drama are generically different and, as it were, incommensurable (imagine, thus, different disciplines describing each of them), whereas quantitative aspects of drama describe the logical structure and the proper *sequence* of the parts of action, leading from a beginning to an end. And action-*praxis* is central to drama, insofar as the narrative is given by the action itself and not by the narration of the author.

61. S. I. Radzig. Op cit., p. 161.

62. *Mar. Par.* 46.

63. See Horace. *Ars poetica* 193–201; Gian Giorgio Trissino. *Poetica*, div. VI: in tragedy chorus comprises 15 people; in Old Comedy 24. In Epicharmus, however,

the chorus probably did not play any role. G. M. Sifakis. *Parabasis and Animal Choruses*, p. 73 sqq.

64. The *choregia* was eliminated after 317, and Menander's first play is staged in 321. Kenneth R. Rothwell, Jr. "The Continuity of the Chorus in Fourth-Century Attic Comedy." In *Beyond Aristophanes*, pp. 99–118.

65. Originally, as Sifakis conjectures, in place of the parabasis there must have existed "a song and epirrhema which were arranged into syzygy by analogy with the epir-rhematic agon." G. M. Sifakis. *Parabasis and Animal Choruses*, pp. 68–69. The full parabasis begins with a kommation (a short introductory piece by the chorus), followed by the anapest (usually, a speech of the coryphaeus on behalf of the author) and the pnigos (a quickly uttered speech, spoken as if "in one breath").

66. Aristotle, *Poet.* 1450a22–25.

67. In the prologue to *The Mother-in-Law* (*Hec.* 46–47), Terence asks the public "not to allow the dramatic art (*artem musicam*) to fall into the hands of a few through your negligence" and thus allow comedy to speak to everyone in all goodness and fairness; cf. *Phorm.* 34. However, five of Plautus's comedies—*Curculio, Epidicus, Mostellaria, Persa,* and *Stichus*—have no prologue. See an excellent discussion of Roman New Comedy, which also traces subtle but important differences between Greek and Roman comedy, as well as the evolution of Roman comedy from Plautus toward the humanism and universality of Terence, in K. Gaiser. "Zur Eigenart der römischen Komödie: Plautus und Terenz gegenüber ihren griechischen Vorbildern." *Aufstieg und Niedergang der Römischen Welt: Geschichte und Kultur Roms im Spiegel der neueren Forschung,* I, 2. Berlin and New York: De Gruyter, 1972, pp. 1027–113; pp. 1047–49, 1104–9 et passim; and also Sander M. Goldberg. *Understanding Terence*. Princeton: Princeton University Press, 1986, pp. 31–60.

68. See N. Frye. *The Anatomy of Criticism*, p. 41.

69. Whitman has argued that the hero of Old Comedy is identical with the one of epic and tragedy on account of the inner structure that is manifest in his "largeness" and "excessiveness." Cedric H. Whitman. *Aristophanes and the Comic Hero*. Cambridge, MA: Harvard University Press, 1964, pp. 21–58, esp. p. 25.

70. R. W. Corrigan. "Aristophanic Comedy: The Conscience of a Conservative," p. 354f.

71. Ibid., p. 358.

72. Stoicism became a leading philosophical tendency through the whole of antiquity, enduring even into modernity.

73. Approximately 342/1–292/1.

74. See Richard L. Hunter. *New Comedy of Greece and Rome*. Cambridge: Cambridge University Press, 1985.

75. G. Meredith. *An Essay on the Idea of Comedy, and of the Uses of the Comic Spirit*. Introduzione e commento a cura di Stefano Bronzini. Bari: Adriatica Editrice, 2001, p. 102: "Without undervaluing other writers of Comedy, I think it may be said that Menander and Molière stand alone specially as comic poets of the feelings and idea."

76. Aristophanes's language "shows much incongruence and dissimilarity: a tragic element and a comic; the pretentious and the prosaic; the obscure and

the commonplace; grandeur and elevation; vulgar garrulity and nauseating nonsense . . . [I]t puts any words in the mouth of any character." Menander, conversely, "has so contrived his language as to make it appropriate to every nature, disposition, and age." Plutarch even goes so far as to ask a rhetorical question: if not for Menander, "what other reason would a cultivated man have to go to the theater?" Plutarch. *Comparationis Aristophanis et Menandri compendium, Moralia* 853A–854D; esp. 853 C–F, 854B. See also Gregory W. Dobrov. "The Poet's Voice in the Evolution of Dramatic Dialogism," in *Beyond Aristophanes*, pp. 47–97 and Erich Segal. *The Death of Comedy*. Cambridge, MA, and London: Harvard University Press, 2001, pp. 153–82. Horace mentions Menander together with Plato as those writers whom one takes along, *Sat.* 2.3.11. Pausanias also testifies that the Athenians of the second century CE venerated Menander, while Aristophanes gets no mention at all. "In the theatre at Athens there are statues of tragic and comic poets, but most of the statues are of poets of little mark. For none of the renowned comic poets was there except Menander." Pausanias I.21.1. *Pausanias's Description of Greece*. Translated with a commentary by J. G. Frazer. New York: Biblo and Tannen, 1965, p. 29.

77. Aristophanes of Byzantium, ap. Syrianus. *In Hermog.* II 23=Menander. Test. 32 KT (*Menandri quae supersunt*, II. Ed. by A. Koerte, with addenda by A. Thierfelder. Leipzig: Teubner, 1959 (2nd ed.)).

78. These include the *Aspis, Epitrepontes, Perikeiromene, Samia*, and others.

79. Menander, vols. I–III. Edited and translated by W. G. Arnott. Cambridge, MA: Harvard University Press, 1997–2001; Menander. *The Plays and Fragments*. Translated with explanatory notes by Maurice Balme, Introduction by Peter Brown. Oxford: Oxford University Press, 2001.

80. While Menander's first play is staged for the first time around 321 BCE, Aristotle's *Poetics* is published about ten years before, around 330 BCE. Therefore, while Aristotle did not know Menander's work, we can be certain that the educated Menander would have known Aristotle's.

81. One should thus agree with Silk that "Aristotle's dramatic norms virtually constitute a prescription for Menandrian New Comedy." M. S. Silk. *Aristophanes and the Definition of Comedy*, p. 13.

82. Cf. Aristotle, *Poet.* 1451b14–15.

83. Aristotle, *NE* 1128a22–24.

84. W. G. Arnott, "Introduction," Menander, vol. I. Cambridge, MA, and London: Harvard University Press, 1997, p. xxxv; cf. pp. xxxv–xxxviii, with appropriate examples from Menander.

85. For example, see Aristophanes, *Thesmoph.* 785–845.

86. Plato, *Symp.* 212d–e.

87. Ibid., 223b.

88. Cf. Horace, *Ars poetica* 189–90.

89. Menander. *Dyskolos*, dramatis personae. Menander, vol. I, p. 183.

90. E. Bakola. *Cratinus and the Art of Comedy*, pp. 177–79.

91. "*skēnikos philosophos*," Athenaeus 4.158e; 13.561a. Interestingly, Aristophanes's hostility toward Euripides is well-known. Euripides's nemesis knows no fatigue

in ridiculing him and criticizing his literary methods, especially in the *Acharnenses*, *Thesmophoriazusae*, and the *Frogs*, where Aristophanes depicts a parody of the comic contest between Aeschylus and Euripides, in which Aeschylus wins, though it should have been Sophocles. Aristophanes, *Ranae* 830 sqq.

92. For example, Quintilian, the Roman rhetorician, says that Menander admired and followed Euripides in his works. Quintilian. *Inst.* 10.1.69=Menander. Test. 38 KT: "(Euripidem) admiratus maxime est, ut saepe testatur, et secutus, quamquam in opere diverso." Thus, in Menander's *Epitrepontes*, we find a direct reference to Euripides's lost tragedy *Auge*. Menander, *Epitrepontes* 1123–225; and further, it is likely that a key scene of arbitration in the *Epitrepontes* was borrowed from Euripides's *Alope*, which also has not been preserved. Ibid., 225 sqq.

93. Cf. Aristophanes, *Ranae* 959.

94. Euripides, *Medea* 539–757.

95. Arnott calls this device the "secularisation of familiar tragic scenes." W. G. Arnott. "Introduction," Menander, vol. I, pp. xxxviii–xliii. Similarly, the opening of Plautus's "Pseudolus" comes from Euripides's "Iphigenia at Aulis"; see R. L. Hunter. *New Comedy of Greece and Rome*, p. 116; cf. also p. 25 et passim.

96. This is done similarly to the "formulaic diction" and "formulae" in epic poetry.

97. Aristotle, *Rhet.* 1404b24–26.

98. Euripides, *Orestes* 1506–26.

99. Aristotle, *Poet.* 1456a26–27.

100. As in the *Hippolytus*, *Andromache*, *Suppliants*, *Electra*, *Ion*, *Iphigenia in Tauris*, *Helen*, and *Orestes*.

101. Such are, for example, Sostratos in Menander's *Dyskolos*; the kind courtesan (*bona meretrix*) Bacchis in *The Mother-in-Law* (*Hecyra*) and the *Self-Tormentor* and Thais in the *Eunuch* (Terence, *Eun.* 880–1); the young man Pamphilus in *The Mother-in-Law*, who is praised for his decent and responsible character (*pium ac pudicum ingenium*) (Terence, *Hec.* 152); the slave Parmeno in *The Mother-in-Law* and Micio in the *Brothers*, who, in particular, is a moving character who can excuse others by saying "that's being rather more human" (*haec magis sunt hominis*) (Terence, *Ad.* 736) and who can make his stiff and conservative brother Demea radically change in his attitude toward fellow humans, recognizing that he's "discovered that in reality nothing is better for a man than to be generous and easygoing" (*re ipsa repperi facilitate nil esse homini melius neque clementia*) (Terence, *Ad.* 860–61; cf. 967).

102. Yet "Terence did not please the rough old conservative Romans; they liked Plautus better, and the recurring mention of the *vetus poeta* in his prologues, who plagued him with the crusty critical view of his productions, has in the end a comic effect on the reader." George Meredith. *An Essay on the Idea of Comedy*, p. 101, footnote h. Cf., however, Horace's critical view of Plautus's comedies, *Ep.* 2.1.168–181.

103. Varro. *De Poetis*, cit. ap. R. W. Corrigan. *Classical Comedy*, p. 241.

104. Cf. Plutarch. *Comp. Aristoph. et Men.*

105. R. W. Corrigan. *Classical Comedy: Greek and Roman*. New York, NY: Applause Theatre Book Publishers, 1987, pp. 241–42.

106. Such are the improvisational Oscan atellana, the Etruscan satura, and the Fescennine verses. The Etruscan satura, though transformed, survived down to the *commedia dell'arte*.

107. Cit. ap. Ben Jonson. Ed. by C. H. Herford and Percy and Evelyn Simpson. Oxford: Clarendon, 1952, vol. XI, p. 289.

108. See Peter Holland. *The Ornament of Action: Text and Performance in Restoration Comedy*. Cambridge: Cambridge University Press, 1979.

109. N. Frye. *A Natural Perspective: The Development of Shakespearean Comedy and Romance*. New York: Columbia University Press, 1965, p. 72; N. Frye. *The Anatomy of Criticism*, pp. 151–52; Elder Olson. *The Theory of Comedy*. Bloomington: Indiana University Press, 1968; Morton Gurewitch. *Comedy: The Irrational Vision*. Ithaca: Cornell University Press, 1975, pp. 43–44; R. W. Corrigan. *Classical Comedy*, p. 341; T. G. A. Nelson. *Comedy: An Introduction to Comedy in Literature, Drama, and Cinema*. Oxford and New York: Oxford University Press, 1990, pp. 19–20; E. Segal. *The Death of Comedy*, passim.

110. Ben Jonson. *Every Man in His Humour*, Induction, 247–70. In Ben Jonson. Ed. by C. H. Herford and Percy Simpson. Oxford: Clarendon, 1927, vol. III, p. 437.

111. Molière. *Les femmes savantes*, 1394.

112. David Konstan. *Greek Comedy and Ideology*. New York: Oxford University Press, 1995, pp. 156–64.

113. "Pour l'amour de moi, aimez Térence." Cit. ap.: G. Meredith. *An Essay on the Idea of Comedy*, p. 99.

114. Horace, *Ars poetica* 89.

115. Ibid., 156–57.

116. This probably included some additions, such as the commentary of fellow grammarian Evanthius.

117. *Aelii Donati quod fertur commentum Terenti. Accedunt Evgraphi commentum et scholia Bembina*. Vol. I–III, rec. Paulus Wessner. Leipzig, 1902–1908 (repr. 1962–1963).

118. These are Turpilius and Lucius Afranius, as well as various types of comedy, such as *comoedia palliata* (in Greek dress), *togata* (treating Roman subjects), *tabernaria* (low comedy), *Attellana* (farce), mime, and *Rhintonica* (travestied tragedy). Evanthius. *De comoedia*. In *Aelii Donati quod fertur commentum Terenti*, vol. I, pp. 22–31; pp. 26–28 (trans. as Donatus. "A Fragment on Comedy and Tragedy." In *Theories of Comedy*. Ed. with an introduction by P. Lauter. Garden City, NY: Anchor Books, Doubleday, 1964, pp. 27–32; pp. 28–29). Cf. Horace. *Ep.* 2.1.57–62.

119. "*Fabula*," which translates the Greek *mythos*.

120. "Comoedia est fabula diuersa institute continens affectuum ciuilium ac priuatorum, quibus discitur, quid sit I uita utile, quid contra euitandum." Evanthius. *De comoedia*, p. 22 (Donatus. *A Fragment on Comedy and Tragedy*, p. 27).

Chapter 2

1. See, for example, Plautus's *Amphitryon*.

2. Paul G. Ruggiers. *Versions of Medieval Comedy*. Norman: University of Oklahoma Press, 1977, p. 7 et passim; Lloyd Bishop. *Comic Literature in France: From the*

Middle Ages to the Twentieth Century. New Orleans: University Press of the South, 2004, p. 58.

3. B. Weinberg. *A History of Literary Criticism in the Italian Renaissance*. 2 vols. Chicago: Chicago University Press, 1961; Marvin T. Herrick. *Comic Theory in the Sixteenth Century*. Urbana: University of Illinois Press, 1964 (first publ. 1950).

4. The Latin translation of Aristotle's *Poetics* was published by Valla in 1498; the Greek text followed in 1508. Renaissance commentators mostly accept Aristotle's distinction of six main constituents of comedy: plot or fable (*fabula*), character (*mores*), thought or intellectual reflection (*sententia*), diction or linguistic expression (*oratio*), spectacle or mode of representation, and music or melody. See Trissino. *Poetica*, in *Theories of Comedy*, pp. 42–47; p. 43; Robortello. *On Comedy*, p. 231 sqq.

5. See Cicero's *De oratore*. Among others were Hermogenes, Evanthius, and Diomedes.

6. B. Weinberg. *A History of Literary Criticism in the Italian Renaissance*, pp. 107–8 et passim; M. T. Herrick. *Comic Theory in the Sixteenth Century*, pp. 190–214.

7. This scholarship encompassed the works of humanists elsewhere in Europe, too, including Erasmus, Melanchton, Muretus, and Willichius, all of whom were still capable of writing, reading, and communicating in the same language.

8. We have at our disposal a list of commentators, together with a brief and simple narrative that could be always expanded further and even developed into a history: Iodocus Badius Ascensius (1500), Pomponio Gaurico (1510), Giovanni Britannico da Brescia (1518), Marco Girolamo Vida (1527), Aulo Giano Parrasio (1531), Filippo Sassetti (1539), Bernardino Tomitano (1545), Francesco Robortello (1548), Vincenzo Maggi (1550), Giacopo Grifoli (1550, 1557), Giason Denores (1553), Francesco Lovisini (1554), Luca Antonio Ridolfi (1557), Bernardino Parthenio (1560), Pietro Angeli (ca. 1560), Julius Caesar Scaliger (1561), Giovanni Battista Pigna (1561), Bartolomeo Maranta (1561), Lilio Gregorio Giraldi (1561), Giovanni Fabrini (1566), Lodovico Castelvetro (1570), Antonio Maria de'Conti (1572), Agnolo Segni (1573), Aldo Manuzio (1576), Lorenzo Gambara (1576), Torquato Tasso (1584), Tommaso Correa (1586), Nicola Colonio (1587), Francesco Patrizi (1587), Federico Ceruti (1588), Antonio Riccoboni (1587, 1591, 1599), and many others (all are discussed by Weinberg and some by Herrick). Note, in particular, that Robortello published his famous commentary on Aristotle's *Poetics* in 1548 and appended to it a short treatise on comedy. See Francesco Robortello. *On Comedy*. Trans. with annotation by Marvin T. Herrick. In: M. T. Herrick. *Comic Theory in the Sixteenth Century*, pp. 227–39.

9. I. G. *A Refutation of the Apology of Actors*, Book III (a response to Thomas Heywood's *An Apology for Actors* [1612]). In *Theories of Comedy*, pp. 127–32, 133–38; p. 135.

10. For examples of this point, see Ben Jonson's "Dedicatory Epistle" to *Volpone* (1605) or Molière's "Preface" and three "Placets" to *Tartuffe* (1664–1669).

11. One can also perhaps develop a poetics of history, although in sixteenth-century discussions, a study of poetics as a discipline is opposed to that of history. See B. Weinberg. *A History of Literary Criticism in the Italian Renaissance*, pp. 41–42.

The two have differences: history, which is not imitative, studies the particular and tells how things were; poetry, which is imitative, studies the universal and narrates how things should be. The two also share similarities: for example, both use narration and "demonstrative" and "deliberative" rhetoric devices.

12. Such is, for example, the Florentine Filippo Sassetti's attempt to define poetry philosophically through Aristotle's four causes: "the efficient cause of poetry was the poet himself, the formal cause the imitation, the material cause the verse, and the final cause pleasure [*il diletto*]." Cit. ap. B. Weinberg. *A History of Literary Criticism in the Italian Renaissance*, p. 48.

13. He placed Menander, "whom our Terence above all has imitated," above Aristophanes. Robortello. *On Comedy*, p. 229.

14. Antonio Sebastiano Minturno. *The Art of Poetry* (1563). In *Theories of Comedy*, pp. 74–86, esp. p. 76.

15. For Riccoboni, "Comedy is a low type of poetry with ridiculous elements, and with abuse that tends to be ridiculous." Antonio Riccoboni. *The Comic Art* (1585). In *Theories of Comedy*, pp. 99–100.

16. Lucio Olimpio Giraldi. *Ragionamento in difesa di Terentio* (1566), cit ap.: Bernard Weinberg. *A History of Literary Criticism in the Italian Renaissance*, p. 289.

17. Minturno. *The Art of Poetry*, p. 77.

18. Riccoboni. *The Comic Art*, p. 99.

19. B. Weinberg. *A History of Literary Criticism in the Italian Renaissance*, p. 800.

20. Minturno. *The Art of Poetry*, p. 82.

21. Ibid., p. 84.

22. E.g., Wilhelm Dilthey. "Die Technik des Dramas." Anhang to: Gustav Freytag. *Die Technik des Dramas*. Leipzig, 1922 (13th ed., first publ. 1863; repr. Darmstadt: Wissenschaftliche Buchgesellschaft, 1975, 1982), pp. 315–50.

23. H.-G. Gadamer. "Mythos und Vernunft." In *Ästhetik und Poetik: Kunst als Aussage. Gesammelte Werke*, vol. 8. Tübingen: Mohr, 1993, pp. 164–69.

24. G. W. F. Hegel. *The Phenomenology of Spirit*. Trans. by A. V. Miller, with "Analysis of the Text and Foreword" by J. N. Findlay. Oxford: Oxford University Press, 1977; G. W. F. Hegel. *Phänomenologie des Geistes*. In *Werke*, Bd. 3. Frankfurt am Main: Suhrkamp, 1986.

25. Rodolphe Gasché argues that the comic lies at the heart of Hegel's understanding of both the epic and tragedy but that he takes comedy as a "light-hearted readiness for self-dissolution," which leads to a comic ridiculousness of an individual. Yet this is a Romantic understanding of comedy that might apply to Aristophanes but not to Menander and later comedy. R. Gasché. "Self-Dissolving Seriousness: On the Comic in the Hegelian Concept of Tragedy." In *Philosophy and Tragedy*. Ed. by Miguel de Beistegui and Simon Sparks. London and New York: Routledge, 2000, pp. 38–56.

26. Before Hegel, August Wilhelm Schlegel made exactly the same division in lecture III of his *Lectures on Dramatic Art and Literature* (1808).

27. Should Hegel have written today, he probably would have reserved this role for film.

28. G. W. F. Hegel. *Aesthetics*, pp. 1235–36.

29. *"Der echte Komiker,"* ibid., p. 1233; *Werke*, Bd. 15, p. 569. See also Karin de Boer. "The Eternal Irony of the Community: Aristophanian Echoes in Hegel's *Phenomenology of Spirit."* *Inquiry* 52 (2009), pp. 311–34.

30. S. Kierkegaard. *The Concept of Irony with Continual Reference to Socrates.* Together with *Notes of Schelling's Berlin Lectures.* Edited and translated with introduction and notes by Howard V. Hong and Edna H. Hong. Princeton: Princeton University Press, 1989 (second printing, with corrections, 1992), pp. 128–53.

31. G. W. F. Hegel. *Werke*, Bd. 14, p. 124; Bd. 15, p. 569; Bd. 18, p. 34.

32. Following Hegel, Bohtz too has argued that the comic stands in opposition to the tragic, particularly in the representation of the beautiful. August Wilhelm Bohtz. *Die Idee des Tragischen.* Göttingen: Georg Kübler, 1836, pp. 48–51.

33. Hegel. *Aesthetics*, p. 192; *Werke*, Bd. 13, pp. 251–52.

34. Similarly, we could ask where Friedrich Nietzsche, a Romantic who was critical of Romanticism, located himself when he criticized the "degenerate slave morality" that apparently substituted the sublime heroic one.

35. Hegel. *Aesthetics*, p. 67; *Werke*, Bd. 13, p. 97. See also Anne Paolucci. "Hegel's Theory of Comedy." In *Comedy: New Perspectives*, pp. 89–108, p. 106.

36. The satyric drama was distinguished from Roman satire, which came as a dissolution of the classical form of art. Hegel. *Aesthetics*, pp. 512–16.

37. Cf. Plautus. *Amphitryon*, 52–61.

38. Ibid., pp. 1204–5; *Werke*, Bd. 15, pp. 531–34.

39. "The pretensions of universal essentiality are uncovered in the self; it shows itself to be entangled in an actual existence, and drops the mask just because it wants to be something genuine. The self, appearing here in its significance as something actual, plays with the mask which it once put on in order to act its part; but it as quickly breaks out again from this illusory character and stands forth in its own nakedness and ordinariness, which it shows to be not distinct from the genuine self, the actor, or from the spectator." Hegel. *Phenomenology*, § 744.

40. Ibid., § 744. See also Patrick Downey. *Serious Comedy: The Philosophical and Theological Significance of Tragic and Comic Writing in the Western Tradition.* Lanham, MD: Lexington Books, 2001, p. 234.

41. Hegel. *Phenomenology*, § 747; *Werke*, Bd. 3, p. 544.

42. Hegel. *Aesthetics*, p. 1194; *Werke*, Bd. 15, p. 521.

43. Hegel. *Phenomenology*, § 752; *Werke*, Bd. 3, p. 547. In a noteworthy study of Hegel's drama, Mark Roche notes that "[t]he greatness of Hegel's theory of comedy is his insight into subjectivity and particularity as the defining features of the genre." Mark William Roche. *Tragedy and Comedy: A Systematic Study and a Critique of Hegel.* Albany, NY: State University of New York Press, 1998, p. 312.

44. R. Schürmann. *Broken Hegemonies.* Trans. by Reginald Lilly. Bloomington and Indianapolis: Indiana University Press, 2003, pp. 408–20.

45. Cf. Hegel. *Phenomenology*, § 465; *Werke*, Bd. 3, p. 343.

46. Hegel. *Aesthetics*, p. 591; *Werke*, Bd. 14, p. 218.

47. Hegel. *Aesthetics*, p. 1201; *Werke*, Bd. 15, p. 530. Comedy is obliged "to bring the absolutely rational into appearance" (*das an und für sich Vernünftige als dasjenige zur Erscheinung zu bringen*).

48. Hegel. *Aesthetics*, p. 1200; *Werke*, Bd. 15, p. 530.
49. Hegel. *Aesthetics*, p. 1199; *Werke*, Bd. 15, p. 527.
50. Hegel. *Werke*, Bd. 15, p. 572.
51. Ibid.
52. Ibid.
53. In his discussion of various types of endings in drama, Schmidt, however, fails to notice the good ending's similarity to the conclusion of a philosophical argument. Henry J. Schmidt. *How Dramas End: Essays on the German* Sturm und Drang, *Büchner, Hauptmann, and Fleisser.* Ann Arbor: The University of Michigan Press, 1992, p. 1–34 et passim.
54. Of course, Schlegel is aware of the existing European tradition of literary criticism, mostly French. But there is also a fruitful and original theoretical reflection on comedy in Germany from the eighteenth to the beginning of the nineteenth century, which was influenced by the English theory—in Georg Friedrich Meier, Moses Mendelssohn, Justus Möser, Gotthold Ephraim Lessing, Friedrich Just Riedel, Johann Georg Sulzer, Johann Georg Heinrich Feder, Carl Friedrich Flögel, Kant, Karl Heinrich Heydenreich, and Jean Paul, August Wilhelm Bohtz, Arnold Ruge, and beyond. See Paul Mallory Haberland. *The Development of Comic Theory in Germany during the Eighteenth Century.* Göppingen: Alfred Kuemmerle, 1971, p. 10 et passim.
55. Lecture XI was dedicated to Old Comedy, lecture XII to Aristophanes, lecture XIII to Greek Middle and New Comedy, and lecture XIV to Terence and Plautus. August Wilhelm von Schlegel. *Sämtliche Werke.* Ed. by Eduard Böcking. Bd. V, *Vorlesungen über dramatische Kunst und Literatur.* Erster Theil; Bd. VI, *Vorlesungen über dramatische Kunst und Literatur.* Zweiter Theil. Leipzig: Weidmann'sche Buchhandlung, 1846³ (repr. Hildesheim-New York: Georg Olms, 1971); Augustus William [*sic*] Schlegel. *Course of Lectures on Dramatic Art and Literature.* Trans. by John Black. Revised, according to the last German edition, by A. J. W. Morrison. New York: AMS Press, 1973 (second printing; first printing 1965, repr. from the original edition, London, 1846). Henceforth cited as *LDAL* followed by page number.
56. *LDAL* 145–46. Quite in line with Schlegel, Schopenhauer too recognizes both the opposition of tragedy to comedy and the superiority of tragedy as the highest poetic genre: Arthur Schopenhauer. *Die Welt als Wille und Vorstellung.* München: Deutscher Taschenbuch Verlag, 1998, Bd. I, Buch 3, § 51, pp. 335–38.
57. In his famous essay, "On Naïve and Sentimental Poetry" (1795), Friedrich Schiller equally opposed comedy to tragedy.
58. *LDAL* 150.
59. Ibid., 147.
60. Ibid., 148.
61. Ibid., 149.
62. Ibid., 152.
63. Ibid., 147.
64. Ibid., 149–50, 304 sqq.
65. Ibid., 150.

66. Ibid., 181–82.
67. Ibid., 193.
68. Ibid., 323.
69. Ibid., 148.
70. A. W. Schlegel. *LDAL* (Lecture XIII) 185; *Vorlesungen über dramatische Kunst und Literatur*, Bd. V, p. 230.
71. Ibid., 233.
72. *LDAL* 185.
73. J.-J. Rousseau. *Politics and the Arts: Letter to M. d'Alembert on the Theatre*. Translated with notes and introduction by Allan Bloom. Ithaca: Cornell University Press, 1968, pp. 35–47.
74. *LDAL* 309.
75. Ibid.
76. Ibid., 311. That is, by reference to "experience" and the "involuntary disclosure of emotions" (ibid., 324).
77. Ibid., 176. Schlegel mentioned the celebrated "Grecian masters" of New Comedy—Diphilus, Philemon, Apollodorus, and Menander (ibid., 191).
78. Ibid., 309.
79. Ibid., 157.
80. Ibid., 150–51, 153; Horace, *Ars poetica* 281–84.
81. *LDAL* 146.
82. Ibid., 175.
83. Ibid., 198.
84. Ibid., 145.
85. Ibid., 148. New Comedy "represents what is amusing in character, and in the contrast of situations and combinations; and it is the more comic the more it is distinguished by a want of aim: cross purposes, mistakes, the vain efforts of ridiculous passion, and especially if all this ends at last in nothing; but still, with all this mirth, the form of the representation itself is serious, and regularly tied down to a certain aim" (ibid., 147–48).
86. "*Ernst . . . Scherz*," i.e., seriousness . . . joke. Ibid., 176.
87. Ibid., 178–79.
88. Ibid., 179.
89. Ibid.
90. A. W. Schlegel. *LDAL* (Lecture XIII) 177; *Vorlesungen über dramatische Kunst und Literatur*, Bd. V, p. 220. Similarly, Kerr has argued that comedy is secondary to and entirely depends upon tragedy and degenerates into "serious" comedy (i.e., turns into Nea) with tragedy's demise: Walter Kerr. *Tragedy and Comedy*. London: The Bodley Head, 1967, pp. 19–35, 146 et passim.
91. For Kierkegaard, the expression of our finitude and the sign of subjectivity is irony. S. Kierkegaard. *The Concept of Irony*, pp. 264, 329. The awareness of finitude allows for an unrestrained—negative—freedom for an always new yet arbitrary beginning: "the salient feature of the irony is the subjective freedom that at all times has in its power the possibility of a beginning and is not handicapped by earlier situations" (ibid., p. 253).

92. Schlegel further subdivides New Comedy according to the measure of reflexivity it displays into the comic of observation (*das Komische der Beobachtung*) and the self-conscious or confessed comic (*das selbstbewußte und eingestandne Komische*); the former represents high, refined comedy, whereas the latter represents low comedy or farce (*Possenspiel*). A. W. Schlegel. *LDAL* 183; *Vorlesungen über dramatische Kunst und Literatur*, Bd. V, p. 228.

93. Schlegel noted that Plautus and Terence influenced Molière (ibid., 310–13) and that Plautus's *Menaechmi* influenced Shakespeare's "The Comedy of Errors" (ibid., 380; the other source is Plautus's *Amphitryon*).

94. Ibid., 188.

95. Ibid., 189. "Plautus was perpetually running out into diffuseness, and he was obliged to remedy in some other way the lengthening this gave to the original; the imitations of Terence, on the other hand, from his lack of invention, turned out somewhat meager, and he filled up the gaps with materials borrowed from other pieces. Even his contemporaries reproached him with having falsified or corrupted a number of Greek pieces, for the purpose of making out of them a few Latin ones. Plautus and Terence are generally mentioned as writers in every respect original. In Romans this was perhaps pardonable: they possessed but little of the true poetic spirit, and their poetical literature owed its origin, for the most part, first to translation [*Uebersetzung*], then to free imitation [*Nachahmung*], and finally to appropriation [*Aneignung*] of new modeling, of the Greek" (ibid., 189).

96. Contemporary literary criticism has produced a number of commendable works that discuss comedy in its various aspects. See the discussion of the phenomenon of the comic in *Das Komische*. Wolfgang Preisedanz, Rainer Warning (eds.). (*Poetik und Hermeneutik* VII.) München: Fink, 1976, with contributions by Hans Blumenberg, Odo Marquard, Jean Starobinski, Dieter Henrich, and others. See also Rainer Warning. "Komik/Komödie." In *Das Fischer Lexikon. Literatur*. Ed. by U. Ricklefs, Band 2, Frankfurt am Main: Fischer, 1996, pp. 897–936.

97. Agnes Heller. *Immortal Comedy: The Comic Phenomenon in Art, Literature, and Life*. Lanham: Lexington, 2005, pp. 6, 8, 15, 204 et passim. L. J. Potts refuses to give a definition of comedy as unnecessary: L. J. Potts. *Comedy*. London: Hutchinson's University Library, 1948, p. 15.

98. Richard Keller Simon. *The Labyrinth of the Comic: Theory and Practice from Fielding to Freud*. Tallahassee: Florida State University Press, 1985, p. 3.

99. Ibid., p. 244.

100. Arnold Ruge. *Neue Vorschule der Ästhetik. Das Komische mit einem Komischen Anhange*. Halle: Verlag der Buchhandlung des Waisenhauses, 1837 (repr. Hildesheim: Georg Olms, 1975), pp. 107–36.

101. Mark William Roche. *Tragedy and Comedy: A Systematic Study and a Critique of Hegel*. Albany: State University of New York Press, 1998. Roche provides a (triadic) classification of comedy into comedy of (1) coincidence, (2a) reduction, (2b) negation, (2c) withdrawal, and (3) intersubjectivity ("The hero reaches intersubjectivity, and thus true subjectivity, after passing through false

subjectivity or negativity," p. 330), to which he also adds the comedy of absolute irony. Ibid., pp. 327–30; cf. pp. 135–246 and 281–83. See also Mark Roche. "Hegel's Theory of Comedy in the Context of Hegelian and Modern Reflections on Comedy." *Revue Internationale de Philosophie* 56 (2002), pp. 411–30. Against the predominant interpretation, which states that Hegel considers tragedy the highest dramatic form, Roche argues that comedy is antithetical to tragedy and is therefore more advanced. Ibid., pp. 421–22.

102. Alenka Zupančič. *The Odd One In: On Comedy*. Cambridge: MIT Press, 2008, pp. 27, 218 et passim.

103. Paul Kottman. "Slipping on Banana Peels, Tumbling into Wells: Philosophy and Comedy." *Diacritics* 38, No. 4, 2010, pp. 3–14.

104. Anja Gerigk. *Literarische Hochkomik in der Moderne: Theorie und Interpretationen*. Tübingen: Francke, 2008, pp. 68–74, 101 et passim.

105. Véronique Sternberg. *La poétique de la comédie*. Paris: Sedes, 1999; Andrew Stott. *Comedy*. New York: Routledge, 2005.

106. R. Keller Simon. *The Labyrinth of the Comic*, pp. 239–40. On many different meanings of the comic, see also Beatrix Müller-Kampel. "Komik und das Komische: Kriterien und Kategorien." *LiTheS: Zeitschrift für Literatur- und Theatersoziologie* 7 (2012), pp. 5–39.

107. E. Segal. *The Death of Comedy*, p. 452.

108. T. G. A. Nelson. *Comedy*, pp. 159–70; A. Heller. *Immortal Comedy*, pp. 94–124; András Horn. *Das Komische im Spiegel der Literatur. Versuch einer systematischen Einführung*. Würzburg, 1988, pp. 265–80. Horn, however, argues for three distinct stages in the development of comedy: Old Comedy (Aristophanes), New Comedy (Menander through the twentieth-century dramas), and modern absurdist comedy.

109. Maurice Charney. *Comedy High and Low*. New York: Oxford University Press, 1978, p. x. Cf. Jan Walsh Hokenson. *The Idea of Comedy. History, Theory, Critique*. Madison-Teaneck: Fairleigh Dickinson University Press, 2006, pp. 23, 120 et passim.

110. M. Charney. *Comedy High and Low*, pp. 10–18.

111. David Farley-Hills. *The Comic in Renaissance Comedy*. Totowa, NJ: Barnes and Noble, 1981, p. 20.

112. Brian Edwards. "*Verbum ludens*, or the Antic Disposition of Words: Toward a Theory of the Comic." In *Comic Relations: Studies in the Comic, Satire, and Parody*. Ed. by Pavel Petr, David Roberts, Philip Thomson. Frankfurt am Main-New York: P. Lang, 1985, pp. 43–49.

113. E. Olson. *The Theory of Comedy*, pp. 61, 65, 82–85.

114. V. Sternberg. *La poétique de la comédie*, pp. 25, 74.

115. M. Gurewitch. *Comedy: The Irrational Vision*, p. 9.

116. Friedrich Georg Jünger. *Über das Komische*. Frankfurt am Main: Vittorio Klostermann, 1948 (3rd ed.; first publ. 1936), p. 14.

117. Umberto Eco. "The Frames of Comic 'Freedom.'" In *Carnival!* Ed. by Thomas A. Sebeok. Berlin et al.: Mouton Publishers, 1984, pp. 1–9; p. 2.

118. R. W. Corrigan. "Comedy and the Comic Spirit." In *Comedy, Meaning and Form*, pp. 1–11, p. 2.

119. Christopher Fry. "Comedy." In *Comedy, Meaning and Form*, pp. 15–17. Comedy "believes in a universal cause for delight, even though knowledge of the cause is always twitched away from under us, which leaves us to rest on our own buoyancy." Ibid., p. 15.
120. H. Arendt. Interview, *New York Review of Books* 25 (October 26, 1978), p. 18.
121. N. Frye. *A Natural Perspective: The Development of Shakespearean Comedy and Romance*. New York: Columbia University Press, 1965, p. 133; see also ibid., pp. 119, 139, 158 et passim and N. Frye. *The Anatomy of Criticism*, pp. 158–182.
122. Robert M. Polhemus. *Comic Faith: The Great Tradition from Austen to Joyce*. Chicago and London: The University of Chicago Press, 1980, p. 20.

Chapter 3

1. Contra Heraclitus, for whom *logos* was not understandable to humans, even upon hearing it, fr. B1 DK.
2. This is evident in dialectic, logic, rhetoric, linguistics, mathematics, and the study of nature and its laws. The same is true for multiple arts, including poetry and drama, painting and architecture, and even cooking, in which one has to follow a measured proportion and order.
3. Terence, *Eun.* 476–78.
4. According to Plutarch, Menander considered a play practically complete once he had produced the general structure and framework of the plot, with a carefully thought through chain ("deduction") of the steps of action, which then needed to be completed by adding the dialogue. Ap.: R. W. Corrigan. *Classical Comedy*, p. 79.
5. Cf. Terence, *Phorm.* 191 sqq.
6. D. Nikulin. *Dialectic and Dialogue*. Stanford: Stanford University Press, 2010, pp. 95–118.
7. Walter J. Ong. *Orality and Literacy: The Technologizing of the Word*. London and New York: Routledge, 1988 (first publ. 1982), pp. 136–48.
8. Donatus. *A Fragment on Comedy and Tragedy*, p. 31: "The actors usually deliver the dialogue."
9. In Plautus, the act of addressing oneself was parodied in a scene with drunken Pseudolus in dialogue with his own legs (*Pseud.* 1246 sqq.).
10. *Poet.* 1450a36–1451b10.
11. There is a difference in meter between Old and New Comedy in that, as John Tzetzes noted, "the New for the most part employs the iambic measure, and other measures but seldom, while in the Old a multiplicity of meters was the great desideratum." Still, meter varied widely in both Plautus and Terence, which made the action engaging and interesting while establishing a fluid rhythm of exchange that changed according to situation. John Tzetzes. Op. cit., p. 33.
12. Perhaps there was a kind of dialogue in *parabasis*, but it was always an exchange between an *ode* (sung by the chorus) and an *epirrhema* (spoken by the coryphaeus) and then between an *ode* and an *antode* and an *epirrhema* and an *antepirrhema*, which correspond to each other in structure.

13. D. Nikulin. *On Dialogue*, pp. 72–93.
14. A. Heller. *Immortal Comedy*, p. 11. Accordingly, to say that comedy is reflective means that comedy (the comic playwright and actors, as well as the spectators or readers) should be aware of the properties and (formal) characteristics of what is parodied. Further, comedy should imitate and reproduce what is parodied in a *different* way, that is, according to its own tasks and properties, of which it should be explicitly aware. Finally, comedy should be aware that what it does is actually a parody.
15. G. W. F. Hegel. *Grundlinien der Philosophie des Rechts*, *Werke*, Bd. 7, p. 24.
16. As examples of practical claims, take the equality of people or the possibility of justice and freedom.
17. As Ben Jonson put it, comic "arte hath an enemy cal'd Ignorance." Ben Jonson. *Every Man Out of His Humour*, Induction, 219. Ben Jonson, vol. III, p. 436.
18. At the risk—and pleasure—of repetition, I quote Cicero again: "An imitation of life, a mirror of custom, an image of truth."
19. See, for example, David Lynch's *Lost Highway* or *Mulholland Drive*, whose plot structures are deliberately not comic.
20. Diogenes Laert. III 48.
21. It always moves (i) step-by-step, (ii) from the beginning that announces and presents the case, (iii) through an argument that (iv) may use various methods and (v) contain identifiable parts or structural subdivisions, (vi) toward a conclusion as the established "good" end (which is finding out what a thing is), (vii) all through questions and answers that (viii) refer to opposites and allow for a simple answer. This movement of thought is done (ix) by means of dialogue, which (x) involves a community of people (at least two, but usually more, including the listeners), one of whom—the dialectician—plays the role of the questioner who directs, though does not always control, the flow of the argument.
22. Plato. *RP* 509b, 531d sqq.
23. Aristotle. *Top.* 100b18 sqq. et al., *Met.* 1061b7–10.
24. "*audi nunc contra*" (Terence. *Phorm.* 699).
25. For example, both love and the strife between children and parents come with suffering and struggle, with a "war," which, nonetheless, can end in reconciliation: "*bellum, pax rursum.*" Terence. *Eun.* 59–63; cf. *Ad.* 899 sqq.
26. Terence. *Haut.* 1003 sqq.
27. Terence. *Eun.* 771 sqq.
28. As portrayed in Plato's *Euthydemus, Protagoras, Gorgias*, and elsewhere.
29. In order to achieve its end, comedy can also employ the battle of the sexes, in which women usually win. Said Gnatho, a hanger-on, "I know how women behave. When you want a thing they don't, and contrariwise when you don't they do (*novi ingenium mulierum: nolunt ubi velis, ubi nolis cupiunt ultro*)." Terence. *Eun.* 812–13.
30. Cf. Terence. *Eun.* 921, 940.
31. Anon. *In Plat. Theaet.* 71.26, ap. DK, vol. I, p. 197.
32. Euripides, *Medea* 465–519, 522–75.
33. Euripides, *Trojan Women* 884–1051.

34. *Nubes* 899 sqq. Interestingly, the monologue given by Truth is a ridicule of didactic moralistic speech. Ibid., 961 sqq.
35. Aristophanes, *Ranae* 1441–50.
36. Menander, *Epitr.* 305 sqq.
37. Terence, *Haut.* 1003 sqq.
38. W. G. Arnott. "Introduction," Menander, vol. I, p. xxxv.
39. "Riddles" translates to "*perplexe*," as a pythia, which is a pun on the maid's name.
40. "*scio nescio*" (*Eun.* 817–18.)
41. "*negat quis, nego; ait, aio*" (Terence. *Eun.* 251–52). Another exchange in the *Eunuch* testifies to parody: Gnatho said to an impoverished man, to whom he professed his art of parasitism, that Gnatho would become the founder of a school similar to a philosophical one. "I told him to enroll as my pupil, in the hope that, just as philosophical schools take their names from their founders, so parasites may be called Gnathonists." Terence. *Eun.* 262–64. There was also a parody of a dialectical conversation between a clever yet immoral Sophist (Gnatho) and Gnatho's ignorant and boastful yet dull patron, the soldier Thraso (Cf. *Eun.* 391 sqq.), duped by his agile interlocutor. The ultimate judgment on this debate was made by the slave Parmeno, who could tell right from wrong and was thus the real dialectician: "What a hopeless wretch [of Thraso, the 'questioned']! And the other one's a scoundrel [of Gnatho, the 'questioner']!" *Eun.* 418–19.
42. "*tradunt operas mutuas*" (*Phorm.* 266–67).
43. Terence, *Phorm.* 441–59.
44. "*quot homines, tot sententiae*" (Ibid., 454).
45. "*nolo, volo; volo, nolo rursum; cape, cedo; quod dictum indictumst; quod modo erat ratum irritumst*" (Ibid., 950–51).
46. W. Shakespeare. *Twelfth Night*, act V, sc. I, 17–23. Cf. an example of "negative" dialectic: Viola: "Thy reason, man?" Clown: "I can yield you none without words, and words are grown so false I am loath to prove reason with them." *Twelfth Night*, act III, sc. I, 23–26. Similarly, Ben Jonson in *Every Man Out of His Humour* entrusted one of the characters to invent a humorous dialectical "definition" of humor, which thereby became humorously reflective: "Why, Humour (as 'tis *ens*) we thus define it / To be a quality of aire or water, / . . . So in euery humane body / The choller, the melancholy, flegme, and bloud, / By reason that they flow continually / In some one part, and are not continent, / Receiue the name of Humours. Now thus farre / It may, by Metaphore, apply it selfe / Vnto the generall disposition: / As when some one peculiar quality / Doth so possesse a man, that it doth draw / All his affects, his spirits, and his powers, / In their confluctions, all to runne one way, / This may be truly said to be a Humour. Ben Jonson. *Every Man Out of His Humour*, Induction, 88–109. Ben Jonson, vol. III, pp. 431–32.
47. Agathon's tragedies appear to prefigure New Comedy. Pierre Lévêque. *Agathon*. Paris: Les belles lettres, 1955, pp. 115–24. Cf. Plato. *Symp.* 175e, 198c.
48. See G. Kennedy's commentary in Aristotle. *On Rhetoric: A Theory of Civic Discourse*. Translated with introduction, notes, and appendices by George

A. Kennedy. New York and Oxford: Oxford University Press, 2007, pp. 293–306 and G. Kennedy. *The Art of Rhetoric in the Roman World, 300 B.C.–A.D. 300.* Princeton: Princeton University Press, 1972.

49. Aristotle. *Rhet.* 1354a1–6; cf. 1355b7–21. See also G. Kennedy, p. 63, pp. 27–30.

50. Aristotle. *Met.* 1004b20; *Top.* 101a36 sqq.; cf. also *Anal. post.* 77a27 sqq.; *Soph. el.* 170a 38–39.

51. Aristotle. *Rhet.* 1355a21–22.

52. Ibid. 1397a8–10; 1400a14–16; 1400b4–5. Trans. G. Kennedy.

53. Plato. *Phaedr.* 266c sqq.

54. Refutative enthymemes are more liked by the listeners, as exposition of an inconsistency makes a more profound impression.

55. Aristotle. *Rhet.* 1355a3–18; 1395b20–1397a6; 1418a37–b4; *Anal. priora* 70a10 sqq.; *Anal. post.* 71a9–10.

56. Aristotle. *Rhet.* 1356a1–4; 1377b21–24; 1404b1 sqq.

57. Cicero. *De oratore* 2.15–16.

58. In a more elaborate version, which came from the practice of speechwriting (in Gorgias, Lysias, Isocrates, Plato, and others) and became more or less mandatory for later writers, including comic playwrights, there were five identifiable parts of speech: (1) The introduction or prologue (*prooimion*), which is the beginning—and thus the origin—of any speech and its brief summary and annunciation; this is the speech's "premise," and remarkably, Aristotle was explicit in the comparison between the introduction to a judicial speech and the prologue to a tragedy or comedy (Aristotle. *Rhet.* 1415a8–10); (2) the narration (*diēgēsis*), an exposition of the material, facts, and actions that constitute the argument (*logos*) of the speech; (3) the proof (*pistis*), which makes the point by demonstrative or apodictic means (including examples and enthymemes) as logically valid; (4) interrogation (*erotēsis*), a well-established practice both in judicial and dialectical questioning, in reference to opposites, through which one can demonstrate the invalidity of the opponent's claim by showing its inherent contradiction; and (5) a conclusion (*epilogos*) that seeks the interlocutors' favorable acceptance of the whole speech and also recapitulates the main steps of the argument (ibid. 1414a30 sqq.). These five parts can be found and discerned in various kinds of speech and reasoning, including judicial, Sophistic, rhetorical, philosophical, and dramatic.

59. In ancient mathematics, an important distinction—to an extent preserved in modern mathematics—existed between theorem and problem, the most famous and detailed account of which came in Proclus's commentary on Euclid (Proclus mentioned various explanations for this division. Proclus. *In primum Euclidis Elemetorum librum commentarii.* Ed. by G. Friedlein. Leipzig: Teubner, 1873, p. 77.7 sqq.). Notably, a theorem presupposes a proof that an object has a particular property, yet the very existence of this object is not questioned, because it is supposed to be already posited or existing. In a theorem, the object's very being is not questioned and is thus bracketed. Conversely, a problem requires a production of an object that cannot be considered to exist until its construction is actually

shown and accomplished step-by-step. In a problem, the object's existence has yet to be achieved. Unlike a theorem, a problem thus requires an *action* of an object's production, its implementation. For instance, the very first proposition in Euclid's Book I was a problem, for in order to show that on a given straight line one can construct an equilateral triangle using only a compass and a ruler, one must actually make a construction that shows how the required triangle is produced. Thus, the statement that all humans *are* equal is a theorem, because it presupposes that there are humans whose being can be described by means of an argument within a political theory. But the statement that all humans in fact *can be* equal is a problem, because one needs to describe how exactly equality can be reached and normatively implemented through various political institutions and social habits.

60. Proclus. *In Eucl.* 208.1–210.5. See also *The Thirteen Books of Euclid's Elements.* Translated with introduction and commentary by Thomas L. Heath. Vol. I–III. New York: Dover, 1956 (2nd ed.), vol. I, pp. 129–31. Enunciation (Greek *protasis*, Latin *propositio*) states what is given and what is being sought; exposition (*ekthesis, expositio*) identifies the given; specification (*diorismos, determinatio*) defines what is sought; construction (*kataskeyē, constructio*) produces what is required; proof (*apodeixis, demonstratio*) shows and explains that the construction does actually accomplish what it claims; and conclusion (*symperasma, conclusio*) explicitly confirms that the end has been achieved and thus returns to the beginning, a beginning that is already implicitly contained in the end.

61. Aristotle. *Rhet.* 1414b16.

62. The premises constitute the beginning, *arkhē*, of the argument, similar to the *protasis*, while the *deductive steps* are similar to the *epitasis.* The proof, then, is the end and the purpose of the proof, *telos*, similar to *catastrophe.*

63. Aristotle. *Poet.* 1450b25–34.

64. Aristotle. *De an.* 407a25–29 (*logos de pas horismos ē apodeixis: hē men oyn apodeixis kai ap' arkhēs kai ekhoysa pōs telos, tov syllogismon ē to symperasma*, 407a25–26).

65. The author of a fourth-century CE commentary on Terence (ascribed to Donatus but probably written by Evanthius) explained, "The protasis is the first action and the beginning of the drama, in which part of the argument is unfolded and part is kept back to hold the expectation of the people. The *epitasis* is the increase and advance of the disturbance, and as I said the tangling of the maze. Catastrophe is the change of the situation to a pleasant outcome, a change made clear to all through the knowledge of what has happened." [Donatus.] *A Fragment on Comedy and Tragedy*, p. 30. Cf. <Evanthius.> *De fabula* IV 5: "est prologus uelut praefatio quaedam fabulae, in quo solo licet praeter argumentum aliquid ad populum uel ex poetae uel ex ipsius fabulae uel auctoris commodo loqui; protasis primus actus initiumque est dramatis; epitasis incrementum processusque turbarum ac totius, ut ita dixerim, nodus erroris; catastrophe conuersio rerum ad iucundos exitus patefacta cunctis cognition gestorum." Evanthius's explanation of the parts was slightly different.

66. Evanthius. *De comoedia* VII 4: "*protasis* est primus actus fabulae, quo pars argumenti explicatur, pars reticetur ad populi expectationem tenendam; *epitasis*

inuolutio argumenti, cuius elegantia conectitur; *catastrophe* explicatio fabulae, per quam euentus eius approbatur."

67. This five-act division was noted, for example, in Trissino and Pino. It was already mentioned in Horace and known to the Greek Nea, though it was not distinct in Plautus and Terence. "Comedy is a kind of composition which, retaining always the same form, changes from time to time its matter; so that it always had five acts, always its complication and its denouement in order to be good." Pino. In *Theories of Comedy*, p. 38 and Trissino. *Poetica*, ibid., pp. 42–47. Cf. J. Barsby. Terence, vol. 2, p. 151, note 9 and K. Gaiser. "Zur Eigenart der römischen Komödie," pp. 1038–41.

68. Walter Ong argued that Freytag's pyramid design is characteristic of written literature, whereas the oral tradition, including epic, "stitches songs" or episodes out of a great repertoire available to the oral poet. Ong. *Orality and Literacy*, pp. 141–42. As drama, comedy is a conceptually written enterprise, although, medially, it can be oral. Yet the structure of comic action does not merely imitate live action: it presents an end not only *descriptive* of human action but also *prescriptive* for it.

69. Indeed, both comic plot and logical argument are understandable at any step of their development but rather hard to remember in their entirety due to their complexity and abundance of subtle, yet important, details. To this end, some of Plautus's and all of Terence's comedies were later supplied with a brief synopsis, which was traditionally placed at the very beginning and whose purpose was to recollect and remind the audience of the comedy's "argument."

70. The number of such constituents vary: besides Aristotle's six (qualitative) constituents of drama and three components of comic plot and five acts in comedy and Freytag's five "pyramidal" constituents of dramatic action, Frye identified six phases of comedy (between the poles of irony and satire, N. Frye. *The Anatomy of Criticism*, pp. 165–73), and Gurewitch identified four major components of comedy (satire, humor, farce, and irony, M. Gurewitch. *Comedy*, p. 9). It seems, however, that a particular classification is always only *a* classification, depending on the underlying principles of classification, which may vary.

71. Such as consummation of marriage, sexual release, or earning an amount of money that secures one's social position.

72. Plato. *Phaedo* 60c–61b.

73. "*poiein mythoys all' oy logoys*," Plato. *Phaedo* 61b4.

74. *Ad.* 22. In Latin, *argumentum* has many different meanings, which include *story, subject matter*, or *content; theatrical piece; picture* or *image; argument* or *proof; sign; truth* or *truthfulness*; and *conclusion*. The term itself comes from the verb *arguo*— "to show, make clear," but also "to accuse, blame." Next, *fabula* may mean *rumors; conversation; story* or *plot*; or *dramatic piece*. Thus, *argumentum fabulae* is probably best translated the way it is rendered above, but in fact it may also suggest a right conclusion of a conversation or of the (whole) story of a (comic) drama. Moreover, the mesh of meanings of *argumentum* and *fabula* intersect at the "theatrical piece" or "drama," where the two are almost synonymous, even if the former shows or presents (as the "form") the latter (as the "content").

75. Terence. *Ad.* 2–24.
76. Cicero provided a useful explanation of the term *narrative*: "The narrative [*narratio*] is the exposition [*expositio*] of events that have occurred or are supposed to have occurred." Further, the exposition of an event occurs in three different forms: *fabula, historia,* and *argumentum. Fabula* "is the term applied to a narrative in which the events are not true and have no verisimilitude." *Historia* "is an account of actual occurrences remote from the recollection of our age." Finally, *argumentum* "is a fictitious narrative (*ficta res*) that nevertheless could have occurred." "Narratio est rerum gestarum aut ut gestarum expositio. Fabula est in qua nec verae nec veri similes res continentur. Historia est gesta res, ab aetatis nostra memoria remota. Argumentum est ficta res, quae tamen fieri potuit." Cicero. *De inventione* I.19.27. Trans. H. M. Hubbell.
77. A. Heller. *Immortal Comedy*, p. 39.
78. Boris Tomashevsky. *Poetica.* Moscow: CC, 1996, pp. 75–77. See also David Bordwell. *Narration in the Fiction Film.* London: Methuen, 1985, pp. 30, 49–50.
79. Ap. Riccoboni. *The Comic Art*, p. 104.
80. Such are, for instance, Kant's transcendental deduction and the plot of Terence's *Phormio.* Yet one must go all the way through in order to achieve the end. One must actually *get there.* Writing, then, is needed so as not to forget every minute detail, so as to retain a comprehensive account of the thought and the said, and so as to avoid confounding the exact order of the steps: otherwise the whole of the argument or plot cannot be gone through and played out.
81. This is the case in Aristophanes's *Plutus*, Menander's *Dyskolos*, Plautus's *Amphitryon*, and Terence's *Phormio* Menander. *Dyskolos* 864–65; cf. Arnott. "Introduction," Menander, vol. I, p. xxxvii. Cf. Minturno. *The Art of Poetry*, p. 83; Riccoboni. *The Comic Art*, pp. 103–5; L. Bishop. *Comic Literature in France*, p. 102.
82. See: R. W. Corrigan. *Classical Comedy*, pp. 69–70; N. Frye. *The Anatomy of the Criticism*, p. 41; David Konstan. *Greek Comedy and Ideology.* New York: Oxford University Press, 1995, p. 15 (similarity of the stories in Aristophanes).
83. Terence, *Hec.* 281. The *senex iratus* became an archetype of New Comedy (e.g., Terence. *Phorm.* 350). As Epicurus said, "For if parents are justifiably angered at their children, it is surely pointless to resist and not ask to be forgiven; but if [their anger] is not justifiable but somewhat irrational, it is ridiculous for someone with irrationality in his heart to appeal to someone set against appeals and not to seek in a spirit of good will to win him over by other means." *Sent. Vat.* 62.
84. V. Shklovsky. *Knight's Move.* Translation and introduction by Richard Sheldon. Normal and London: Dalkey Archive Press, 2005, p. 23.
85. As in *Andr., Eun., Haut., Ad.*
86. Eckard Lefèvre. *Der Phormio des Terenz und der Epidikazomenos des Apollodor von Karystos.* München: Beck, 1978, pp. 5–7, 92–96 et passim. See also: K. Gaiser. "Zur Eigenart der römischen Komödie", pp. 1058–66.
87. *Andr.* 21; *Haut.* 16–19.
88. *Ad.* 13–14.
89. *Eun.* 23–34, 41–42; *Ad.* 6–14.

90. "qui bene vortendo et easdem scribendo male ex / Graecis bonis Latinas fecit non bonas." Terence. *Eun.* 7–8.
91. Plato. *Phaedr.* 274b; Alcidamas. *Peri Sophistōn* 27–28. In *Orationes et fragmenta, adiunctis Gorgiae Antisthenis Alcidamantis declamationibus*. Ed. by F. Blass. Leipzig: Teubner, 1908 (2nd ed.), p. 193–205.
92. A. Heller. *Immortal Comedy*, p. 14. See also W. J. Ong. *Orality and Literacy*, pp. 144–47.
93. Frye was thus wrong in taking the detective story as a form of melodrama: N. Frye. *The Anatomy of Criticism*, p. 44.

Chapter 4

1. These clearly fall within the tradition of making distinctions in a speech or argument.
2. Evanthius. *De comoedia* VII 2: "prologus est prima dictio, a Graecis dicta *prōtos logos*, uel antecedens ueram fabulae compositionem elocutio." Evanthius also added that "some have wished that there be this difference between 'prologue' and 'prologium': 'prologue' is a kind of preface to the fable, in which alone something besides the argument is said to the audience, either from the poet or due to the needs of the fable itself or the needs of the actor. But in the 'prologium' only the argument is spoken of." ([Donatus]. *A Fragment on Comedy and Tragedy*, pp. 29–30) ("inter prologum et prologium quidam hoc interesse uoluerunt, quod prologus est, ubi aut poeta excusatur aut fabula commendatur, prologium autem est, cum tantum de argumento dicitur." *De comoedia* VII 3).
3. See, for example, *Hippolytus* 1–68, where the plot is expounded by Aphrodite.
4. Aristophanes ridiculed Euripides's prologue in the *Frogs* (*Ranae* 946).
5. Terence. *Hec.* 9 sqq.
6. These, however, were only added later by Gaius Sulpicius Apollinaris.
7. G. M. Sifakis. *Parabasis and Animal Choruses*, pp. 7–9.
8. R. W. Corrigan. *Classical Comedy*, p. 245: "[T]he plot is usually revealed in the prologue. The audience was not concerned with what happened: their interest was in how things were worked out and the form of the performance itself."
9. Thus, at the end of the prologue in the *Brothers*, Terence noted, "Do not expect [in this prologue] an outline of the plot [*argumentum fabulae*]. The old men who come on first [*sc.* the two main characters of the comedy] will in part explain it [*aperient*] and in part reveal it in the course of the action [*in agendo*]" (*Ad.* 22–24, trans. Barsby).
10. Vladimir Propp. *Morphology of the Folktale*. Edited with an introduction by Svatava Pirkova-Jakobson. Trans. by Laurence Scott. Bloomington: Indiana University Press, 1958, pp. 68–71, 130–31.
11. Terence. *Eun.* 873–75.
12. *Ad.* 26–80.
13. Ibid.
14. This was the case in Terence's *Brothers, Ad.* 26 sqq.

15. See Michael von Albrecht. *A History of Roman Literature: From Livius Andronicus to Boethius, with Special Regard to Its Influence on World Literature*. Vol. 1. Leiden: Brill, 1997, p. 219.
16. Aristotle. *Anal. priora* 24a16–17.
17. Aristotle. *De caelo* 288a19.
18. Aristotle. *Rhet.* 1397a7 sqq.
19. An example that applied this *topos* ran as follows: "A priestess did not allow her son to engage in public debate: 'For,' she said, 'if you say what is just, the people will hate you, but if what is unjust, the gods will. On the other hand, you should engage in public debate; for if you speak what is just, the gods will love you, if what is unjust, the people will.'" Ibid. 1399a20–25.
20. To provide an exhaustive classification of all the comic topics would imply solving the problem of whether such a classification is at all possible. Plato does not provide a general classification of the dialectical methods he uses in his dialogues, nor does Aristotle explain why there are exactly 28 rhetorical *topoi* and whether they all can be derived from a single simple principle of classification. Modern philosophy still lingers on this question, which I leave open here, supposing that human life and action take certain forms that are universally applicable, though there can always be new yet unused and undiscovered ways of thinking and action.
21. Hegel thinks that gnome belongs primarily to epic. G. W. F. Hegel. *Vorlesungen über die Ästhetik, Werke*, Bd. 15, p. 326.
22. It was seen, for example, in Theognis: *Iambi et elegi Graeci*, p. 174 sqq. The early Pythagorean doctrine was preserved and orally transmitted as apophthegms.
23. "*gnōmologei*," fr. B 8–46 DK, fr. A3 DK, ap. Diog. Laert. 8.78; cf. A5 DK=Anon. *de com.* 2.4.
24. Fr. B4 DK.
25. "*communia esse amicorum inter se omnia*," *Ad.* 804.
26. "*tacent: satis laudant*," Terence. *Eun.* 476.
27. "*tacitus citius audies*," Ibid., 571.
28. "*brevitas laudabilis absoluta*," Alexander Gottlieb Baumgarten. *Ästhetik*. Übersetz, mit einer Einführung, Anmerkungen und Registern herausgegeben von Dagmar Mirbach. Bd. 1–2. Hamburg: Felix Meiner Verlag, 2007. Bd. 1, § 158, pp. 134–35; see also § 158–66, pp. 134–45, *Absoluta brevitas*). Baumgarten cites *Hec.* 848.
29. Terence. *Haut.* 77.
30. "*phtheiroysin ēthē khrēsta homiliai kakai*," 1 Corinthians 15:33.
31. LSJ.
32. Aristotle. *Rhet.* 1418a15–16.
33. Ibid., I 21.
34. Ibid., 1394a19–1395b19.
35. Cf. Aristotle. *Rhet.* 1395a3.
36. "La douceur de la gloire est si grande qu'à quelque objet qu'on l'attache, même la mort, on l'aime," fr. 500 Brunschvicg.
37. Terence. *Eun.* 335–39.
38. Plato. *Gorg.* 449b–c.

39. Molière. *Femmes savantes* 559–614, act II, sc. VII.
40. See, for example, Terence. *Eun.* 345 sqq.
41. Terence. *Phorm.* 510–11.
42. Terence. *Andr.* 184.
43. V. Propp. *Morphology of the Folktale*, pp. 133–34.
44. Cf. Shakespeare's *Taming of the Shrew.*
45. Plato. *RP* 586c; *Phaedr.* 243a–b.
46. "*repente*," "suddenly," Terence. *Ad.* 984.
47. See Axel Honneth. *Kampf um Anerkennung. Zur moralischen Grammatik sozialer Konflikte.* Frankfurt am Main: Suhrkamp, 1992, pp. 274–87.
48. A sign might appear as material evidence, such as a token, ring (*anulus*), necklace, layette, or letter. The testimony might be given by a nurse or a stranger, for example. Menander. *Epitr.* 387–88; *Perikeiromene* 742 sqq.; Terence. *Haut.* 614; *Eun.* 808; *Hec.* 574, 811, 821–32, 846; *Ad.* 348. The sign can also be a bodily feature associated with an event, such as a scar from the childhood, which is already used by Euripides (*Electra* 573–74).
49. W. Shakespeare. *Twelfth Night*, act V, sc. I, 270.
50. This same device was used by Euripides in his lost tragedies, *Alexandros*, *Alope*, *Auge*, *Wise Melanippe*, and *Hypsipyle*, now known only in fragments.
51. The token might be, for example, a knucklebone, coin, or seal impression on wax.
52. Menander. *Epitr.* 294 sqq.
53. "*cistella cum monumentis*," Terence. *Eun.* 753
54. Aristotle. *Rhet.* 1400b34 sqq.; cf. *Soph. el.* 165b23 sqq.
55. Terence. *Eun.* 923 sqq.
56. "*defessa sum iam misera te ridendo*," *Eun.* 1008.
57. There were, however, two women in the *Thesmophoriazusae*, whose paired appearance was justified by their interaction with the chorus in parodistic philippics against Euripides.
58. There were, for example, two women, two young men, two old men, a girl and her servant, two servants (a good country slave and a sly town slave, in Plautus's *Menaechmi* and *Mostellaria*), two lovers (a lover and beloved), son and father, daughter and mother, husband and wife, slave and master, two brothers, etc. In Menander's *Epitrepontes* we find two rhetorically sophisticated slaves who are constantly disputing and keep interrupting each other (218 sqq.).
59. See W. Görler. "Doppelhandlung, Intrige und Anagnorismos bei Terenz." *Poetica* 5 (1972), pp. 164–82.
60. Descartes. *Oeuvres de Descartes.* Publiées par Charles Adam et Paul Tannery. Paris: Vrin, 1996. Vol. XI, pp. 661–62; cf. Vol. V, p. 459.
61. Terence, *Haut.* 624–25. Or yet, first there was deceit and then trust; hatred and then love; desperation and then hope; fear and then joy; blame and then praise. Ibid., 810–11; 825 et al.
62. "*ita animus commotust metu, spe, gaudio*," Terence. *Andr.* 937–38.
63. Terence, *Hec.* 343.
64. "*maneto. curre*," Terence, *Hec.* 443.

65. "*amo et odi*," Terence. *Carm.* 85.
66. For Menander's use of double scenes, see the discussion of "parallelism" in W. G. Arnott, "Introduction," Menander, vol. I, pp. xxxix–xl.
67. Terence. *Andr.* 412–31.
68. Ibid., 764–95.
69. "Never mind what I know. Tell me what I ask." Ibid., 764.
70. Ibid., 792–93.
71. "*de industria*," Ibid., 795.
72. Ibid., 863.
73. As Phormio, a parasite and trickster, says, "Now I must put on a new face and change my role." Terence. *Phorm.* 890.
74. Terence, *Haut.* 533–35.
75. Ibid., 537–42.
76. "*non est mentiri meum*," Ibid., 547–49.
77. Such was also the good and smart courtesan in New Comedy, represented by Bacchis in *The Mother-in-Law*, who selflessly helped others in love and assumed features of the comic thinker—those of the smart maid (cf. Terence. *Hec.* 816–40). In her capacity as a lover who turned into a friend, she (and not Shakespearean characters, as Cavell argued) appears to prefigure the main female character in the Hollywood comedy of remarriage who makes love possible (again), as the result of her scheming. Cf. Stanley Cavell. *Pursuits of Happiness: The Hollywood Comedy of Remarriage.* Cambridge, MA: Harvard University Press, 1981, pp. 19–20, 48–50 et passim.
78. Terence. *Haut.* 701.
79. Ibid., 709–11.
80. Ibid., 886–87.
81. This is similar to Sid Caesar's "double-talk."
82. "quam uterque est similis sui!" Terence. *Phorm.* 501.
83. The fool becomes wise, and the wise become fools; the servant becomes a master, and the master a servant.
84. Dio Chrysostom. *Disc.* 4.108.
85. *Eun.* 612, "*mutare*," "to change" (clothes).
86. *La Calandria* was written under the influence of Plautus's *Menaechmi*. Bernardo Dovizi da Bibbiena. *The Follies of Calandro.* In *The Genius of the Italian Theatre.* Ed. by Eric Bentley. New York: Mentor Books, 1964, pp. 34–98.
87. "A sportful malice," *Twelfth Night*, act V, sc. I, 392.
88. Shakespeare. *Twelfth Night*, act V, sc. I, 229–30.
89. Molière. *Sganarelle ou le cocu imaginaire.* In J.-B. Molière. *Oeuvres complètes.* Préface de Pierre-Aimé Touchard. Paris: Seuil, 1962, pp.112–21.
90. A. Heller. *Immortal Comedy*, pp. 44, 49–51, 65.
91. Terence. *Haut.* 469–71.
92. Ibid., 495–96.
93. Terence. *Eun.* 1067 sqq.
94. Perhaps every oppression is a result of a commonly shared misrecognition.

95. P. Lauter. *Theories of Comedy*, p. 305.
96. In modern drama, this began with Jonson. See P. Holland. *The Ornament of Action*, pp. 103–4.
97. Only very rarely are characters made to realize their nonexistence.
98. We see this in Aristophanes's *Clouds* (345 sqq., 1095, 1202, 1299); Plautus's *Pseudolus* (720, 1081–82, 1240, 1333), *Amphitryon* (151), and *Poenulus* (126); Terence's *The Mother-in-Law* (866–68). In Romantic comedy, a good example is Tieck's *Der gestiefelte Kater*.
99. Even trees are subject to fate, "per voi risplenda il fato," as Xerxes suggests in Händel.
100. This is as *Fortuna Primigenia*, "First Bearer," in Praeneste.
101. Menander. *Asp.* 100–148.
102. *pantōn kyria toytōn brabeysai kai dioikēsai*, Menander. *Aspis* 147–48.
103. "*apista*." "*poll' estin erg' apista . . . tykhēs*," Menander. *Perikeiromene* 372 (802 Arnott).
104. "*fortis fortuna adiuvat*," said by the slave Geta. Terence. *Phorm.* 203.
105. As a young man in Menander's *Women Drinking Hemlock* said, "[I've] not [done] right [to rail at] Lady Luck. I have perhaps abused [her, called her blind (bad). But now she's saved me]—clearly she can see! [I really toiled], but my toils achieved [nothing worthwhile]. I'd not have gained success [without her help]. And so let no one, please, ever be too despondent if he fails. That may become an agent of good fortune!" Menander. *Koneiazomenai* 13–20, trans. Arnott.
106. Terence. *Phorm.* 757–59.
107. Cf.: "Do not be afraid. Together we will bear both good and bad (*noli metuere: una tecum bona mala tolerabimus*)," said Antipho to Geta, who was about to weave a complex intrigue but was afraid of unexpected consequences. Terence. *Phorm.* 556.
108. Terence. *Ad.* 739–41.

Chapter 5

1. Aristotle. *Poet.* 1453a36–39.
2. W. Shakespeare. *Twelfth Night*, act V, sc. I, 174–75. In Shakespeare's comedy, the jealous Orsino is ready to kill Cesario (ibid., 123), the impostor with whom Olivia falls in love and who is actually Viola, presenting herself as a young man. Shakespeare is referring to a precedent from Heliodorus's *Aethiopica* (third century CE), which was popular in the Renaissance; there, Theagenes attempts to kill his beloved Chariclea, rather than let her be captured. Nevertheless, the *Aethiopica* has a comic ending: the inevitable marriage of the protagonists.
3. An example in Menander's *Perikeiromene* was the shaving of a woman's head, which was a humiliation and serious offense.
4. R. W. Corrigan. *Classical Comedy*, p. 70.
5. Cf.: Ctesipho in Terence: "I'm desperately keen to spend the whole day in happiness, as I've begun." *Ad.* 521–22.

6. Well-being or happiness should be considered from the perspective of the whole of one's life. See Aristotle. *NE* 1098a15–20.

7. As Antonio Sebastiano Minturno remarked in *The Art of Poetry*, "[I]t is typical of the comic poet to give a pleasing and gay ending to his fable, which would not be possible unless he were able to induce surprise; things happening outside of our expectation are considered surprising." In *Theories of Comedy*, p. 84.

8. An example is Terence's *Brothers*.

9. A. Heller. *Immortal Comedy*, pp. 13–14.

10. "*aequo animo*," Terence, *Ad.* 503.

11. "Comedy usually moves toward a happy ending, and the normal response of the audience to a happy ending is 'this should be'," N. Frye. *The Anatomy of Criticism*, p. 155.

12. T. G. A. Nelson. *Comedy*, p. 97; Ben Jonson. *Volpone, or the Foxe*, act V, sc. XII. In Ben Jonson. Ed. by C. H. Herford and Percy Simpson. Oxford: Clarendon, 1937, vol. V, pp. 130–36. *Volpone* is an example of a type of comedy where the evildoer is excluded from sharing well-being with others, which is the sense of punishment. Other examples are Molière's *Tartuffe, L'Avare, Le Misanthrope*, Congreve's *The Double Dealer*, Sheridan's *The School for Scandal*, Goldoni's *Il bugiardo*, Kleist's *Der zerbrochene Krug*, Hautpmann's *Der Biberpelz* and Schnitzler's *Anatol*. I am grateful to Mark Roche for pointing out this distinction.

13. Terence. *Hec.* 866–68, trans. J. Barsby.

14. The end of judicial speech is the just (*dikaion*); the end of deliberative, or advisory, speech is the good (*agathon*); and the end of epideictic, or declamatory, speech is the beautiful (*kalon*). Aristotle. *Rhet.* 1358a36–1359a2; 1391b18–1392a.

15. See: Heidegger on *Sein zum Tode*: M. Heidegger. *Sein und Zeit*. Tübingen: Max Niemeyer, 1993 (17. Aufl.), pp. 235–67 (sect. 46–53). E.g., "Der Tod ist *eigenste* Möglichkeit des Daseins." p. 263, etc.

16. Or, in Schopenhauer's terms, comedy is the assertion of the will to live, whereas tragedy is its denial: op. cit.

17. "*prius . . . disce quid sit vivere*," Terence. *Haut.* 971–72.

18. A. Heller. *Immortal Comedy*, pp. 3, 38.

19. See: F. G. Jünger. *Über das Komische*, p. 68 sqq.

20. *Tractatus Coislinianus*, IV. See Walter Watson. *The Lost Second Book of Aristotle's Poetics*. Chicago: The University of Chicago Press, 2012, p. 183 sqq.

21. John Tzetzes. *First Proem to Aristophanes*. In *Theories of Comedy*, pp. 33–34; p. 33: "Comedy is an imitation of an action [that is ridiculous] . . . purgative of emotions, constructive of life, moulded by laughter and pleasure. Tragedy differs from comedy in that tragedy has a story, and a report of things [or 'deeds'] that are past, although it represents them as taking place in the present, but comedy embraces fictions of the affairs of everyday life; and in that the aim of tragedy is to move the hearers to lamentation, while the aim of comedy is to move them to laughter." See also Stephen Halliwell. *Greek Laughter. A Study of Cultural Psychology from Homer to Early Christianity*. Cambridge: Cambridge University Press, 2008, pp. 243–63.

22. See, for instance, W. H. Auden. "Notes on the Comic." In *Comedy, Meaning and Form*, pp. 61–72; Helmuth Plessner. *Philosophische Anthropologie. Lachen und*

Weinen; Lächeln; Anthropologie der Sinne. Herausgegeben und mit einem Nachwort von Günter Dix. Frankfurt am Main: S. Fischer Verlag, 1970, pp. 88–101; V. Sternberg. *La poétique de la comédie,* p. 140; and Michel Meyer. *Le comique et le tragique. Penser le théâtre et son histoire.* Paris: PUF, 2003, p. 71 sqq. See also *Das Komische.* Ed. by Rainer Warning und Wolfgang Preisendanz. München: Fink, 1976.

23. Monro lists (1) superiority, (2) release from restraint (relief), (3) incongruity, and (4) ambivalence. Incongruity and ambivalence stand rather close, as Morreall argued, and thus we can consider them under the same rubric. D. H. Monro. *Argument of Laughter.* Melbourne: Melbourne University Press, 1951, pp. 83–231. See also John Morreall. *Taking Laughter Seriously.* Albany: State University of New York Press, 1983, pp. 15–19. Manfred Frank showed that for Tieck the comic arises out of a contradiction in the subject's perception of his purposes or intentions. Manfred Frank. "Vom Lachen. Über Komik, Witz und Ironie. Überlegungen im Ausgang von der Frühromantik." In *Vom Lachen. Einem Phänomen auf der Spur.* Ed. By Thomas Vogel. Tübingen: Attempto, 1992, pp. 211–31.

24. D. H. Monro. Op. cit., pp. 83–84. Hobbes famously said that laughter is "a kind of sudden glory," that is, vainglory. For the relief theory, see S. Freud. *Jokes and their Relation to the Unconscious.* Trans. by James Strachey. New York: Norton, 1960.

25. Lessing, twenty-eighth piece of his *Hamburgische Dramaturgie* (August 4, 1767). See Paul Mallory Haberland. *The Development of Comic Theory in Germany during the Eighteenth Century.* Göppingen: Verlag Alfred Kuemmerle, 1971, pp. 84–85.

26. The comic fight for freedom against political and social oppression is usually delegated to satire. Cf. Cynthia Willett. *Irony in the Age of Empire: Comic Perspectives on Democracy and Freedom.* Bloomington: Indiana University Press, 2009; and Andrew Cutrofello. "It Takes a Village Idiot: And Other Lessons Cynthia Willett Teaches Us." *Journal of Speculative Philosophy* 24 (2010), pp. 87–95.

27. "*ouai hymin hoi gelōntes nyn, hoti penthēsete kai klaysethe,*" Luke 6:25.

28. H. Bergson. *Laughter: An Essay on the Meaning of the Comic.* Trans. by Cloudesely Brereton and Fred Rothwell. New York: Macmillan, 1921 (first publ. 1911), pp. 9, 58, 69 et passim.

29. A. Heller. *Immortal Comedy,* pp. 201, 206, 213–14.

30. A. Heller. *Immortal Comedy,* pp. 11, 14, 24–26, 65.

31. E. Olson. *The Theory of Comedy,* p. 61.

32. Molière. *Les femmes savantes.* Act II, sc. VI, 64–65.

33. Charles Baudelaire. "On the Essence of Laughter, and, in General, on the Comic in the Plastic Arts." In *Comedy, Meaning and Form,* pp. 448–65; pp. 454–55.

34. G. Bataille. "*Conférences sur le non-savoir.*" *Tel Qel* 10 (1962), pp. 3–20. George Bataille. "Un-Knowing: Laughter and Tears." October 36 (1986), pp. 89–102, p. 90: "That which is laughable may simply be *the unknowable . . . the unknown makes us laugh.*"

35. Simon Critchley. *On Humour.* London: Routledge, 2002.

36. Aristotle's *aiskhron,* Cicero's *turpitudo* (*De oratore* 2.236).

37. A. Riccoboni. *The Comic Art* (1585). In *Theories of Comedy*, p. 106. As Ben Jonson put it, "the moving of laughter is a fault of comedy." *Discoveries*, 2625–77, cf. Ben Jonson. Ed. by C. H. Herford, Percy and Evelyn Simpson. Oxford: Clarendon, 1952, vol. XI, p. 289.

38. Lisa Trahair. *The Comedy of Philosophy: Sense and Non-Sense in Early Cinematic Slapstick*. Albany: State University of New York Press, 2007, p. 13 et passim. In Terence's *Brothers* a pimp Sannio, after being beaten by a young man, sighs, "We're both totally exhausted [*defessi*], him with beating and me with being beaten." *Ad.* 213.

39. This is *deformitas* in Cicero.

40. Cf. Terence. *Ad.* 126.

41. H. Plessner. "Das Lächeln." In H. Plessner. *Philosophische Anhtropologie*, pp. 175–86.

42. A. Heller. *Immortal Comedy*, p. 26.

43. T. G. A. Nelson. *Comedy*, p. 123: "The most obvious and distinctive feature of comic dialogue and narrative is, of course, joke."

44. W. Shakespeare. *Twelfth Night*, act III, sc. I, 62–70.

45. This is how it is presented in Baldassare Castiglione's *Il Cortegiano*. A. Stott. *Comedy*, pp. 56–57.

46. Ben Jonson. The Dedicatory Epistle to *Volpone*. In Ben Jonson, vol. V, pp. 17–21.

47. E. Olson. *The Theory of Comedy*, p. 21.

48. G. Meredith. *An Essay on the Idea of Comedy*, p. 125; cf.: "to touch and kindle the mind through laughter, demands more than sprightliness, a most subtle delicacy." Ibid., p. 74.

49. It appeared in Hippocrates and Galen and was taken over by Paracelsus.

50. S. Critchley. *On Humour*, p. 79. Cf. Antony Earl of Shaftesbury. "Sensus communis: An Essay on the Freedom of Wit and Humour." In *Characteristicks of Men, Manners, Opinions, Times*. Ed. by Philip Ayers. Vol. 1. Oxford: Clarendon Press, 1999, pp. 37–81.

51. For Hegel, humor is only subjective and as such has nothing to do with comedy: G. W. F. Hegel. *Aesthetics*, pp. 600–601.

52. L. J. Potts. *Comedy*, pp. 19–20; D. Farley-Hills. *The Comic in Renaissance Comedy*, p. 3.

53. Menander. *Dysk.* 341–47.

54. Greek antiquity distinguishes between the courtesan (*hetaira*), the concubine (*pallakē*), and the wife (*akoitis*). "In New Comedy . . . the concubine is associated with the hetaera by the foreclosure of any possibility of marriage, on the basis of her civic status; and she is associated with the wife in her participation in a household, represented as a unique association free of mercenary motives." David Konstan. *Greek Comedy and Ideology*, p. 121. See also L. A. Post. "Woman's Place in Menander's Athens." *Transactions of the American Philological Association* 71 (1941), pp. 420–59; pp. 443–46.

55. "*ita plerique ingenio sumus omnes: nostri nosmet paenitet*," Terence. *Phorm.* 172.

56. "I'm beside myself [*non sum apud me*]," recognized Antipho, a young man in love. Terence. *Phorm.* 204.

57. Demipho, an old man irritated by his son having married without asking his permission, says, "I'm so angry [irritated] I can't get any thoughts together [*ita sum irritatus animum ut nequeam ad cogitandum instituere*]." Terence. *Phorm.* 240.
58. "*amare, odisse, suspicari,*" Terence. *Eun.* 40.
59. See David Farley-Hills. *The Comic in Renaissance Comedy*, p. 12.
60. R. W. Corrigan. *Classical Comedy*, p. 70.
61. "It's a common fault (*vitium commune*) of all of us that in old age we are too worried about money." Terence. *Ad.* 953–54.
62. "*ipset sibi,*" Terence. *Ad.* 35–39.
63. When Protagoras famously claimed that man is the measure of all things (in Plato. *Theaet.* 152a), *pantōn khrēmatōn metron*, he might have meant not the things we come to know but possession or money, which is the meaning of *khrēmata*. Hence, man is the measure of everything that we come to acknowledge as a possession capable of being owned, valued, and exchanged, which, in the case of Protagoras himself, was also knowledge that could be sold.
64. D. Konstan. *Greek Comedy and Ideology*, p. 161.
65. Friedrich Schlegel. "Vom ästhetischen Werte der griechischen Komödie," in *Dichtungen und Aufsätze*. Ed. by W. Rasch. München: Hanser, 1984, pp. 256–67, p. 259.
66. F. G. Jünger. *Über das Komische*, pp. 16–17.
67. See D. Nikulin. *On Dialogue*, pp. 111–19.
68. "Jag föddes fri, levde fri ock skall dö frigjord."
69. Terence. *Phorm.* 271.
70. Thus, the girl in Terence's *The Mother-in-Law* never said a word.
71. As did Parmeno in Terence's *Eunuch* and Alceste in Molière's *Le Misanthrope* (considered "*fort singulier*"), 1163.
72. See A. Heller. *Immortal Comedy*, p. 41.
73. Such were the courtesan Habrotonon in Menander's *Epitrepontes* (538 sqq.) and the slaves Doris in Menander's *Perikeiromene* (982–83) and Syrus in Terence's *Brothers* (960).
74. Friedrich Schiller. "Naïve and Sentimental Poetry" (ch. "Satirical Poetry"). In F. Schiller. *Naive and Sentimental Poetry: On the Sublime*. Translated with introduction and notes by Julius A. Elias. New York: Frederick Ungar Publishing Co., 1966, p. 122.

Chapter 6

1. Aristotle. *Poet.* 1450a15–23, 1450b9–10.
2. To assert a strong primacy of the plot leads to claims of this kind: "The technical hero and heroine are not often very interesting people: the *adulescentes* of Plautus and Terence are all alike . . ." N. Frye. *The Anatomy of Criticism*, p. 155. Or: "character types are so rigidly defined that their behaviours are entirely predictable within given situations . . . human identity is stripped of its subtlety or ambiguity, leaving only monstrous activity." A. Stott. *Comedy*, p. 44.

3. For Ludwig, this was seen in dramatic dialogue, and for Grossman and Bakhtin not in comedy but in Dostoevsky's novels, which present an original psychological version of the (comic) detective story.

4. M. Bakhtin. *Problems of Dostoevsky's Poetics*. Ed. and trans. by C. Emerson. Introduction by W. C. Booth. Minneapolis: University Of Minnesota Press, 1984, pp. 36–43.

5. See A. Heller. *Immortal comedy*, pp. 49–50.

6. To be sure, spectators *watch* a drama, whereas listeners *listen to* a comedy read by others (and readers listen to themselves). Spectators *see more*, because they attain not only to the audible but also to the visual, which does not fit within the text (such as gestures, grimaces, costumes, decorations, etc.). But listeners *hear more*, because they hear the voice of others and thus can *be* with them, if to be is to be in dialogue.

7. M. S. Silk. *Aristophanes and the Definition of Comedy*, p. 232.

8. E. Olson. *The Theory of Comedy*, p. 85. Cf. A. W. Schlegel. *LDAL* 174.

9. Other examples include *Eunomia*, "Good Order," in Plautus's *Dyskolos*; *Glykeria*, "Sweet," in Terence's *Andria*; *Lysander*, "Man-releaser" in Shakespeare's *A Midsummer Night's Dream*; and *Harpagon*, "Plunderer" in Molière's *L'avare*, who comes out of Plautus's *Pseudolus*. Importantly, many speaking names are Greek, which suggests that Roman comedy wanted to stress its continuity with the Greek dramatic tradition. In this respect, modern comedy then followed in the footsteps of Roman comedy, although names also came from other languages, including Latin, Spanish, Italian, Arabic, and the native tongues of the playwrights themselves, such as the colorful *Sir Toby Belch* in Shakespeare's *Twelfth Night*. Further, the tradition of "speaking names" testifies to the fact that the Roman and later spectators and readers were sufficiently educated to understand the meaning, or at least the hints of the meaning, of these names.

10. Theophrastus. *Characteres*. Rec. H. Diels. Oxford: Clarendon, 1909. See also R. L. Hunter. *New Comedy of Greece and Rome*, pp.148–49.

11. Theophrastus. *Char.* I.6.

12. "Moral characters" is a literal rendering of the Greek *Ēthikoi kharaktēres*.

13. This is seen with the mosaics in the House of Menander in Mytilene, as well as from costumes that would suggest a typical character.

14. As Sheila D'Atri aptly observed, "Menander was particularly adept at revealing character through dialogue." Sheila D'Atri. "Introduction" to Menander's *Grouch*. In Robert Willoughby Corrigan. *Classical Comedy*, pp. 161–66; p. 161.

15. For example, in Menander (e.g., Parmeno in the *Samia*), Plautus (Chrysalus in the *Bacchides* and Epidicus in *Epidicus*), and Terence (Davos and Mysis in the *Andria*, Pythias in the *Eunuch*, et al).

16. Such as Toinette in Molière's *Le malade imaginaire* or Dorine in *Tartuffe*.

17. "*rufus*," Terence, *Phorm.* 51; cf. Plautus, *Pseud.* 1218. Red was the usual hair color of a slave in ancient comedy. J. Barsby. Terence, vol. 2, p. 17, note 14.

18. Plautus, *Pseud.* 1218–20.

19. For example, *Geta, Syrus, Mysis, Dorias*, and *Pythias*.

20. Terence, *Phorm.* 291–93.
21. "*doylois . . . kai xenois*," *Legg.* 816e.
22. H. Blumenberg. *Das Lachen der Thrakerin. Eine Urgeschichte der Theorie.* Frankfurt am Main: Suhrkamp, 1987, pp. 33–41 et passim; A. Heller. *Immortal Comedy,* p. 65.
23. "*fides et taciturnitas*," Terence, *Andr.* 34.
24. See, for example, *Ranae* 738–813.
25. "*illud mihi vitiumst maxumum*," *Hec.* 112.
26. As was Doris in Menander's *Perikeiromene* (1004–8 et passim).
27. "*scies, modo ut tacere possis*," Terence. *Phorm.* 58–59.
28. "*caput*," Terence, *Ad.* 568.
29. "*dedit consilium*," Terence, *Eun.* 1045.
30. Terence, *Phorm.* 616.
31. And yet, "in Aristophanes the word *pharmakos* means simply scoundrel, with no nonsense about it." Northrop Frye. *The Anatomy of Criticism,* p. 43.
32. Examples of the smart comic fool are aplenty, pervasive in all cultures at all times. As a *universal* figure, the smart fool appears under the guise of a jester, trickster, prankster, buffoon, clown, *alazon*, and *eiron*, among others. See V. Sternberg. *La poétique de la comédie,* p. 182–85 and T. G. A. Nelson. *Comedy: An Introduction to Comedy in Literature, Drama, and Cinema.* Oxford and New York: Oxford University Press, 1990, pp. 89–102, 112–22; "though rogue and trickster differ, the line between them can never be sharp." Ibid., p. 93. Such were the thievish but loyal Cario in Aristophanes's *Plutus*, Palaestrio in Plautus's *Miles gloriosus*, the ingenious Syrus in Terence's *Self-Tormentor* and *The Brothers*, the deceiving Geta and the insolent Phormio (*homo confidens, Phorm.* 123) in Terence's *Phormio*, medieval jesters and fools (Diego Lanza. *Lo stolto: Di Socrate, Eulenspiegel, Pinocchio e altri trasgressori del senso comune.* Turin: Einaudi, 1997 and J. W. Hokenson. *The Idea of Comedy,* pp. 150–62 ["The Medieval Fool Tradition"]), Till Eulenspiegel, Ivan the Fool of Russian folktales, Hoja Nasreddin from Bukhara, Karagöz of Turkish shadow theater, Andare of Sinhalese literature, Hanswurst of the German Stegreiftheater, Pietro Gonnella, the famous Florentine buffoon of the fifteenth century (also mentioned in *Don Quixote*), Callimaco in Machiavelli's *La Mandragola*, Puck in Shakespeare's *A Midsummer Night's Dream*, the Clown in *Twelfth Night* (called a "foolish Greek," which is a clear reminiscence of the Greek origin of [New] comedy), the smart yet devious *picaro* of the picaresque novel, the seventeenth- through eighteenth-century comic Spanish *graciosos*, the court *bufones* subtly depicted by Velázquez, the boorish drunkards Jodelet, Guillot, and Ragotin, the Italian *zanni*, the roguish and unscrupulous Philipin, Arlequin, Sganarelle, Mascarille, Scapin, Crispin, Merlin, and Frontin, Goethe's Lustige Person, Count Myshkin in Dostoevsky, the Good Soldier Švejk in Jaroslav Hašek, Beckett's Clov, and many others.
33. Here, again, comedy is similar to the detective story. The detective is inconspicuously smart and capable of solving complex problems, which involve both reasoning and practical action. Yet simultaneously, he often seems strange, eccentric,

and extravagant, to the point of appearing almost foolish—that is, incomprehensible from an ordinary perspective—while in fact he is profoundly moving and humane, as are Father Brown and Lieutenant Columbo.

34. When reading a letter from Malvolio, whom everyone considered mad but who in fact was fooled by others (and who signed his letter as *The madly used Malvolio*), a clown said: "Look, then, to be well edified when the fool delivers the madman." W. Shakespeare. *Twelfth Night*, act V, sc. I, 287. The intended pun of *deliver* here is both *to present the message of* and *to liberate* the poor madman. If I am right that Theophrastus's *Characters* described comic types, it is then no accident that the list began with the definition of irony as a paramount type of character.

35. For Hegel, however, the fool of comedy was just simplistic and naïve: "The fools are such naïve fools . . . [Die Toren sind so unbefangene Toren]." G. W. F. Hegel. *Aesthetics*, p. 1222; *Werke*, Bd. 15, p. 554. In this case, Hegel, otherwise a smart dialectician, was himself rather naïve.

36. Viola about the clown: "This fellow is wise enough to play the fool, / And to do that well craves a kind of wit. / He must observe their mood on whom he jests, / The quality of persons, and the time; / Not, like the haggard, check at every feather / That comes before his eye. This is a practice / As full of labor as a wise man's art; / For folly that he wisely shows, is fit; / But wise men, folly-fall'n, quite taint their wit." W. Shakespeare. *Twelfth Night*, act III, sc. I, 62–70.

37. "*stultus*" and "*callidus*," Terence, *Phorm.* 591; cf. *astutia*, *Andr.* 723.

38. Terence, *Haut.* 874–78.

39. W. Shakespeare. *Twelfth Night*, act I, sc. V, 32–36. Quinapalus is an ironically invented authority.

40. This was also a favorite fable character, as B'rer Rabbit or the Fox, which shows again comedy's proximity to fable.

41. According to Schlegel, "The knavish servant is generally also the buffoon, who takes pleasure in avowing, and even exaggerating, his own sensuality and want of principle, and who jokes at the expense of the other characters, and occasionally even addresses the pit. This is the origin of the comic servants of the moderns, but I am inclined to doubt whether, with our manners, there is propriety and truth in introducing such characters." A. W. Schlegel. *LDAL* 195. See also Peter Berger. *Redeeming Laughter: The Comic Dimension of Human Experience.* Berlin and New York: De Gruyter, 1997, pp. 190–96.

42. Aelian. *Varia hist.* X 14.

43. Euripides. *Ion* 854–56.

44. Euripides. *Aves* 157.

45. Ibid., 70–75.

46. Ibid., 764–65.

47. Terence should have known this better than others, being himself a freed slave. As Moschion in Menander's *Samia* said, "I think there's no distinction when one's born, / But if you test them fairly, good men are / Legitimate, bad men are bastards and / slaves." Menander. *Samia* 140–43, trans. Arnott.

48. Plautus, *Pseud.* 23–24.
49. This later became a privilege of a jester: "There is no slander in an allowed fool, though he do nothing but rail; nor no railing in a known discreet man, though he do nothing but reprove." W. Shakespeare. *Twelfth Night*, act I, sc. V, 95–98.
50. Diogenes, who owned less property than most, did this in the face of Alexander Dio Chrysostom. *Disc.* 4.1–35.
51. G. W. F. Hegel. *Phenomenology*, § 190 sqq.; *Werke*, Bd. 3, p. 150 sqq.; see also A. Kojève. *Introduction to the Reading of Hegel.* Ed. by Allan Bloom. Ithaca and London: Cornell University Press, 1969, pp. 45–67.
52. Astonishingly, a power distribution similar to the stone-scissor-paper type is not only present in comedy but also commonly found in nature, particularly in the phenomenon of sexual male trimorphism, which has been observed in different species of beetles, isopods, fish, lizards, and birds (ruff). Thus, beetles have three distinct forms and sizes of horns, ruffs have three different sizes and feather colors, and the *Uta stansburiana* lizards, common in the western part of the United States, have three distinct types of throat coloration. The orange-colored lizards hold and control big territory, blue-colored small territory, and yellow-colored no territory at all. In other words, the orange have much, the blue have a little, and the yellow have nothing. Yet within the triangular rochambeau kind of power checks and balances, the orange overpower the blue; the blue overpower the yellow; and the yellow overpower the orange by outsmarting the orange, using parts of their territory when the orange are busy defending other parts of it. In this way, nobody has the absolute upper hand.
53. *Gnōmē* or *pistis*. Proof further comprised oaths, agreements, testimonies, ordeals, and laws. *Tractatus Coislinianus*, XIII.
54. B. Weinberg. *A History of Literary Criticism in the Italian Renaissance*, p. 804.
55. A. Schmitt. *Kommentar* zu: Aristoteles, pp. 354–60, 581–85. See also Mary Whitlock Blundell. "*Ēthos* and *Dianoia* Reconsidered." In *Essays on Aristotle's Poetics*, pp. 155–75 (esp. pp. 156–57, 166–68), who stresses the role of purposeful choice (*prohairesis*), which requires both *ēthos* and *dianoia* and becomes central in the constitution of action.
56. Aristotle. *Poet.* 1149b38; *NE* 1107a1, 1138b18 sqq.
57. Aristotle. *Poet.* 1450b5–12, 1456a34–37; *NE* 1139a21–36, 1142b12.
58. Eric A. Havelock. *The Muse Learns to Write.* Yale: Yale University Press, 1986, p. 95: "A character in Greek drama does not theorize himself out of an unpleasant situation. He walks into it with motives that are specific and, if he has to, later accepts it when he recognizes what has actually happened."
59. "*loquarne? incendam. taceam? Instigem,*" Terence, *Phorm.* 185–86.
60. R. Jakobson. "Beitrag zur allgemeinen Kasuslehre." In *Travaux du cercle linguistique de Prague*, 1936, vol. 6 (repr. Nendeln, Liechtenstein: Kraus Reprint, 1968), pp. 240–88.
61. "*istuc est sapere, non quod ante pedes modost videre sed etiam illa quae futura sunt prospicere,*" Terence. *Ad.* 386–68. This was another aphorism coined by a slave.
62. "*feci imprudens quam sciens,*" Terence, *Hec.* 875–80.

63. "*ta prosēkonta*," Plato. *Euthyd.* 301 c–d. Cf. also *Gorg.* 462a–466a, where Plato draws an unfavorable parallel between Sophistic reasoning and the art of cooking.
64. Aelian, *Var. hist.* IV 16.
65. Ec. 1169–75.
66. As in Aesop's "The Dog and the Butcher," Babrius's "The Oxen and the Butcher" and "The Departure of a Well-Sated Guest," Phaedrus's "The Wethers and the Butcher," and Krylov's "The Cat and the Cook." Aesop 256, 295; Babrius 21, 42.
67. N. Frye. *The Anatomy of Criticism*, pp. 152, 163.
68. As, for example, the cook Sikon in Menander's *Dyskolos* and the *cuisinier maître* Jacque in Molière's *L'avare*.
69. "[C]uriosity is a stock trait of the comic cook." R. L. Hunter. *New Comedy of Greece and Rome*, p. 54.
70. Food is a powerful comic aphrodisiac, which was explored by Archestratus in his (now lost) gastronomic poem Athenaeus (Archestratus. The Life of Luxury: Europe's Oldest Cookery Book. Translated with introduction and commentary by John Wilkins and Shaun Hill. Totnes: Prospect Books, 1994, 8.335b–e) and by Rabelais in *Gargantua and Pantagruel.*
71. Or at least, in the end, the mastermind of the plot would have the fulfillment of his wishes. Terence. *Phorm.* 1050–1.
72. Plato. *Meno* 82b sqq.
73. Plato. *Phaedo* 70c sqq.
74. For example, in the figure of Phormio in Terence.
75. Diogenes opposed such a life to three kinds of "inauthentic" life: self-indulgence, avariciousness, and honor. Dio Chrysostom. *Disc.* 4.83–138. Cf. Diogenes Laert. VI 20–81.
76. Aelian. *Varia hist.* II 43, IV 11, cf. II 13.
77. Aesop's characters very much resembled Aristophanes's choreuts.
78. Plato. *Phaedo* 60d–61b. Aesop, the most imaginative author of fables, was also the author of gnomes and abundant sententiae.
79. Plautus. *Pseud.* 464–65.
80. Ibid., 480.
81. Ibid., 687.

Conclusions

1. Molière. *Les femmes savantes*, act III, sc. II.
2. "*quod fors feret feremus aequo animo,*" Terence, *Phorm.* 138.
3. *pros ta aproaireta tharrein, eylabeisthai ta proairetika.* Epictetus. *Disc.* II.1.30, cf. 40. Thus, "How wise it is to entertain desires that can easily be cured when things go wrong! (*quam scitumst eius modi in animo parare cupiditates quas, quom res advorsae sient, paullo mederi possis!*)" (Terence. *Phorm.* 821–22) is clearly a parody of the Stoic moral attitude (cf. also *Phorm.* 247–52).
4. That is, Arcesilaus in the Middle Academy, the next generation after Menander, and Carneades in the New Academy.

5. I should therefore disagree with Gurewitsch, who took skepticism to be an ironic response to the inevitable absurdity of life: "A Pyrrhonic ironist . . . may be described as a radical skeptic whose awareness of the absurd prompts him, under the aegis of comedy, to ruin reverence, desanctify values, and collapse ideals, all of which are, of course, rather wormy to begin with." M. Gurewitsch. "From Pyrrhonic to Vomedic Irony." In *Comedy: New Perspectives*. Ed. by Maurice Charney. New York: New York Literary Forum, 1978, pp. 45–57; p. 47. And: "Exposed to the facts of disenchantment—nature is mutable; man, corruptible; the universe, chaotic—one had better learn to laugh; for in the face of unavoidable calamities, it is more enlightened to be flippant than furious, wiser to be mocking than miserable." Ibid., p. 55. Such a response is not comic but rather tragic and sarcastic.

6. Diogenes, ap. Stobaeus IX 49 (*mēte phoboymenon mēte aiskhynomenon*).

7. This motif is also taken up by Epicurus. Epicurus. *KD* 13, 14.

8. They knew each other as synephebes. *Der Kleine Pauly*. Bd. 2, col. 314–18.

9. A. W. Schlegel. *LDAL* 190.

10. Epicurus. *Ep. Menoec.* 124–26; *KD* 2.

11. "*symphilosophein*," Epicurus. *KD* 20, cf. 2, 3, 5; *Ep. Menoec.* 132.

Bibliography

Albrecht, Michael von. *A History of Roman Literature: From Livius Andronicus to Boethius, with Special Regard to Its Influence on World Literature*, vol. 1 (Leiden: Brill, 1997).

Alcidamas. *Peri Sophistōn*, in *Orationes et fragmenta, adiunctis Gorgiae Antisthenis Alcidamantis declamationibus*, ed. F. Blass (Leipzig: Teubner, 1908; 2nd ed.).

Archestratus. *The Life of Luxury: Europe's Oldest Cookery Book*, trans. and ed. John Wilkins and Shaun Hill (Totnes: Prospect Books, 1994).

Arendt, Hannah. Interview, *New York Review of Books* 25 (October 26, 1978).

Aristophanes. *Aristophanes*, trans. Jeffrey Henderson, 5 vols. (Cambridge: Harvard University Press, 1998–2008).

Aristotle. *Opera*, ed. Immanuel Bekker (Berlin: Reimer, 1831).

———. *On Rhetoric: A Theory of Civic Discourse*, trans. George A. Kennedy (Oxford: Oxford University Press, 2007).

Arnott, W. G. "Introduction," in vol. 1 of *Menander*, ed. W. G. Arnott (Cambridge: Harvard University Press, 1997).

Auden, W. H. "Notes on the Comic," in *Comedy, Meaning and Form*, ed. Robert Willoughby Corrigan (San Francisco: Chandler Publishing Company, 1965).

Bakhtin, Mikhail. *Rabelais and His World*, trans. Hélène Iswolsky (Cambridge: MIT Press, 1984).

———. *Problems of Dostoevsky's Poetics*, ed. and trans. C. Emerson (Minneapolis: University of Minnesota Press, 1984).

Bakola, Emmanuela. *Cratinus and the Art of Comedy* (Oxford: Oxford University Press, 2010).

Bataille, Georges. "*Conférences sur le non-savoir*," *Tel Qel* 10 (1962), pp. 3–20.

———. "Un-Knowing: Laughter and Tears," *October* 36 (1986), pp. 89–102.

Baudelaire, Charles. "On the Essence of Laughter, and, in General, on the Comic in the Plastic Arts," in *Comedy, Meaning and Form*, ed. Robert Willoughby Corrigan (San Francisco: Chandler Publishing Company, 1965).

Baumgarten, Alexander Gottlieb. *Ästhetik*, ed. Dagmar Mirbach, 2 vols. (Hamburg: Felix Meiner Verlag, 2007).

Benjamin, Walter. "Molière: Der eingebildete Kranke," in vol. 2, part 2 of *Gesammelte Schriften*, ed. Rolf Tiedemann and Hermann Schweppenhäuser (Frankfurt: Suhrkamp, 1972).

Bentley, Eric, ed. *The Genius of the Italian Theatre* (New York: Mentor Books, 1964).

Berger, Peter. *Redeeming Laughter: The Comic Dimension of Human Experience* (Berlin and New York: De Gruyter, 1997).

Bergson, Henri. *Laughter: An Essay on the Meaning of the Comic*, trans. Cloudesely Brereton and Fred Rothwell (New York: Macmillan, 1921; first publ. 1911).

Bishop, Lloyd. *Comic Literature in France: From the Middle Ages to the Twentieth Century* (New Orleans: University Press of the South, 2004).

Blumenberg, Hans. *Das Lachen der Thrakerin: Eine Urgeschichte der Theorie* (Frankfurt: Suhrkamp, 1987).

Blundell, Mary Whitlock. "*Éthos* and *Dianoia* Reconsidered," in *Essays on Aristotle's Poetics*, ed. Amélie Oksenberg Rorty (Princeton: Princeton University Press, 1992).

Bohtz, August Wilhelm. *Die Idee des Tragischen* (Göttingen: Georg Kübler, 1836).

Bordwell, David. *Narration in the Fiction Film* (London: Methuen, 1985).

Cavell, Stanley. *Pursuit of Happiness: The Hollywood Comedy of Remarriage* (Cambridge: Harvard University Press, 1981).

Charney, Maurice. *Comedy High and Low* (Oxford: Oxford University Press, 1978).

Cicero. *On the Orator: Books 1–2*, trans. E. W. Sutton (Cambridge: Harvard University Press, 1942).

———. *On the Orator: Book 3. On Fate. Stoic Paradoxes. Divisions of Oratory*, trans. H. Rackham (Cambridge: Harvard University Press, 1942).

———. *On Invention. The Best Kind of Orator. Topics. A. Rhetorical Treatises*, trans. H. M. Hubbell (Cambridge: Harvard University Press, 1949).

Cooper, Lane. *An Aristotelian Theory of Comedy* (New York: Harcourt Brace, 1922).

Corrigan, Robert Willoughby. "Aristophanic Comedy: The Conscience of a Conservative," in *Comedy, Meaning and Form*, ed. Robert Willoughby Corrigan (San Francisco: Chandler Publishing Company, 1965).

———. *Classical Comedy: Greek and Roman* (New York: Applause Theatre Book Publishers, 1987).

Critchley, Simon. *On Humour* (London and New York: Routledge, 2002).

Cutrofello, Andrew. "It Takes a Village Idiot: And Other Lessons Cynthia Willett Teaches Us," *Journal of Speculative Philosophy* 24 (2010), pp. 85–95.

de Boer, Karin. "The Eternal Irony of the Community: Aristophanian Echoes in Hegel's *Phenomenology of Spirit*," *Inquiry* 52 (2009), pp. 311–34.

Descartes, René. *Oeuvres de Descartes*, ed. Charles Adam and Paul Tannery, 11 vols. (Paris: Vrin, 1996).

Diels, Hermann, and Walther Kranz, eds. *Die Fragmente der Vorsokratiker*, 3 vols. (Zürich: Weidmann, 1996).

Dilthey, Wilhelm. "Die Technik des Dramas," appendix to Gustav Freytag, *Die Technik des Dramas* (Darmstadt: Wissenschaftliche Buchgesellschaft, 1982; first publ. 1863).

Dobrov, Gregory W. "The Poet's Voice in the Evolution of Dramatic Dialogism," in *Beyond Aristophanes: Transition and Diversity in Greek Comedy*, ed. Gregory W. Dobrov (Atlanta: Scholars Press, 1995).

———, ed. *Beyond Aristophanes: Transition and Diversity in Greek Comedy* (Atlanta: Scholars Press, 1995).

Donatus. "A Fragment on Comedy and Tragedy," in *Theories of Comedy*, trans. and ed. Paul Lauter (Garden City, NY: Anchor Books/Doubleday, 1964).

Downey, Patrick. *Serious Comedy: The Philosophical and Theological Significance of Tragic and Comic Writing in the Western Tradition* (Lanham, MD: Lexington Books, 2001).

Eco, Umberto. "The Frames of Comic 'Freedom,'" in *Carnival!*, ed. Thomas A. Sebeok (Berlin: Mouton Publishers, 1984).

Edwards, Brian. "*Verbum ludens*, or the Antic Disposition of Words: Toward a Theory of the Comic," in *Comic Relations: Studies in the Comic, Satire, and Parody*, ed. Pavel Petr, David Roberts, and Philip Thomson (Frankfurt and New York: P. Lang, 1985).

Epictetus. *Discourses 3–4. The Encheiridion*, trans. W. A. Oldfather (Cambridge: Harvard University Press, 1928).

Euclid. *The Thirteen Books of Euclid's Elements*, trans. and ed. Thomas L. Heath, 3 vols. (New York: Dover, 1956).

Farley-Hills, David. *The Comic in Renaissance Comedy* (Totowa, NJ: Barnes and Noble, 1981).

Foucault, Michel. *Fearless Speech*, ed. Joseph Pearson (Los Angeles: Semiotext(e), 2001).

Frank, Manfred. "Vom Lachen. Über Komik, Witz und Ironie. Überlegungen im Ausgang von der Frühromantik," in *Vom Lachen. Einem Phänomen auf der Spur*, ed. Thomas Vogel (Tübingen: Attempto, 1992).

Freud, Sigmund. *Jokes and Their Relation to the Unconscious*, trans. James Strachey (New York: W. W. Norton & Co., 1960).

Freytag, Gustav. *Die Technik des Dramas* (Darmstadt: Wissenschaftliche Buchgesellschaft, 1982; 13th ed., first publ. 1863).

Fry, Christopher. "Comedy," in *Comedy, Meaning and Form*, ed. Robert Willoughby Corrigan (San Francisco: Chandler Publishing Company, 1965).

Frye, Northrop. *The Anatomy of Criticism: Four Essays*, vol. 22 of *The Collected Works of Northrop Frye*, ed. Robert D. Denham (Toronto, Buffalo, and London: University of Toronto Press, 2006).

———. *A Natural Perspective: The Development of Shakespearean Comedy and Romance* (New York: Columbia University Press, 1965).

Gadamer, Hans-Georg. "Mythos und Vernunft," in *Ästhetik und Poetik: Kunst als Aussage*, vol. 8 of *Gesammelte Werke* (Tübingen: Mohr, 1993).

Gaiser, Konrad. "Zur Eigenart der römischen Komödie: Plautus und Terenz gegenüber ihren griechischen Vorbildern," in *Aufstieg und Niedergang der Römischen Welt: Geschichte und Kultur Roms im Spiegel der neueren Forschung* (Berlin and New York: De Gruyter, 1972).

Gasché, Rodolphe. "Self-Dissolving Seriousness: On the Comic in the Hegelian Concept of Tragedy," in *Philosophy and Tragedy*, ed. Miguel de Beistegui and Simon Sparks (London and New York: Routledge, 2000).

Gerigk, Anja. *Literarische Hochkomik in der Moderne: Theorie und Interpretationen* (Tübingen: Francke, 2008).

Goldberg, Sander M. *Understanding Terence* (Princeton: Princeton University Press, 1986).

Gurewitsch, Morton. *Comedy: The Irrational Vision* (Ithaca: Cornell University Press, 1975).

———. "From Pyrrhonic to Vomedic Irony," in *Comedy: New Perspectives*, ed. Maurice Charney (New York: New York Literary Forum, 1978).

Haberland, Paul Mallory. *The Development of Comic Theory in Germany during the Eighteenth Century* (Göppingen: Alfred Kuemmerle, 1971).

Halliwell, Stephen. *Greek Laughter: A Study of Cultural Psychology from Homer to Early Christianity* (Cambridge: Cambridge University Press, 2008).

Havelock, Eric A. *The Muse Learns to Write* (New Haven: Yale University Press, 1986).

Hegel, Georg Wilhelm Friedrich. *The Phenomenology of Spirit*, trans. A. V. Miller (Oxford: Oxford University Press, 1977).

———. *Phänomenologie des Geistes*, vol. 3 of *Werke* (Frankfurt: Suhrkamp, 1986).

———. *Aesthetics: Lectures on Fine Art*, trans. T. M. Knox, 2 vols. (Oxford: Clarendon Press, 1975).

———. *Vorlesungen über die Ästhetik*, vols. 13–15 of *Werke* (Frankfurt: Suhrkamp, 1986).

———. *Grundlinien der Philosophie des Rechts*, vol. 7 of *Werke* (Frankfurt: Suhrkamp, 1986).

Heidegger, Martin. *Sein und Zeit* (Tübingen: Max Niemeyer, 1993).

———. *Being and Time*, trans. Joan Stambaugh, rev. Dennis J. Schmidt (Albany: State University of New York Press, 2010).

Heller, Agnes. *Immortal Comedy: The Comic Phenomenon in Art, Literature, and Life* (Lanham, MD: Lexington, 2005).

Herrick, Marvin T. *Comic Theory in the Sixteenth Century* (Urbana: University of Illinois Press, 1964; first publ. 1950).

Hokenson, Jan Walsh. *The Idea of Comedy: History, Theory, Critique* (Madison and Teaneck: Fairleigh Dickinson University Press, 2006).

Holland, Peter. *The Ornament of Action: Text and Performance in Restoration Comedy* (Cambridge: Cambridge University Press, 1979).

Honneth, Axel. *Kampf um Anerkennung. Zur moralischen Grammatik sozialer Konflikte* (Frankfurt: Suhrkamp, 1992).

Horace. *Satires, Epistles, and Ars Poetica*, trans. H. Rushton Fairclough (Cambridge: Harvard University Press, 1929).

Horn, András. *Das Komische im Spiegel der Literatur: Versuch einer systematischen Einführung* (Würzburg: Konigshausen & Neumann, 1988).

Hunter, Richard L. *New Comedy of Greece and Rome* (Cambridge: Cambridge University Press, 1985).

Jakobson, Roman. "Beitrag zur allgemeinen Kasuslehre," in vol. 6 of *Travaux du cercle linguistique de Prague* (Nendeln and Liechtenstein: Kraus Reprint, 1968).

Janko, Richard. "From Catharsis to the Aristotelian Mean," in *Essays on Aristotle's Poetics*, ed. Amélie Oksenberg Rorty (Princeton: Princeton University Press, 1992).

———. *Aristotle on Comedy: Towards a Reconstruction of Poetics II* (Berkley: University of California Press, 1984).

Jonson, Ben. *Ben Jonson*, ed. C. H. Herford, Percy Simpson, and Evelyn Simpson, 11 vols. (Oxford: Clarendon Press, 1925–1952).

Jünger, Friedich Georg. *Über das Komische* (Frankfurt: Vittorio Klostermann, 1948; first publ. 1936).

Kennedy, George A. *The Art of Rhetoric in the Roman World, 300 B.C–A.D. 300* (Princeton: Princeton University Press, 1972).

Kerr, Walter. *Tragedy and Comedy* (London: The Bodley Head, 1967).

Kierkegaard, Søren. *The Concept of Irony with Continual Reference to Socrates; Notes of Schelling's Berlin Lectures*, ed. and trans. Howard V. Hong and Edna H. Hong (Princeton: Princeton University Press, 1989; second printing, with corrections, 1992).

Kock, Theodorus, ed. *Comicorum Atticorum Fragmenta*, 3 vols. (Leipzig: Teubner, 1880–1887).

Koerte, A. and A. Thierfelder, eds. *Menandri quae supersunt* (Leipzig: Teubner, 1959; 2nd ed.).

Kojève, Alexandre. *Introduction to the Reading of Hegel*, ed. Allan Bloom (Ithaca: Cornell University Press, 1969).

Konstan, David. *Greek Comedy and Ideology* (Oxford: Oxford University Press, 1995).

Koster, W. J. W., ed. *Prolegomena de Comoedia*, pt. 1, fasc. 1A of *Scholia in Aristophanem* (Groningen: Bouma, 1975).

Kottman, Paul. "Slipping on Banana Peels, Tumbling into Wells: Philosophy and Comedy," *Diacritics* 38:4 (2010), pp. 3–14.

Lanza, Diego. *Lo stolto: Di Socrate, Eulenspiegel, Pinocchio e altri trasgressori del senso commune* (Turin: Einaudi, 1997).

Latacz, Joachim, ed. *Archaische Periode*, vol. 1 of *Die griechische Literatur in Text und Darstellung* (Stuttgart: Philipp Reclam, 1991).

Lauter, Paul, ed. *Theories of Comedy* (Garden City, NY: Anchor Books/Doubleday, 1964).

Lefèvre, Eckard. *Der Phormio des Terenz und der Epidikazomenos des Apollodor von Karystos* (München: Beck, 1978).

Lévêque, Pierre. *Agathon* (Paris: Les belles lettres, 1955).

Lévinas, Emmnauel. *Le temps et l'autre* (Paris: Presses Universitaires de France, 1983).

———. *Time and the Other*, trans. Richard A. Cohen (Pittsburgh: Duquesne University Press, 1990).

Meineke, August, ed. *Fragmenta Comicorum Graecorum*, 3 vols. (Berlin: Reimer 1840).

Menander. *The Plays and Fragments*, trans. and ed. Maurice Balme (Oxford: Oxford University Press, 2001).

———. *Menander*, trans. and ed. W. G. Arnott, 3 vols. (Cambridge: Harvard University Press, 1997–2001).

Meredith, George. *An Essay on the Idea of Comedy, and of the Uses of the Comic Spirit*, ed. Stefano Bronzini (Bari: Adriatica Editrice, 2001).

Meyer, Michel. *Le comique et le tragique. Penser le théâtre et son histoire* (Paris: Presses Universitaires de France, 2003).

Molière, Jean-Baptiste. *Oeuvres complètes*. Préface de Pierre-Aimé Touchard (Paris: Seuil, 1962).

Monro, D. H. *Argument of Laughter* (Melbourne: Melbourne University Press, 1951).

Morreall, John. *Taking Laughter Seriously*. (Albany: State University of New York Press, 1983).

Müller-Kampel, Beatrix. "Komik und das Komische: Kriterien und Kategorien," *LiTheS: Zeitschrift für Literatur- und Theatersoziologie* 7 (2012), pp. 5–39.

Nelson, T. G. A. *Comedy: An Introduction to Comedy in Literature, Drama, and Cinema* (Oxford: Oxford University Press, 1990).

Nikulin, Dmitri. *On Dialogue* (Lanham, MD: Lexington, 2005).

———. "Richard Rorty, Cynic: Philosophy in the Conversation of Humankind," *Graduate Faculty Philosophy Journal* 29:2 (2008), pp. 85–111.

———. "The Comedy of Philosophy," in *Engaging Agnes Heller: A Critical* Companion, ed. Katie Terezakis (Lanham: Lexington, 2009)

———. *Dialectic and Dialogue* (Stanford: Stanford University Press, 2010).

Olson, Elder. *The Theory of Comedy* (Bloomington: Indiana University Press, 1968).

Ong, Walter J. *Orality and Literacy: The Technologizing of the Word* (London and New York: Routledge, 1988; first publ. 1982).

Paolucci, Anne. "Hegel's Theory of Comedy," in *Comedy: New Perspectives*, ed. Maurice Charney (New York: New York Literary Forum, 1978).

Parry, Milman. "Studies in the Epic Technique of Oral Verse-Making," in *The Making of the Homeric Verse: The Collected Papers of Milman Parry* (Oxford: Clarendon Press, 1971).

Pausanias. *Pausanias's Description of Greece*, trans. and ed. J. G. Frazer (New York: Biblo and Tannen, 1965).

Plato. *Platonis Opera*, ed. John Burnet, 5 vols. (Oxford: Clarendon Press, 1900–1907).

Plautus. *Plautus*, trans. Wolfgang de Melo, 4 vols. (Cambridge: Harvard University Press, 2011–2012).

Plessner, Helmuth. *Philosophische Anthropologie. Lachen und Weinen; Lächeln; Anthropologie der Sinne*, ed. Günter Dix (Frankfurt: S. Fischer Verlag, 1970).

Plutarch. *Moralia*, ed. Bernadotte Perrin et al., 16 vols. (Cambridge: Harvard University Press, 1927–2004).

Polhemus, Robert M. *Comic Faith: The Great Tradition from Austen to Joyce* (Chicago: The University of Chicago Press, 1980).

Potts, L. J. *Comedy* (London: Hutchinson's University Library, 1948).

Post, L. A. "Woman's Place in Menander's Athens," *Transactions of the American Philological Association* 71 (1941), pp. 420–59.

Proclus. *In primum Euclidis Elemetorum librum commentarii*, ed. G. Friedlein (Leipzig: Teubner, 1873).

———. *Procli Diadochi in Platonis rem publicam commentarii*, ed. W. Kroll, 2 vols. (Leipzig: Teubner, 1899–1901).

Propp, Vladimir. *Morphology of the Folktale*, trans. Laurence Scott, ed. Svatava Pirkova-Jakobson (Bloomington: Indiana University Press, 1958).

Radzig, S. I. *History Ancient Greek Literature* [*Istoriya drevnegrecheskoy literatury*] (Moscow: Vysshaya shkola, 1982; 5th ed.; first publ. 1940).

Roche, Mark William. *Tragedy and Comedy: A Systematic Study and a Critique of Hegel* (Albany, NY: State University of New York Press, 1998).

———. "Hegel's Theory of Comedy in the Context of Hegelian and Modern Reflections on Comedy," *Revue Internationale de Philosophie* 56 (2002), pp. 411–30.

Rorty, Amélie Oksenberg, ed. *Essays on Aristotle's Poetics* (Princeton: Princeton University Press, 1992).

Rosen, Ralph M. "Plato Comicus," in *Beyond Aristophanes: Transition and Diversity in Greek Comedy*, ed. Gregory W. Dobrov (Atlanta: Scholars Press, 1995).

Rothwell, Jr., Kenneth S. "The Continuity of the Chorus in Fourth-Century Attic Comedy," in *Beyond Aristophanes: Transition and Diversity in Greek Comedy*, ed. Gregory W. Dobrov (Atlanta: Scholars Press, 1995).

Rousseau, Jean-Jacques. *Politics and the Arts: Letter to M. d'Alembert on the Theatre*, trans. Allan Bloom (Ithaca: Cornell University Press, 1968).

Ruge, Arnold. *Neue Vorschule der Ästhetik: Das Komische mit einem Komischen Anhange* (Halle: Verlag der Buchhandlung des Waisenhauses, 1837; repr. Hildesheim: Georg Olms, 1975).

Ruggiers, Paul G. *Versions of Medieval Comedy* (Norman: University of Oklahoma Press, 1977).

Schiller, Friedrich. "Naïve and Sentimental Poetry," in *Naïve and Sentimental Poetry. On the Sublime*, trans. and ed. Julius A. Elias (New York: Frederick Ungar Publishing Co., 1966).

Schlegel, August Wilhelm. *Course of Lectures on Dramatic Art and Literature*, trans. John Black, Rev. A. J. W. Morrison (New York: AMS Press, 1973; repr. from the original edition, London, 1846).

———. *Sämtliche Werke*, ed. Eduard Böcking (Leipzig: Weidmannsche Buchhandlung 1846; repr. Hildesheim and New York: Georg Olms, 1971).

Schlegel, Friedrich. "Vom ästhetischen Werte der griechischen Komödie," in *Dichtungen und Aufsätze*, ed. W. Rasch (München: Hanser, 1984).

Schmidt, Henry J. *How Dramas End: Essays on the German* Sturm und Drang, *Büchner, Hauptmann, and Fleisser* (Ann Arbor: The University of Michigan Press, 1992).

Schmitt, Arbogast. "Kommentar zu: Aristoteles. *Poetik*," in vol. 5 of *Werke in deutscher Übersetzung*, trans. Arbogast Schmitt (Berlin: Akademie, 2008).

Schopenhauer, Arthur. *Die Welt als Wille und Vorstellung* (München: Deutscher Taschenbuch Verlag, 1998).

Schürmann, Reiner. *Broken Hegemonies*, trans. Reginald Lilly (Bloomington: Indiana University Press, 2003).

Seaford, Richard. "Tragedy and Dionysus," in *A Companion to Tragedy*, ed. Rebecca Bushnell (Oxford: Blackwell, 2005).

Segal, Erich. *The Death of Comedy* (Cambridge: Harvard University Press, 2001).

Shaftesbury, Antony Earl of. "Sensus communis: An Essay on the Freedom of Wit and Humour," in vol. 1 of *Characteristicks of Men, Manners, Opinions, Times*, ed. Philip Ayers (Oxford: Clarendon Press, 1999).

Shklovsky, Viktor. *Knight's Move*, trans. Richard Sheldon (Normal and London: Dalkey Archive Press, 2005).

Sifakis, Gregory Michael. *Parabasis and Animal Choruses: A Contribution to the History of Attic Comedy* (London: Athlone Press, 1971).

Silk, Michael Stephen. *Aristophanes and the Definition of Comedy* (Oxford: Oxford University Press, 2000).

Simon, Richard Keller. *The Labyrinth of the Comic: Theory and Practice from Fielding to Freud* (Tallahassee: Florida State University Press, 1985).

Sternberg, Véronique. *La poétique de la comédie* (Paris: Sedes, 1999).

Storey, Ian C. *Eupolis: Poet of Old Comedy* (Oxford: Oxford University Press, 2003).

Stott, Andrew. *Comedy* (New York: Routledge, 2005).

Terence. *Terence*, trans. John Barsby, 2 vols. (Cambridge: Harvard University Press, 2001).

Theophrastus. *Characters*, ed. Hermann Diels (Oxford: Clarendon Press, 1909).

Tomashevsky, Boris. *Poetica* (Moscow: CC, 1996).

Trahair, Lisa. *The Comedy of Philosophy: Sense and Non-Sense in Early Cinematic Slapstick* (Albany: State University of New York Press, 2007).

Warning, Rainer. "Komik/Komödie," in vol. 2 of *Das Fischer Lexikon. Literatur*, ed. U. Ricklefs (Frankfurt: Fischer, 1996).

Warning, Rainer, and Wolfgang Preisendanz, eds. *Das Komische* (München: Fink, 1976).

Watson, Walter. *The Lost Second Book of Aristotle's Poetics* (Chicago: The University of Chicago Press, 2012).

Weinberg, Bernard. *A History of Literary Criticism in the Italian Renaissance*, 2 vols. (Chicago: The University of Chicago Press, 1961).

Wessner, Paulus, ed. *Aelii Donati quod fertur commentum Terenti. Accedunt Evgraphi commentum et scholia Bembina*, 3 vols. (Leipzig, 1902–1908; repr. 1962–1963).

West, Martin L. *Studies in Greek Elegy and Iambus* (Berlin and New York: De Gruyter, 1974).

———, ed. *Iambi et elegi Graeci ante Alexandrum cantata* (Oxford: Oxford University Press, 1989; 2nd ed.).

———, ed. *Homeric Hymns. Homeric Apocrypha. Lives of Homer*, trans. Martin L. West (Cambridge: Harvard University Press, 2003).

Whitman, Cedric H. *Aristophanes and the Comic Hero* (Cambridge: Harvard University Press, 1964).

Willett, Cynthia. *Irony in the Age of Empire: Comic Perspectives on Democracy and Freedom* (Bloomington: Indiana University Press, 2009).

Ziegler, Konrad, Walther Sontheimer, and Hans Gärtner, eds., *Der Kleine Pauly. Lexikon der Antike* (München: Deutscher Taschenbuch Verlag, 1979).

Zupančič, Alenka. *The Odd One In: On Comedy* (Cambridge: MIT Press, 2008).

Index

Fichte, Johann Gottlieb xii
flyax 5
fool ix, xii–xiii, 18, 24, 32, 101, 109,
        113, 117–120, 124, 131,
        139n12, 164n83, 171n32,
        172n33, 172n35
    see also servant; comic character
Fonvizin, Denis 19
Ford, John 68
Formalism 63, 64
    see also Shklovsky, Victor
Formalists *see* Formalism
fragment 5, 9, 14, 29, 38, 73, 74,
        75–77
    see also aphorism; gnome
Freytag's pyramid 60–61, 159n68,
        159n70
Frye, Northrop 7, 43, 159n70,
        161n93
free speech (*parrhēsia*) 4, 89, 122, 131,
        135
freedom viii–xiii, 12, 30, 32, 34–38, 42,
        61, 64, 65, 66, 84, 92, 95, 105,
        106, 107–110, 120–122, 125,
        127, 129, 134, 135, 151n91,
        155n16, 167n26
Freud, Sigmund 40, 41, 119

Gaiser, Konrad 143n67, 159n67
Gerigk, Anja 41
Gogol, Nikolai 18, 115
goodness ix, 26, 58, 86, 91, 95, 97, 120,
        127, 135, 143n67
good ending viii–xii, 16, 26, 44, 47,
        62, 68, 69, 76, 81, 85, 88,
        92, 93–110, 113, 118, 119,
        121, 124, 127, 129, 130, 131,
        133–135, 150n53
    see also well-being
Giraldi, Lucio Olimpio 7
gnome 44, 73–77, 91, 125, 162n21,
        174n78
    see also aphorism; fragment
Green, John 24
Gurewitch, Morton 43, 159n70

Hegel, G. W. F. viii, 26, 27–34, 36,
        37, 40, 50, 115, 122, 137n2,
        148n25, 148n26, 148n27
Heidegger, Martin 13, 26
Heraclitus 5, 6, 154n1
Heller, Agnes 19, 39, 40, 42, 50, 63, 88,
        95, 99, 117, 118, 155n14
Herrick, Marvin T. 23
Hobbes, Thomas 98, 167n24
Homer 4, 5, 6, 26, 73, 79, 138n12
Honoratus 23
Horace 19, 20, 23, 24, 37, 144n76,
        145n102, 159n67
Horn, András 42, 153n108
Huxley, Aldous 7, 140n35
humor 98–102, 156n46, 159n70, 168n51

iambus 4–5, 7, 138n11, 141n54
imitation (*mimēsis*) 6–8, 18, 21, 25, 39,
        42, 49, 55, 125, 135
    and Plato 5, 25
    and laughter 102
intellect (*noys*) 124, 125
Ionesco, Eugène 42
    The Chairs 82
irony 30, 43, 78, 85, 115, 119
    and subjectivity 151n91
    see also Socratic irony

Jakobson, Roman 127
Jonson, Ben xii, 19, 96, 101, 147n10,
        165n96, 168n37
    Epicoene, or The Silent Women 63
    Every Man Out of His Humour
        156n46
    Volpone, or the Foxe 96
joke xii, 7, 12, 17, 43, 62, 74, 98–102,
        118, 122, 172n41
    and comic plot 44
    see also laughter
Jünger, Friedrich Georg 43, 107
justice ix, xi–xiii, 3, 86, 96
    and fate 91
    and good ending 68, 97, 107, 155n16
    and slave xiii

190 • Index

CPSIA information can be obtained at www.ICGtesting.com
Printed in the USA
LVOW04*0905120715

445927LV00009B/161/P